Fashion Victim

Fashion Victim

DRESSING,

'LE

Michelle Lee

BROADWAY BOOKS

NEW YORK

For my family and EMV

FASHION VICTIM. Copyright © 2003 by Michelle Lee.
All rights reserved. No part of this book may be reproduced or
transmitted in any form or by any means, electronic or
mechanical, including photocopying, recording, or by any
information storage and retrieval system, without written
permission from the publisher. For information, address
Broadway Books, a division of Random House, Inc.,
1745 Broadway, New York, NY 10019.

Broadway Books titles may be purchased for business or
promotional use or for special sales. For information, please
write to: Special Markets Department, Random House, Inc.,
1745 Broadway, New York, NY 10019.

PRINTED IN THE UNITED STATES OF AMERICA

BROADWAY BOOKS and its logo, a letter B bisected on the diago-
nal, are trademarks of Broadway Books, a division of Random
House, Inc.

Visit our website at www.broadwaybooks.com

First edition published 2003

Book design by Scott Santoro/Worksight

The Cataloging-in-Publication Data is on file
with the Library of Congress.

ISBN 0-7679-1048-6

10 9 8 7 6 5 4 3 2 1

Contents

Acknowledgments

Just as most garments today aren't created solely from the work of one person, neither is a book the product of a single individual. I'd like to thank the editors, designers, stylists, photographers, doctors, businesspeople, professors, activists, and all the other gracious people who allowed me to interview them for this book.

I'm infinitely grateful to William Clark, an incredible agent and all-around great guy who believed in this book from Day One. Since that first day when I met him for lunch at Balthazar (where I got a glimpse of how popular he is!), he was always there to field any questions I had about the business or about the book.

My original editor at Broadway Books, Suzanne Oaks, was instrumental in helping me focus the vision of *Fashion Victim*. Suzanne left the business, and I was incredibly sad to see her go. But I was elated upon meeting my new editor, Ann Campbell. Writers all dream of working with an editor like Ann, who offered much-appreciated encouragement and keen observations that helped the book enormously. Her assistant Jenny Cookson was also a big help throughout the process. Then Brian Jones and Julia Coblentz lent their publicity and marketing genuis in the latter part of the project.

I thank my wonderful journalism teacher Randy Miller, who was a key player in getting me to move to New York all those years ago, and my magazine friends—Lisa, Lauren, Beth, Rachel, Marisa, Elizabeth, Kim—who've offered genuine support and positive feedback. My German friends Oli and Sabine helped me kick off some of my stress by being my gracious hosts in Spain. Shalini, my partner in crime since middle school, has always been a welcome voice on the phone, as has my longtime friend Faith. Ben and Terry Valencia, who've been like a second set of parents to me, were kind enough to lend me a place where I could write for a few months.

In the beginning of my career, I was fortunate to work with a great editor, Susan Dix. She took a chance and hired me as a staff writer at a paper in Florida. Had it not been for that first journalism break, I might have gone into an entirely different line of work. I count Susan as a dear friend and great mentor. I've also been so fortunate to write for other fabulous magazine editors, like Bonnie Fuller of *Us Weekly*, Cindi Leive of *Glamour*, Jon Durbin of *Paper*, Christene Barberich of *City*, my old editors at *Mademoiselle*, plus so many others.

My sister Jennifer, probably the most fashion-savvy and word-savvy math teacher in the world, has offered priceless advice and guidance. And absolutely none of this would have been possible without the support of my parents, Benny and Sue Lee, who've always encouraged me to do my best. My family has seen me in my most embarrassing fashion victim stages through the years—I also thank them for not showing anyone all those old pictures.

And I thank my lucky stars that I have the love and support of my boyfriend Erwin, who put up with my late nights, daytime pajamas, and writer's mood swings for a year. I consider him my silent partner on this book for the unbelievable insight he's given me not only about topics in the book but also about life itself.

Introduction

Fashion makes fools of some, sinners of others, and slaves of all.
—Josh Billings, nineteenth-century humorist

She'd taken a whirl in the style blender, and it wasn't pretty. The glass door to a bank in midtown Manhattan swung open, and out she strolled . . . a sturdy redhead of about thirty-five, whose look reflected her apparent belief that the more trends you pile on your body the better. I counted four: detachable faux-fur collar, leather pants, multicolored snakeskin boots, and the real showstopper, a sequined cowboy hat, all of which made for an amalgam on a par with taking different colors of Play-Doh and mashing them together. Two tourists—who presumably hadn't beheld anything quite as flashy since the matinee of *Cabaret* at Studio 54 the day before—snickered and pointed as she walked by.

Now, *that's* a Fashion Victim, I thought as I passed her. But as I continued on my way, the question struck me: Was I any better? I mentally scanned my own outfit—cashmere Calvin Klein turtleneck, black pants I'd impulse-bought at Club Monaco the weekend before, pointy ankle boots with a three-inch heel and viselike toe box that shortened my stride to baby steps, and a tiny Fendi bag, a holiday present from my editor-in-chief at *Mademoiselle,* just roomy enough to accommodate a lipstick and bundle of four keys (but not five). In the days and weeks that followed, I began to realize that I—like everyone around me—was a Fashion Victim. I may not have been decked out in head-to-toe animal prints or swathed in huge designer decals, but I was just as guilty of bowing to fashion as the Play-Doh woman at the bank.

But how could I help it? We're a society hooked on—and bombarded with—fashion. Style, once a commodity reserved for the elite, is being marketed to the masses at an ever-quickening pace. In 2000, once-pricey designer Mossimo struck an exclusive deal with Target, the cool consumer's Kmart, which will sell one billion dollars' worth of his clothes over the next three years. The late Carrie Donovan, who spent decades hobnobbing with upper-echelon designers like Giorgio Armani and Christian Lacroix as fashion editor of the *New York Times,* became better known as "that lady with the glasses" thanks to her TV spots for Old Navy. And fêted supermodels like Gisele Bündchen (who can command up to $30,000 per runway show) now grace millions of mailboxes courtesy of catalogs like Victoria's Secret, a medium once viewed strictly as busywork for the modeling B-List. Today, even the least knowledgeable consumers know the names Valentino, Dior, and Versace if they watch the Oscar preshows, or Jimmy Choo, Manolo Blahnik, and Fendi if they watch *Sex and the City*. Fashion has not only begun to meld with the mainstream, it *is* the mainstream.

We're crazy about fashion . . . literally. Rational people are driven to near lunacy in their pursuit of style. You can see it in the eyes of shoppers as they tussle for designer bargains at New York's legendary Barney's Warehouse Sale. You can hear it in the grumbling stomachs of dieting men and women on the quest for the perfect body. And you can smell it on the wrists of fashionistas who dutifully buy a designer's perfume solely for the name on the bottle. You can feel it every time you cram your feet into uncomfortable shoes and tell the salesperson, "I'll take them."

WHO IS A FASHION VICTIM?

By most accepted definitions, a Fashion Victim is someone who fol-
lows trends slavishly, a person who is not necessarily captivated by the
beauty of a new garment so much as by the mere novelty of it and the
social standing it conveys. In everyday life, the people we typically
refer to as Fashion Victims are tagged as such for one simple reason:
they don't look good. The Fashion Victim is the balding small-town
male hairdresser who pours himself into tight leather pants, wild
imported silk shirts, and fluorescent-green alligator boots; the
bulbous-bellied talk-show guest in stripper-esque spandex who slaps
her own behind while howling, "I look *good*"; the high school typing
teacher still stuck in her disco youth with wide polyester lapel,
mushroom-printed shirt, and high-waisted flares; the A-List actress
who struts down the red carpet at the Oscars in a pair of unflattering
bike shorts (somewhere in Idaho, Demi Moore is *still* embarrassed).
We catch one glimpse of these misguided souls and can't help but proclaim them Fashion Victims. But these eyesores aren't the only ones
who deserve the label.

One day, on a sidewalk in Manhattan's Nolita shopping district,
an ultra-hip neighborhood nook lined with cafés and cutesy boutiques, a chic twentysomething walked out in front of me dressed
entirely in Burberry plaid, from her bucket cap to her jacket to her
skirt, right down to her shoes. She was the type of girl nearly anyone
who laid eyes on would agree was cool, although being wrapped in the
trademark checks was obvious overkill. In the same way that fashion
darlings like Chloë Sevigny and Kate Moss can pull off outfits that
would make a good number of other people look foolish, this girl made
it work. Did she look good? Yes. Was she still a raging Fashion Victim?
Absolutely. The point is: We are all slaves to fashion . . . some just do a
better job of conforming to the socially accepted norms of good taste.

The Fashion Victim is all around us. The Hollywood starlet who's
personally dressed by Donatella Versace is no less a Fashion Victim
than the small-town salesgirl who hops on every fad at her local JC
Penney. The genteel lady in the Chanel suit toting her toy poodle in his
Louis Vuitton carrier is no less a Fashion Victim than the Japanese

teen swathed in full-body Dolce & Gabbana with ankle socks and white pumps. The Latin crooner in the long Armani jacket and collarless shirt is no less an offender than the club kid squeezed into silver pleather pants and sparkly jacket. The hipster with the Prada sneakers and Hermès bag is no less a Fashion Victim than the soccer mom with the faux snakeskin pants and bad Fendi knockoff.

A Fashion Victim is anyone who has ever looked back at old pictures and cringed—a reflex induced by the realization that fashion at some point in their lives had been able to manipulate their brain waves with some sort of ninja mind control. It's anyone who has ever worn a scratchy sweater, tight jeans, a stiff collar, or unyielding shoes just because it looked good. It's anyone who owns more clothing than they reasonably need (I'd venture to guess that this includes about 99.9 percent of you reading right now). But most of all, Fashion Victims are people who, no matter how many frustrations they can list about fashion—the cost, the tyranny of style, the ridiculousness of trends—heartily continue to play along.

All this being said, fashion is not some mighty force that sweeps over us, leaving us incapable of making rational decisions. Throughout history, people—women, in particular—have been regarded as slaves of fashion, whose concern with dress branded them as vain or foolish. Modern theorists have put forth the image of malleable consumers pushed in certain directions by an oppressive fashion system, and even today, there's a tinge of shame associated with caring too much about fashion. In the August 2002 issue of *Vogue,* Chloë Sevigny—upon seeing a dress with a leaping stallion across the front at a 1930s costume-design exhibit—remarked, "How Stella McCartney," adding, "it's so sad that I know that." But for the most part, we are far from being defenseless victims. On the contrary, we are Fashion Victims by our own volition—style masochists, if you will. We jump into the sometimes ridiculous world of fashion head first. Even an article of clothing as excruciating as the corset was not something thrust upon unsuspecting wearers. For years, fashion historians referred to the tight-laced garments as a sort of torture chamber imposed on women by men in the wicked hopes of making them quite literally the weaker sex. But as Valerie Steele argues in her book *The Corset: A Cultural History,* it was actually a tool women willingly used to make themselves *more* powerful. Likewise, the modern woman who dresses in slinky minis and low-cut blouses isn't necessarily succumbing to the masculine power structure, but may instead be exerting her own feminine force through self-expression.

Why do we allow ourselves to be taken in by such ridiculousness? "Fashion is a constant search for the perfect look," says Marilyn Kirschner, editor-in-chief of *The Look On-Line* and former senior market editor of *Harper's Bazaar*. "Each season we can reinvent ourselves, and achieve our own degree of perfection. It's also about being 'brainwashed.' Fashion intimidates us into thinking we never look good enough, are never adequate enough until that new thing comes along: Prada show, Gucci bag, Chanel jacket, YSL peasant blouse. And in a few months—presto change-O—it's something else."

There's little question as to why fashion has become such a huge part of our lives. After all, our clothing is one of the few things we can readily change about ourselves. Our clothes are visible symbols of who we are and who we want to be. Just take a look at your shoe collection one day. Lisa Greenstein of El Cerrito, California, paints still-life portraits of people's shoes as visual representations of their personalities. The shoes we buy—sexy, athletic, comfy, quirky—speak volumes about us, she says. Nearly every piece of your wardrobe can do the same: Are you a free spirit? A trend junkie? An uptown society girl? An artsy Bohemian? The styles and labels we wear reveal our membership in certain groups. A jacket is not just a jacket, but also a lifestyle ingredient. As Ralph Lauren once said, "I don't design clothes. I design dreams." When a man buys the flat-front linen Regent pant and Yarmouth shirt in gingham twill from the Polo store, he's not just buying an outfit; he's buying an attitude. Another reason that fashion has lured so many avid followers over the years is that it's an attractive world associated with glamour—a fusion of art, entertainment, and business, all rolled into one. We're drawn to the sheer excitement of everything we think it stands for.

Fashion is built on contradictions. It's fun, but frustrating. It's creative, but commercial. Fashion brings people closer together, but also drives them farther apart. It can make us feel beautiful—or ugly when we can't live up to the established ideals. Fashion makes us strive to attain more, but it also makes us think about everything we *don't* have. Thanks to these contradictions, most of us harbor a love-hate attitude toward clothing. We love how a nice outfit can brighten our mood one day, but hate the frustration of having "nothing to wear" the next. We love shopping for clothes to relieve stress, but hate looking at our credit card statements at the end of the month. We love how high heels make our legs look, but hate covering our blisters with Band-Aids the next morning. Fashion, as enjoyable as it can be at times, often highlights how warped society's priorities can be. Today, being well dressed can elevate a person to mythic proportions. How many times have we seen a so-so actress rise to the rank of screen idol simply because she shows up to events in designer gowns? On the flip side, fabulously talented people are sometimes swept aside because they don't play the fashion game. Unglamorous Sissy Spacek, for instance, gave a knockout performance in the 2001 film *In the Bedroom*, but her presence on the red carpet at every awards show was severely overshadowed by her couture-wearing competitors.

For all the crazy things fashion encourages us to do, many of us simply accept the directions it steers us in without questioning why it carries so much weight in our lives. We have the power to change how we feel about our clothes, but we rarely do it. Can't stand swimsuit shopping? Then why buy a new one every year? Hate exorbitant price tags? Then why continue to spend so much money? Tired of seeing everyone wearing the same clothes you see in stores? Why shop at the mall? Frustrated by the pace at which handbag shapes come and go? Why snatch up the latest styles? Sick of rail-thin models and celebrities in magazine layouts? Then why subscribe to three different fashion glossies?

This year, the average American will spend $1,729 on clothing, racking up more than $200 billion in annual sales for the industry. That same average Joe (or Josephine) will make four trips to the mall each month (interestingly, the same number of times the average American has sex per month). Hundreds of millions of people around the world buy clothes every year. They'll spend a good chunk of their mornings pondering which pants to pair with which shirts, but few ever truly contemplate their own motives for having those clothes in the first place,

Millions of research dollars are poured into understanding the basic human drives of hunger, thirst, sex, and security, but what about the drive to be fashionable, which in some people is just as strong? It's not as though fashion is something that's easily overlooked; in fact we seem to have formed a dysfunctional bond with it. Our modern-day hunger for more clothes and the latest trends, together with the premium we put on looking good, has undermined our self-esteem, our health, the environment, our finances, our morals—but we continue to be more ravenous than ever.

The purpose of this book is to examine how fashion has become enmeshed in our everyday lives and to illuminate the many ways it has affected society, both good and bad. While I cast a critical eye on the industry and on the concept of fashion itself, I certainly don't undervalue the ways in which fashion enriches our lives. Who can deny that a bride glows ten times brighter when she's wearing her dream gown? (When my boyfriend and I get married, we're going to register for gifts at Gucci—who needs silverware and fancy china when you can have leather loafers and finely crafted Italian pants?) Fashion has also contributed aesthetic beauty and extraordinary art to the world. Many designers, like Vivienne Westwood and John Galliano, are artists who happen to work with the medium of fabric on bodies. And clothes serve the purpose of memorializing many wonderful times in our lives—the dress you wore on the day you met the love of your life, the fuzzy yellow jumper your child toddled around in when he took his first step, the outfit you were wearing the day someone asked, "Aren't you that famous model?" My father's favorite shirt in the 1970s was a cornflower-blue T-shirt with his name, "Benny," ironed on the front. To this day, the mere thought of that shirt makes me smile.

. . .

Clothing itself has been around in one form or another since early man wrapped himself in animal pelts. Fashion, on the other hand, is a slightly more modern invention, though not as novel a concept as once believed. In 1999, three anthropologists reexamined the "Venus" figurines, the portly six-inch statuettes of female bodies carved up to 27,000 years ago that are believed to be the world's oldest surviving works of art created in the human image. Through careful inspection, the researchers found evidence that the women of the Upper Paleolithic era may have worn caps, belts, skirts, and rather stylish bandeaux fashioned out of a woven, linenlike cloth, offering groundbreaking evidence that the taste for fashion as well as function dates back to the Ice Age. Over time, people began to use their attire as a means of communication—and often exclusion—rather than just for warmth and protection. By the European Renaissance, dress had evolved into a fully developed art form and status symbol. Restrictive corsets, stiff fabrics, and high heels painted an accurate picture of their wearer: he or she clearly didn't work . . . and didn't *have* to work. By the late nineteenth century, ready-to-wear had begun to take the place of tailor-made clothing and removed many boundaries between the classes—what some call the democratization of fashion.

Today, dress is still used to some extent to distinguish groups—rich/poor, liberal/conservative, hip/unhip—only the dividing lines have blurred. The ostentation still exists, just not always in the same overt way. Some of the most stripped-down, minimalist clothing, like Prada and Helmut Lang, is now among the most expensive and coveted. Haute couture, while highly ogled, caters to less than two thousand buyers worldwide (some argue less than one thousand), only two hundred of whom are regular customers. Although designer originals are still restricted to the wealthy, those designs now serve as templates for numerous knockoffs sold to the masses—a practice that has further watered down the separation of upper- and lower-class style. With $30 imitations arriving in stores at the same time as $500 originals, the difference between the two begins to dissipate. This widespread accessibility to fashion for the general populace has opened the way to an era in which the trend rules—a time when even the most ridiculous fads have an opportunity to shine.

Today, trends don't just trickle down, they *gush*. Technological advances in manufacturing, along with increased media attention to fashion, now make it possible for trends to spread within days, creating a new attitude within the fashion community—one of Speed Chic. This accelerated time frame has created a perpetual cycle of flash trends. As nineteenth-century writer Marie von Ebner-Eschenbach once wrote, "So soon as a fashion is universal, it is out of date." Only today, a trend doesn't need to go global before becoming outmoded. While the trends of yesteryear lasted several seasons before fizzling out, today's wear out their welcome within a matter of months or even weeks. The fedora, for example, experienced a surge in popularity in late 2001. After the classic hat was featured prominently in several music videos and then in Banana Republic's fall ad campaign, a few Fashion Victims scooped them up early on. But by the time most consumers saw the hats in stores, the trend was already nearly dead.

The speed of trends hasn't snowballed without wreaking a little havoc along the way. Consumers, swept up in a sort of collective insanity, are driven to purchase merchandise they have no rational use for. Still, as much as they spend, they can't shake the frustration of never being able to keep up with the trend treadmill. What's more, we're so busy going with the flow that we never develop our own personal style. Instead, we've become a culture of copycats, always letting the current carry us to and fro without sticking our necks out and testing truly provocative looks. As Marc Berger, fashion director of *GQ*, once lamented to me, "Dressing well is a lost art."

One of the greatest strengths of fashion is its ability to make the ridiculous seem hopelessly cool. Through fashion's tutelage, we adopt and make mockeries of looks that were once associated with social and political statements. Any woman who bought a $400 "Bohemian" dress or blouse when the look was all the rage in 2002 was essentially going against what it meant to be a Bohemian. Likewise, the grunge and punk movements were based on individuality, low income, and the drive against commercialism. Yet the fashion world reinterpreted the styles of both groups and spit out a series of expensive combat boots, flannel shirts, leather jackets, and rock T-shirts at consumers. The poor pioneers of punk, whose subversive style, recycled, has appeared on many a modern mall-going teenager in the form of baby tees that say "Punk Rocker" in silver glitter. The same kind of thing has happened to nearly every major social group. Being a hippie in the sixties wasn't simply about bell-bottoms and peasant tops, just as being a beatnik wasn't only about wearing a black turtleneck. At some point, dressing in these ways was an honest, pure, and uncontrived expression of a way of life, a shared attitude. And the fashion industry diminishes the value of those beliefs by reducing them to mere fashion statements.

With so many new trends circulating, you'd think there would at least be some variety in dress. But the offerings available to most people are sadly homogeneous, and in fact only a handful of mass-market retailers sell a majority of the clothes. One Saturday morning, I was flipping through TV channels when I landed on a "Bollywood" movie, one of those kitschy, feel-good Indian musicals with the elaborate song and dance numbers. The women, singing in high-pitched Hindi, were dressed in matching orange saris, except for the film's female star, who was wearing a gossamer black one. Some of the men were bare chested, wearing only exotic black sarongs. The sets, choreography, songs, makeup, jewelry—all spoke of Indian culture. Then, the camera broke away to a scene of the two lead characters frolicking hand in hand and singing on a grassy hill—the woman in her black sari, the man in a navy blue hooded sweatshirt with the word *GAP* emblazoned across the front. Traditional ethnic costume had sadly been replaced by a boring assembly-line hoodie.

Today, mass-market retailers have reached nearly every nook and cranny of the globe. Over eighteen thousand clothes makers (not to mention countless importers) and eighteen hundred enclosed shopping malls feed our hunger for fashion in the U.S. In the late 1990s and into the new millennium, new Gap stores were opening at a rate of one per day. The proliferation of standardized mass-market fashion around the world mirrors that of McDonald's, creating something I call McFashion. (It's interesting that longtime Gap CEO Millard Drexler, who retired in 2002, goes by the nickname Mickey, as in Mickey D. Coincidence?) Thanks to McFashion, safe, socially acceptable style can be effortlessly obtained by nearly anyone around the world. But on the downside, McFashion stores, like McDonald's restaurants, have spread across the globe, rubbing out regional and cultural looks and replacing them with homogeneous ones. In the past

two decades, fashion has increasingly moved downmarket to accommodate this more lucrative mass-market segment. Discount chains
like Target and Wal-Mart are reaping the benefits. After many successful partnerships like those of Mossimo and Todd Oldham with Target,
and Joe Boxer at Kmart, established designers are actually pursuing
the *retailers*, not the other way around. "We get calls every week,"
Michael Francis, senior vice president of marketing at Target, told the
Wall Street Journal in 2002. In 2000, discounters' apparel sales reached
about sixty billion dollars, a 15 percent increase over 1998, according
to the International Mass Retail Association.

For the average consumer today, partaking of fashion is the
equivalent of buying an Eiffel Tower souvenir at Epcot Center instead
of buying one in Paris. It's what Tang is to orange juice; what Las
Vegas's Venetian Hotel is to Venice—a watered-down, manufactured
experience that's slightly removed from the real thing. Shoppers can
feel like they're participating in fashion even though it's in a dumbed-
down form. Shopping for clothes today is entertainment, a national
pastime, even a tourist attraction. The Mall of America, nestled like a
gargantuan shrine to consumerism on seventy-eight acres in
Bloomington, Minnesota, attracts forty-two million people a year—
more annual visitors than Disney World, Graceland, and the Grand
Canyon combined. Twelve states rank malls among their top three
tourist attractions.

Even if a consumer never took a conscious interest in fashion,
he or she would still learn by osmosis. Fashion and media have
merged, creating a form of veiled advertising. We can't ignore trends
because they're all around us. Designers have become celebrities;
celebrities have become designers. Fashion's popularity has been
fueled significantly by its bond with Hollywood, which has produced a
multitude of television programs like MTV's *House of Style*, E!'s *Fashion
File*, the offerings on the Style Network, and CNN's venerated but can-
celed *Style with Elsa Klensch*, which broadcast a steady stream of fashion into people's homes. In the mid-1990s, celebrities officially
replaced supermodels as the most sought-after faces for magazine
covers and solidified their status as the world's fashion icons. When
Sharon Stone boldly arrived on the red carpet at the 1996 Oscars in a

Gap mock turtleneck, she caused more of a splash than she would have had she shown up in full designer regalia. And when ubiquitous hipster fashion muse Chloë Sevigny was photographed wearing a gray thrift-store sweatshirt while seated in the audience at a fall 2000 runway show, fashionistas didn't retch at the sight . . . they praised the schlumpy look as a chic new trend ("What can *we* pair with a sweatshirt?" they pondered). Famous fashion plates like Madonna, Gwyneth Paltrow, and Julia Roberts can not only *afford* to dress well, they get a lot of clothes for free. Designers court stars for months before big events to persuade them to wear their gowns and tuxedos, making awards shows as much about fashion as they are about the winners. Furthermore, with the popularity of paparazzi shots in much of the media today, designers have realized that outfitting stars every day—not just for special events—can be a beneficial way of displaying their clothes. This may have made Hollywood more fashionable, but it's also created a potentially dangerous form of real-life product placement, in which sneaky advertising messages are being pitched to us at all times.

Being surrounded 24/7 by fashion is bound to have consequences. One of the most visible social problems that fashion has contributed to is warped body image. The link between fashion and body image has always been somewhat of a chicken-and-egg debate. (Did corsets create the tiny-waist ideal? Or did the tiny-waist ideal create corsets?) In a 1995 *Psychology Today* study, just three minutes spent looking at models in a fashion magazine caused 70 percent of the subjects to feel depressed, guilty, and shameful. In Britain, where an estimated 1.15 million people suffer from eating disorders, the government actually ordered an official investigation in 2000 to determine if it should order a countrywide ban on skinny models. To make things worse, consumers are now given mixed messages—the same industry that presents thinness as the beauty ideal turns around and tells them to "Love Your Body." Fashion ideals and real body shapes have butted heads for centuries, but now more than at any other time in history, people are turning to drastic measures. Today, Americans spend $34 billion annually on weight-loss products and services. Liposuction procedures increased 118 percent between 1991 and 2001 in the U.S. and are on the rise in nearly every other country, including Great Britain, Korea, Brazil, South Africa, and Austria.

Most experts agree that fashion is not the sole cause of distorted body image but that it can influence a person who already has low self-esteem. Fashion's true power, though, lies in the fact that the Fashion Victim is fully aware of this but, instead of fighting against it, continues to buy into the insanity. Fashion not only makes us self-conscious about our size but also makes us catty about others' skinniness—in tearing them down we hope to make ourselves feel better. We mope when styles don't suit our body shapes and pout when sizes don't fit, but instead of turning away from fashion, we self-medicate our moods with the thing that made us miserable in the first place: we go shopping.

Fashion is a self-centered pursuit—it makes us think about ourselves rather than others. This Me-Me-Me mentality has had major effects on the global economy and on people around the world. Compared to all the money that's spent to buy clothing, the amount that the workers who make those garments receive is notoriously little. Take a look at the tags on five items of clothing in your closet one day and see where they came from. Chances are, your wardrobe is far worldlier than you are. Over the past forty years, thanks to free-trade agreements, clothing manufacturers have fled the U.S. at a staggering pace. The reason for their departure? The constant search for lower prices to satisfy the Fashion Victim's hunger for inexpensive trends and—you guessed it—Speed Chic, that driving force behind fashion's accelerating fickleness. The flight of manufacturers from our shores has not only harmed the U.S. economy but also hastened the race to the bottom of the pay scale, effectively driving workers' wages down even more. The numbers are shocking: the average American garment worker earns $7 per hour, according to the Bureau of Labor Statistics, compared to 15¢ per hour for workers in Indonesia. But clothing companies argue that they couldn't afford to change operations without drastically increasing prices for consumers. And while surveys show that American shoppers would be willing to pay an extra dollar for a $20 garment if they could be assured that it wasn't made in a sweatshop, consumers tend to be far more generous when they're talking about hypothetical money than when they're reaching into their wallets. One might question how ready average shoppers truly are to part with their hard-earned money for the sake of sewing-machine operators in distant countries.

Average consumers are blissfully unaware of where clothes come from. Most have never heard the gruesome tales of how New York garment workers suffered intimidation, beatings, and even murder at the hands of the mob starting in the 1930s. For nearly three-quarters of a century, La Cosa Nostra's grip on the city's once-burgeoning Garment Center strangled business, causing hikes in retail prices and stimulating the exit of many manufacturers to foreign lands.

Just as fashion blinds us to the plight of those who make our clothes, it also renders us careless about other things, including our own health and safety. Fashion through the years has driven people to do some pretty outlandish things. According to David Louis's *2201 Fascinating Facts*, some women in eighteenth-century England wore wigs that were up to four feet high and matted with lard, often attracting mice and insects. Special pillows had to be constructed to hold these giant creations, and rat-resistant caps made of gilt wire were common. For centuries, Fashion Victims have squeezed their bodies into garments that don't fit properly for the sake of style, from corsets and girdles to tight acid-washed jeans. Controversial studies have blamed tight clothing for a variety of health problems, including infertility, endometriosis, indigestion, and even cancer. And who can overlook the pain and danger women put up with for cute shoes? Several fatal accidents caused by platform shoes spurred some cities in Japan to prohibit wearing "skyscraper shoes" while driving. Countless women have taken nasty spills teetering down the sidewalk on stiltlike high heels and have damaged their feet from squeezing into too-tight shoes. Podiatrists say that the deformities seen in women's feet today from high heels are similar to those seen in the grisly X-rays of Chinese women who'd had their feet bound. Does it stop us? Not a chance.

Ugly trends may turn your stomach at times but who ever thought clothes could literally make you ill? Our voracious appetite for fashion has created the need for a massive garment-manufacturing industry, and the proliferation of major industrial sites poses environmental and health concerns. Even those cool thrift and vintage clothes we're snagging for that retro-cool look may be giving us more than we bargained for. A recent report by the Panafrican News Agency warned that millions of people might be exposing themselves to serious health problems including scabies, radioactivity, ringworm, skin infections, and tuberculosis, by wearing secondhand clothes without washing them. Chemicals that are used to make textiles wrinkle free and solvents used to clean stains put workers at risk and pollute water and air. The dry-cleaning solvent perchlorethylene (perc) was recently classified as a probable human carcinogen by the International Agency for Research on Cancer and has been linked to a whole host of health problems, including breast cancer and liver and kidney damage, yet is still used by 85 percent of dry cleaners in the U.S. Most of us have heard about the possible health risks but inexplicably weigh the pros of crisp, clean dry-cleaned clothes as higher than the cons.

Fashion shields us from our own common sense. It also has the uncanny ability to brainwash us into overlooking our moral convictions. Fur fell out of vogue after the 1980s, no doubt fueled in part by animal activists' attacks on fur wearers but mostly because skins had simply fallen out of vogue. In 1988 there were more than a thousand mink farms in the U.S. By 1997, there were about half that number. But in the late 1990s, fur began to make a comeback, showing up in a number of fashion shows, not just as coats but also as decorative trim on everything from dresses to shoes. Suddenly, Fashion Victims who considered themselves moderately anti-fur were faced with the difficult choice between following fashion or their consciences—and in many cases, fashion won. Supermodel Naomi Campbell, a spokesperson for People for the Ethical Treatment of Animals (PETA) in the early 1990s, now wears fur and has publicly criticized PETA. Leather, while historically less disputed than fur, since most of it comes from farming by-products, has also been the focus of greater attention in recent years. In 2000, PETA protesters convinced the Gap to stop using leather from cows that are cruelly killed for the black market in India. Still, sales of leather apparel grew about 8.5 percent in 2001—twice the rate of regular apparel, according to market research firm NPD Group.

The animal rights versus fashion debate has grown uglier in recent years. Anti-fur protests have escalated to assaults on fur farms and related businesses, costing millions of dollars in property damage. But the shocking stories seem only to strengthen the pro-fur side, as it launches multimillion-dollar PR and marketing campaigns to gain public support. The more that fur is promoted as cool, the more Fashion Victims grasp at straws, rationalizing actions they believe deep down to be wrong. Fur's inclusion in this book is less a sign of fur's renewed popularity than it is evidence of fashion's power to make sure that fur keeps popping up as an issue in the first place. Whether wearing fur is actually right or wrong seems to get lost in the shuffle.

Under fashion's spell, our vision of right and wrong blurs. Like good art, fashion is often best when it pushes the envelope. But it sometimes crosses the line, offending individuals, groups, religions, even entire cultures. Some innocent political incorrectness that upsets a few overly sensitive people is understandable. But what should we think of a company that makes money by exploiting a belief or symbol that a group of people holds dear?—for instance, the designer who prints a drawing of the Buddha on the backside of jeans. When Buddhists protest that this is disrespectful to their religion, should the company be forced to remove its product from stores? Who decides who's right and wrong when fashion offends?

. . .

Today, fashion isn't reserved simply for those who seek it out. It's entered into nearly every facet of life. Airports in Europe, once relegated to junky duty-free stores that sold tobacco and perfume, now house upscale fashion retailers like Gucci, Chanel, Hugo Boss, DKNY, Gaultier, and Bally. Versace, Todd Oldham, and the Italian luxury jeweler Bulgari have forged business ties with hotels. During Paris Fashion Week in January 2002, Vertu, the world's first-ever luxury mobile-phone company, introduced its line of handmade cell phones adorned with platinum, gold, precious stones, and steel, priced at over $20,000 apiece for the seriously moneyed Fashion Victim. Fashion will even follow us into outerspace: Throughout 2000, Donatella Versace was involved in negotiations to pay the Russian space program $750,000 for the opportunity to design new space suits for cosmonauts. (The deal never came through, but can't you just imagine astronauts floating through the solar system in gold suits with mink collars?) We move through our lives, blissfully unaware and content to play the role of consumer and disciple.

And who ever said you can't take it with you? In ancient Egypt, the dead were often buried with their finest possessions, including clothing, so they would have plenty to wear in the afterlife. In Iceland, hunters found the remains of eight mummies buried since 1475 with seventy-eight items of clothing for their journey to the other side. And upon the death of Madame Xin Zhui, the Marquise of Dai, who lived some 2,100 years ago in Han Dynasty China, she was entombed with forty-nine articles of exquisite clothing to ensure that her stay in the next world was a fashionable one (talk about overpacking). So when our time here ends and we leave this world as lifelong Fashion Victims, we'll enter the next . . . and fashion will no doubt make us crazy there, too.

1

The Fashion Victim's Ten Commandments

We Fashion Victims hold certain truths to be self-evident. Without so much as a raised eyebrow, we allow a set of ridiculous, yet compelling, rules to govern our wardrobes, our purchases, our desires, even our own sense of self-worth. It's these unquestioned tenets that have helped bring us to the sorry state we find ourselves in today.

❶

THOU SHALT PAY MORE TO APPEAR POOR

It takes a great deal of time and money to look as though you put no effort into dressing. Since a garment today rarely remains a popular item in our wardrobes beyond a few months, we require it to be worn out before we buy it. Fabrics are prewashed and grayed out to appear less new. Designers sew on decorative patches, slash gaping holes into the knees of jeans, and fray the hems. Dresses and shirts are prewrinkled. Jeans are stonewashed, sandblasted, acid-washed, and lightened; they're iron-creased and bleached to "whisker" at the upper-thigh as if they were passed down to you by your mother, who inherited them

1

from her father, who had worn them in the wheat fields a century ago. Designers add "character" to clothes by messing them up, like Helmut Lang's famous $270 paint-spattered jeans. Jeans, blasted and stained dust-brown, by CK, Levi's, and Dolce & Gabbana, cost up to $200. In fact, Calvin Klein's "dirty" jeans sold for $20 more than a pair of his basic, unblemished ones. In 2001, Commes des Garçons produced a peasant dress, priced at a very unpeasantlike $495, described by discount shopping website Bluefly.com as "given a chic tattered look."

Fashion may be bent on newness, but we apparently can't stand it when something looks *too* new (who can bear the blinding whiteness of new sneakers?). The industry has taken to calling the shabby, imperfect look "distressed"—a word that carries a connotation of pain and suffering. This fashion agony doesn't come cheap, from Jean-Paul Gaultier's distressed leather pants for $1,560 and two-piece distressed leather jacket and bustier for $2,740 to Versace's distressed ball gowns and midpriced shoe maker Aldo's distressed leather pumps for $70.

On most new clothes, a flaw is reason to return a garment to the store; on others, it's a reason to love the garment with even more fervor. The Fashion Victim understands that ready-to-wear clothes are mostly mass produced, and that a handsewn article somehow possesses more soul and uniqueness. Minute blemishes in a fabric's color prove that a gown was hand-dipped by a dressmaker in Paris; slightly raised threads on a vest attest that it was handcrafted by the real wives of authentic sherpas in Nepal. Some clothes, like a sweater I bought years ago, come with tags explaining how the pills and flecks you may see in the fabric are not flaws at all but rather intentional imperfections, there to add to the garment's charm.

In our hunt for substance in style, we covet clothes that evoke the blue-collar world, like the Authentic Prison Blues shirts (actually made by inmates!) that Bruce Willis and Billy Bob Thornton wore in the 2001 movie *Bandits*. Why do we do it? Fashion is our way of visually signaling to others how we want to be seen, and even though we all want to be considered stylish, we don't want to look like we've put too much planning and money into doing so. Glamour and neatness have their place, but premeditated nonchalance is the Fashion Victim's

Holy Grail. We shop at stores like Filthmart, the Manhattan vintage store co-owned by Drea de Matteo of *The Sopranos* and featuring Hell's Angels–meets–Jewel wares. Hip-hop fans spend exorbitant amounts of cash on urbanwear to prove they're still "street": a pair of denim and Ultrasuede pants from Phat Farm for $150, an Enyce "bulletproof" nylon vest for $97, puffy down jackets from the North Face for $199. Even a simple wifebeater tank top can sell for over $100 if it has the right label. We buy peasant blouses at faux-boho Anthropologie because we want to look like we churn butter on a farm in Provence, or grungy $80 pants at Urban Outfitters to show our downtown cool. For his fall 2002 Marc by Marc Jacobs show, Jacobs sent models down the runway in mismatched grandma knits, oversized seventies scarves, rainbow-striped sweaters, jeans, and corduroys—the ultimate home-grown poor-girl look for the woman who has everything. In early 2000, John Galliano took the dressed-down look one step further: he stunned the fashion crowd in Paris with his Homeless Chic couture show for Christian Dior, featuring models draped in torn clothes held together by string and strewn with kitchen utensils and miniature liquor bottles.

In the world of the Fashion Victim, shopping at a thrift store is cool . . . unless you're actually on welfare and have to buy *all* your clothes there. Some hard-core fashionistas insist they only shop second hand. But it's usually not all from the buck-a-pound bin at the local thrift store. In recent years, designers like Imitation of Christ who rework vintage and thrift have become hip. The Fashion Victim drools over these born-again garments, which still possess some of the old, dirty charm but at twenty times the price. Today, even the mere implication that a garment is old can suffice. Gap and Abercrombie & Fitch have pilfered the word "vintage" for use on their fresh-from-the-factory shirts and jeans to suggest classic style. Are we really fooled by a crisp new T-shirt that spells Gap Vintage in faded letters?

Today, it's fun to think you're shopping downmarket. "Cheap chic" stores like H&M, Target, Japan's Uniqlo, and Spain's Mango have made fortunes in recent years selling cut-rate trends. But no true fashionista worth her salt would buy her entire wardrobe at one of these stores, so she engages in cheap chic in her own way, to the point at which "cheap" becomes a completely relative term. Moschino's lower-priced line, called Moschino Cheap & Chic, is far from cheap for most shoppers. A "Leopard" coat and scarf retails for $1,340, and a Petal Trim Sweater for $615. Frugality at its finest, indeed.

❷
THOU SHALT COVET USELESS UTILITY

To the Fashion Victim, there's nothing wrong with clothes that serve no purpose other than looking cool. But if a garment can create the illusion that it's functional as well, it's all the better. A part of us knows that fashion is frivolous, so we attempt to justify our participation in it by making our clothes seem useful. We're grasping at straws to rationalize making some of our unnecessary purchases. Shirts come with hoods whose sole purpose is to hang behind one's neck. The polar fleece vest was pitched as functional in a climbing-the-Alps sort of way, but if you really wanted something to keep you warm, wouldn't you give it sleeves? Cargo pants, with their multitude of pockets, seemed infinitely useful . . . imagine all the odds and ends you could carry. Countless designers, including Calvin Klein, Gucci, and Versace, interpreted the military style for the runway, and mall retailers followed suit with their versions, like Abercrombie's Paratroops and American Eagle's Cargo Trek Pant. Ralph Lauren even produced an army-green cargo bikini with pockets at the hip (for toting beach grenades?). The fashion world's idealized image of the utilitarian future appears to involve lots of zippers, buckles, Velcro, pull closures, straps, and strings—no matter if they actually serve a purpose or not.

Judging by the creations we've seen of late, fashions of the future won't serve just one purpose—they'll serve purposes we never knew needed serving. In 2001, women's magazines touted a new pair of panty hose that dispense a tiny bit of lotion onto the legs with each wearing. The Fuji Spinning Company in Japan has developed a T-shirt and lace underwear that will give wearers their daily dose of vitamin C. Newly developed shirts can monitor vital signs like heart rate and breathing patterns by using optical fibers that send and receive electrical impulses. For years, techies have drooled over the advent of "smart clothes," ultramodern garments with fully operational computers implanted in them. The first samples, furnished with round-the-clock Internet access, have been revealed in fashion shows at tech conferences, with models wearing headset microphones and built-in keyboard sleeves. For all the innovation that's been shoveled into fashion, you'd think inventors would be able to come up with something truly useful—like snag-proof cashmere sweaters. Is that so much to ask?

③

THOU SHALT OWN MINUTELY DIFFERING
VARIATIONS OF THE SAME THING

At least part of the Fashion Victim's closet looks like that of a cartoon character, with rows of essentially identical items hanging next to one another. There are multiple pairs of sneakers: a pair for running, a pair for walking, a pair for shopping, a pair for going out, a pair for jeans, a pair for shorts. Then there are the multiple pairs of black pants: wide-legged, skinny-legged, fitted, baggy, flat-front, zipper, button-fly, pleated, wool, stretch, rayon, linen. Former Filipino first lady Imelda Marcos, who once famously defended herself by stating, "I did not have three thousand pairs of shoes, I had one thousand and sixty," surely had some overlapping styles hanging in her gigantic closet.

Fashion Victims own duplicates of items that are just different enough to not be *exactly* the same. The average American owns seven pairs of blue jeans. Certainly, each pair could be cut and colored differently, but are those seven pairs really that different? Rosa, a twenty-six-year-old office manager in Chicago, owns more than fifteen pairs of navy-blue jeans that she's amassed over the last two years, picking up one or two pairs a month. "Some are regular-waisted, some are boot-cut, others are tapered, one has red stitching on the sides and on the pockets, some are button-fly, some are a bit darker," she explains. "Even though they all look the same, they each have their special style." All that variety means she doesn't wear each pair very often. "I have a few clothes that I have in my closet that I've only worn once or twice," she says. "But it's hard to part with them because I always feel like, 'Maybe I'll wear it *one* more time.'" Fashion Victims all share in this mind-set, and as a result, we could have two walk-in closets stuffed to the gills and still never feel like we have enough. So we continue to buy.

Fashion Victims convince themselves that they need variety in their wardrobes; often they aren't aware of how similar all their clothes really are. "Many of my clients are really surprised at the end of an organizing project to learn they own five pairs of black slacks," says Debbie Williams, a personal organizing coach in Houston, Texas, and publisher of *Organized Times*. "They wouldn't dream of wearing black slacks each and every day of the work week, so having five pairs is overkill to say the least—they really could get by with two or three pairs." When the time comes that our closets begin to burst at the seams and a clean-out is necessary, we moan about the effort it takes to dispose of all our unwanted items.

Nevertheless, it's the nature of the Fashion Victim to be a clothing pack rat, to act as an apparel archivist, to collect superfluous garments for the sake of collecting superfluous garments, to fool herself into thinking she needs a new jacket—even though she already owns its lookalike.

● 4

THOU SHALT BELIEVE SUBMISSIVELY IN
THE FASHION LABEL'S REACH

Today when you buy a designer's clothes, you're also buying a lifestyle. Ralph Lauren (a.k.a. Ralph Lifschitz from the Bronx) knew this when he created Polo, a brand meant to evoke the image of the affluent, holiday-in-Hyannisport set. As a result, our favorite clothing brands can sell us practically anything else—hand cream, lipstick, perfume, nail polish, dishes, pillows, candles, duvets, music. You can not only wear Ralph Lauren, Calvin Klein, Banana Republic, Eddie Bauer, Donna Karan, Liz Claiborne, Nautica, and Versace, but you can dress your bedroom in them, too. Love how Club Monaco clothes look? Buy the retailer's line of cosmetics. Hooked on Victoria's Secret bras? Well, they must have good skin-care products if they make good bras, right? Like Armani suits? Buy their line of gourmet chocolates. Just as automakers like Jaguar, Vespa, and Harley-Davidson have their own branded clothing lines, retailers and designers have left their mark on the automotive world with special-edition cars like the Eddie Bauer Ford Explorer and Expedition, the Coach-edition Lexus, the Subaru Outback LL Bean edition, the Joseph Abboud Special Edition Buick Regal, and the Louis Vuitton edition of Chrysler's PT Cruiser.

A fashion label may be able to excel at auxiliary products, but don't always assume they're made by who you think they are. For decades, designers have known that their illustrious names alone can sell nearly anything, so they engage in multimillion-dollar licensing deals, offering their names for use by others to make and promote a variety of products. In the 1970s, designers like Valentino and Pierre Cardin began to license their names for everything from sheets to luggage to toilet-seat covers (by 1970, the House of Cardin had licensed its name for use on more than six hundred products). Donna Karan reported that its fastest growth segment was in its licensing division— including accessories, jeans, home, and bath—which grew to over a billion dollars in sales in 2000. Kenneth Cole has admitted that his company licenses out most of what it does, except for shoes and women's handbags.

Some well-known brands actually make the products of *other* well-known brands. Fossil designs, manufactures, markets, and distributes Burberry watches. Perry Ellis manufactures apparel, bags, and accessories under the Nautica label. Liz Claiborne holds the exclusive license to design and produce DKNY jeans. Estée Lauder holds exclusive licensing agreements to make fragrances for both Tommy Hilfiger and Donna Karan. Procter and Gamble, home of Noxzema, Oil of Olay, and Old Spice, also holds licenses for Hugo Boss, Giorgio, Helmut Lang, and Hervé Leger fragrances. Luxottica makes eyewear for Armani, Brooks Brothers, Anne Klein, Moschino, Ungaro, and Ferragamo. Women's outerwear for Kenneth Cole and Nine West is made by the same company—G-III Apparel, which also holds the license for Tommy Hilfiger's leather outerwear for men.

Licensing may help designers expand their businesses, but it's historically been frowned upon in the fashion world. Cardin's newfound middle-brow appeal made him the world's richest couturier but also got him booted out of the Chambre Syndicale, the exclusive supervisory body for haute couture in Paris. By the late 1990s, licensing had fallen out of favor with many luxury designers, with many like Gucci and Armani beginning to buy back their licensing agreements in an attempt to regain brand control. Then there was the much-publicized lawsuit between Calvin Klein and licensee Warnaco in 2000. In his countersuit, Klein alleged that Warnaco CEO Linda Wachner damaged his brand's image by selling to discount stores and putting his name on designs he hadn't approved. Prior to the lawsuit, an unbelievable 90 percent of Klein's revenues came from licenses. The case shed much unwanted light on the practice of licensing. Consumers fretted, "Could our designer clothes actually be made by lesser manufacturers?" Quite the contrary, say designers—licensing actually improves the quality of products, because they pair with the pros. For instance, an expert in hosiery may do a better job at creating a line of silk stockings under the designer's name than the designer could do himself. Frankly, it works both ways. A good number of licensed products are well made while others are essentially generics with designer labels slapped on them. Luckily for them, either will do just fine for the Fashion Victim.

5

THOU SHALT REQUIRE VALIDATION OF THINE OWN STYLISHNESS

I've always wondered how people felt after they appeared in one of those "On the Street" photos in the *New York Times* Sunday Styles section, taken by fashion historian/scholar/journalist Bill Cunningham, a thirty-year veteran of the paper, a man whose job it is to catch the latest fashion trends on real people on the street. Clotheshorses are snapped as they're walking to Saks during their lunch break or browsing an outdoor vendor or exiting a bistro with co-workers. Some of the subjects are unknown; others, like Ivana Trump, *Vogue* editor Anna Wintour, and socialite/painter Anh Duong are career fashion plates. Some are clearly posing for the camera; others are caught unexpectedly, typically engaging in the Manhattanite's favorite outdoor pas-time—nattering on the cell phone.

Cunningham, who camps out on the sidewalk day in and day out for up to a month just to photograph enough subjects for one story, says he never consciously goes out with a specific trend in mind. During Spring Fashion Week 2001, his discerning lens fell upon a for-mer co-worker of mine outside one of the shows as she flaunted her cute metal-studded handbag. It was perhaps the least flattering angle at which I've ever seen her, but ego stroking nonetheless, in a "you have good enough taste in bags to be in the *New York Times*" kind of way. Many "On the Street" subjects are proud to be featured there. Cunningham has photographed Patrick McDonald, a public-relations director for a dressmaker, at least a dozen times. McDonald, who keeps a book of all his clips, told *New York* magazine in 2000, "I have friends who say, 'I look in the Style section as soon as I get home from the Hamptons to see if you're in it.' "

The art of dress is quite frequently built on the opinions of oth-ers. We may like to think that how we dress is an extension of how we see ourselves, but more commonly, it's an expression of how we want *others* to see us. "We dress to communicate our social identities to oth-ers," says Kim Johnson, Ph.D., a professor at the University of Minnesota who teaches courses on the social psychology of clothing. "Dress informs others of how willing you are to participate in fashion and at what levels you're playing." In our appearance-centered society, one of the most common ways we butter up strangers and acquain-tances is to compliment them on their clothes. We shower people with praise for their sense of style and expect to receive praise in return, like the sometimes sincere "You look great," which never fails to elicit the awkward yet gushing "You do *too*."

Fashion Victims dress deliberately, and whether the validation of their stylishness comes in the form of a photograph or a random com-pliment, that confirmation is all they need to keep going. A few years back I attended *Paper* magazine's "Beautiful People Party," held at the ultra-swanky restaurant of the moment, The Park, in Manhattan's meatpacking district. As guests entered, a photographer selected cer-tain fashionable people to snap, letting others pass. To be waved through sans photo was like being dissed by the doorman at some snooty nightclub. I was swept up into the crowd and ended up standing next to a six-foot-five-inch gentleman dressed in full Dandy garb, complete with white jacket and chapeau. Sure enough, the photographer thought I was the dapper Dandy's date and encouraged us to smile for the camera. Was it because I, in my rather plain strapless dress, looked particularly smashing that night? Unfortunately, no. I had simply become fashionable by association. Did I feel like one of the Beautiful People that night? You bet.

⑥
THOU SHALT DRESS VICARIOUSLY THROUGH
THY CHILDREN AND PETS

It's not enough for Fashion Victims to dress themselves in designer clothes; they often feel it necessary to share their impeccable taste with others. Someone once told me, "You give what you want to receive." People choose items for others that reflect their own taste, rather than the recipient's. We Fashion Victims live by this. We dress our kids (and others' children when we buy gifts) in mini-me lines like Moschino kids, GapKids, babyGap, Old Navy Kids, Diesel Kids, Ralph Lauren kids, Prada kids, and Guess? Kids. Small sizes don't mean small prices. A baby leather jacket costs $200 at Polo. A jean jacket from Diesel Kids costs $109—more than a grown-up size at many stores. Then there's the $125 tulle dress for girls by Christian Dior, the $175 sweater by Missoni Kids, the pink knit pant set by Baby Dior, $93 trousers by Young Versace, and $68 bootleg jeans by Diesel. Before Dolce & Gabbana's kiddy line, D&G Junior, ran into some trouble in 2000 when its licensee Nilva went belly up, it carried several categories of clothing like "Denim Rock Star," "Lord Rapper," and "Logomania." There were gold denim jackets, tiny shearling coats, and a red leather racing-team jacket for $599. With most kids' clothes, there's not even the possibility of an outfit becoming a long-lasting part of a wardrobe because they outgrow things so quickly, so laying out exorbitant amounts of cash is truly like throwing money into a bottomless pit.

Fashion Victims also know that true style must rub off on one's pets. We ooh and ahh over cutesy pet fashions, not just the doggy sweaters, bandannas, and plastic booties sold in most pet stores, but rather real designer duds that mirror our own dress. Illustrious labels like Hermès, Louis Vuitton, Prada, Salvatore Ferragamo, and Gucci have gotten in on the act, offering high-priced beds, bags, collars, and leashes. Gucci ignited the trend in 1997 when it released a collar and leash. Louis Vuitton and Prada followed in 1998, and Coach and Burberry in the following years. Gucci sells a brown doggy raincoat for $117. Louis Vuitton introduced LV-monogram leather dog carriers in the seventies; they are still available today for just under $1,000. And for those with financial constraints, there's always Old Navy's line of poochy fashions. In L.A., Hollywood's pet owners shop at chi-chi Fifi & Romeo, a luxurious boutique that sells a line of hand-knitted cashmere sweaters and wool coats for little dogs that come in sizes like "teacup" and "mini," priced from $100 to $300.

Models tote their grapefruit-sized Yorkies in their Fendi bags as they sit in the makeup chairs at fashion shows. And fashionable folk dine at sidewalk cafés with their debonair doggies fastened to a table leg with $300 leashes. If it's true what they say about dogs looking like their owners, the Fashion Victim must be quite the pampered human.

⑦

THOU SHALT FEIGN ATHLETICISM

Today, our fascination with sports goes beyond wearing the jerseys and caps of athletes and teams we like. Shoppers at American Eagle Outfitters can lounge around the house on a Sunday afternoon wearing one of the store's football shirts, a Vintage Rugby, Spin Cycle Trek T, or Motocross T. Few of us have ever taken a hit on the rugby field, but we can dress like those robust lads with rugby shirts from stores like J. Crew, Polo Ralph Lauren, H&M, and the Gap.

Abercrombie & Fitch carries such faux-sporty wares as the Morrill Athletic Knit with a number eight stitched over the heart, Field Events Vintage Track Pants, Mountaineering Windpant, Rock Climbing Crew, Sculling Hooded Fleece (basically just a hooded sweatshirt with a big green 9 sewn on), and the Goal Keeper Nylon

Pant for women. Gap carries an entire Gap Athletic line. There's Prada Sport, Polo Sport, and Tommy Sport. Designers even create sport perfumes and colognes that emit clean scents fitting for the fashion-conscious wannabe athlete, like Escada Sport, Benetton Sport, Boss Sport, and Liz Sport. We wear shoes with technical-sounding names like Reebok's Trailzilla III and Nike's Air Terra Humara Slip-on. Fila's Pininfarina shoe was designed in conjunction with the sports car manufacturer of the same name.

Most of our lives are wholly un-rugged, so we attempt to reinsert that missing ruggedness through our wardrobes. Labels like the North Face and Patagonia, which create functional garb for the mountaineering über-athlete, have become fashionable brands to traipse around town in. Timberland boots are as ideal for digging through CDs at the Virgin Megastore as they are for hiking through backwoods Montana. Columbia Sportswear recently produced a parka that detects when the wearer's skin temperature has dropped and releases stored body heat, which will no doubt become a must-have item for those climbing the Himalayas—or picking up an iced latte at Starbucks (*brrrr*).

Those of us who aren't triathletes or marathoners still enjoy examining the sole of a sneaker and seeing very scientific-looking springs, air pockets, gel, and pumps. Employees at the Nike Sport Research Laboratory hold Ph.D.'s or master's degrees in human bio-mechanics and bioengineering. In March 2002, Adidas introduced ClimaCool sneakers, designed to keep feet cool with a "360-degree ventilation system." Athletic shoe makers spend millions of dollars on research to develop supersneakers that add more bounce, absorb shock, improve traction, and cushion arches. And when the Fashion Victim buys these supersneakers, he is delighted over his purchase and can't wait to wear them when he meets his buddies for a drink, no doubt at the local sports bar.

⑧

THOU SHALT BE A WALKING BILLBOARD

The fashion industry is filled with bright ideas thought up by marketing opportunists, from the famous logo print of Louis Vuitton to the ubiquitous Polo emblem, the conspicuous A/X printed on Armani Exchange T-shirts, the unmistakable Nike swoosh, and the name of skatewear company Fuct emblazoned on a sweatshirt. In 2001, Kenneth Cole, Tommy Hilfiger, and Aldo shoes released lines of handbags that touted their designers' names in Steven Sprouse–like graffiti. When Ja Rule wears Burberry's signature plaid in his videos, he provides the company with a free subliminal ad that reaches millions of people, without even uttering the word *Burberry*.

Logophilia hit a high in the 1980s, then dipped in the less showy 1990s. But in 2000, it kicked into full gear again with brand names and logo prints splashed across everything from the most downmarket to the most luxurious items. "Quite a bizarre trend if you analyze it too deeply," says Shelly Vella, fashion director of *Cosmopolitan* UK. "People normally associate wearing logoed merchandise with the need to advertise wealth and buying power: 'Look at my Versace sweatshirt, Gucci jeans, etc.' In decades past, sophisticated designer-ism was about quiet elegance and style—connoisseurs could recognize the cut of a good designer garment. Somehow, in the late nineties, Louis Vuitton logo-itis caught on and everything from Macs to bags, shoes, and tops bore a logo. I saw that whole trend as an attempt—very successful—by designers to reestablish the 'cult of the designer' and to market conspicuous consumption as cool."

In a way, wearing a logo is like wearing gang colors. Just as the Bloods and Crips brandish red and blue bandannas, the Fashion Victim wears the designer logo as a proud badge of membership. It's an act that's tribal at its core. "It's like schoolchildren all nagging for the coolest trainers [sneakers, for you non-Anglophiles]," says Vella. "If you're seen to be wearing the right thing, you're in."

A brand name can add immediate "worth" to two identical products. "Branding is unfortunately the cornerstone of many fashion labels today—not the design, the innovation, the cut, or any other skill honed by the designer. And what the brand stands for is everything," says Debi Hall, fashion-branding strategist for JY&A Consulting in London. "As the Japanese say, name is the first thing—without a name, a garment in today's highly capitalistic, value-added culture is worth very little. Take the vintage phenomenon: even if a secondhand YSL dress is without a label, because it once had a name, it is still worth something. If, however, it is simply a secondhand dress with a name nobody has heard of, then it will go for pennies."

Still, not every Fashion Victim is so taken with the visible logo. Some fashion-conscious folk have been known to consider a visible label such a dealbreaker that they'll take the time to remove it. A few years back, hipsters in London started a trend by tearing the *N* off their New Balance sneakers. And according to *New York* magazine, the late Carolyn Bessette Kennedy once had employees cut the labels out of skiwear she had bought. Emily Cinader Woods, cofounder and chairman of J. Crew, says that unlike her friend Michael Jeffries—CEO of Abercrombie & Fitch, a company notorious for slapping its name conspicuously on everything—she's always been adamant about no logos. "There are so many brands that you might love an item or the color but the logo keeps you from buying it," she says. On the other hand, when you're around people who are familiar with various brands—as is typical for the Fashion Victim—it's possible to be a walking billboard without ever displaying the brand name on your body. I once wore a sleeveless J. Crew top to the office, and two co-workers that day remarked in passing, "I like that—J. Crew?" The brand's familiar look and prevalence in their mail-order catalogs had made the clothes recognizable enough that they didn't need an obvious swoosh, polo player, or little green alligator sewn across the chest. I had been a moving J. Crew billboard all day without the presence of any visible logos.

9

THOU SHALT CARE ABOUT PARIS HILTON'S GAULTIER MICRO-MINI

Although some might argue that the socialite as we once knew her is dead, her successor's social calendar is still jam packed, and her list of contacts in the fashion industry is growing by the New York minute. Fashion glossies like *W* and *Vogue* regularly feature young butterflies like Alexandra Von Furstenberg, Rena Sindi, Aerin Lauder, Brooke de Ocampo, and the Hilton sisters mugging for photographers amid the hip DJs, models, movie stars, and artists who are typically their fellow revelers. The Fashion Victim devours the photos with delight, checking out the Dior gown that Karen Groos wore to an AIDS benefit or the Celine sheath that Pia Getty wore to a summer soiree, knowing little about who these people are except that they're in a magazine, they're rich, and they're incredibly well dressed.

Our fascination with the Junior Jet-setter is somewhat puzzling. She sometimes holds a glamorous job, like contributing editor at a magazine, or even perhaps heads up a relative's business empire, but it's an occupation that would not necessarily garner the same level of press attention for some other person in a similar position. For example, Aerin Lauder may be the executive director of creative marketing for family biz Estée Lauder, but you certainly wouldn't see someone with the same title at Lancôme or Elizabeth Arden in the pages of *Vogue* eight times a year. The Junior Jet-setter often has a famous last name, like Rockefeller or Von Furstenberg, but, again, a well-known surname on its own doesn't necessarily guarantee anyone an overwhelming number of glam photo ops (just look at Sean Lennon).

The socialite's role in the fashion game is to look stunning at events in couture gowns, and casually upper class when attending a summer soiree in the Hamptons. A gossipworthy socialite should be trailed by at least one rumor of out-of-control partying, like making out with someone other than her date or accidentally letting her Galliano gown slip down and flashing her fellow partygoers. Her job is to *be* the answer to the question: "Who actually wears those clothes?" These are the women who can afford the Fendi furs and Gucci pant-suits, but like celebrities, they are also the frequent recipients of loans and freebies from designers—residing below the A-List celebrity, but above B-List TV actresses and pop stars in the fashion hierarchy. In magazines, they seem somehow superhuman. Mostly whippet-thin (perfect for fitting into the sample size), the pretty and privileged attend trunk shows, where they're wined, dined, and shown exquisite new designs. Their job description also includes sitting front row at catwalk shows. Of course, these women are expected to do something in return: they are obliged to wear (and showcase) the designer's clothes. It would be social suicide for a Junior Jet-setter to show up in a Gucci dress at a Versace show. The smart socialite knows this: a few seasons back in Paris, Brooke de Ocampo was seen in Celine at the Celine show and then Dior at the Dior show—both on the same day.

The fashion system is built on want. Looking at socialites' clothes in *Vogue* is like drooling over the estates in *Architectural Digest* or flipping through the *DuPont Registry* to catch a glimpse of the Bentleys and Aston Martins you'll never be able to afford. We live vicariously through the socialite—who has deep enough pockets to buy designer threads of a caliber most of us will never even see in person. Perplexing as our interest may be, the Fashion Victim eats up every morsel, but not without a tinge of jealousy, of course. "I *love* looking at those rich bitches," says Rita, a forty-nine-year-old website editor in Stamford, Connecticut. "But what kills me is that a lot of them don't really have great taste—they just have great resources. If they had to put together a wardrobe like the rest of us mere mortals—from the Gap, Banana Republic, etc.—I doubt they'd be so fabulous. But you do get good fashion ideas from looking and it's nice to daydream."

⑩ THOU SHALT WANT WITHOUT SEEING

Curiously, selling clothes today does not always require actually *showing* the clothes. "Sex sells, sells, and keeps selling," says Marc Berger, fashion director of *GQ*. "A sexy woman in an ad will always grab the attention of a man. It's a great marketing ploy." The no-show advertising technique is frequently justified with "We're selling an image." Ads are another example of fashion's hypnotic power over us. All a company needs to do is get our attention—whether or not we love the clothes is insignificant. In recent years, Abercrombie & Fitch's controversial magalog, the *A&F Quarterly*, has raised eyebrows with its photos of tanned all-American dudes and dudettes, often with zero body fat and zero clothing—a buff naked guy holding a film reel in front of his privates, a couple wearing nothing but body paint, a group of disrobed guys flashing their smiles (and nearly everything else) by the pool. The image: cool, horny coeds. In 1999, a Sisley campaign shot by Terry Richardson simply showed the faces of two female mod-els in a half-sexy, half-goofy liplock. Two years later, an ad for the retailer featured a self-portrait of the moustached Richardson wearing a snake around his neck and nothing else. The image: sexy, slightly dirty. Then there was an Ungaro print ad a few years back showing a werewolf licking a woman's bare body, which was widely condemned for being overly graphic. The image? Anyone's guess. Perhaps the most controversial campaign of late comes from French Connection. To announce the opening of its largest store ever, the retailer took out a full-page ad in a London paper that read, "The World's Biggest FCUK," flaunting the company's easily misread acronym (think of the poor dyslexics!).

Some industry experts think the sex pitch has gone too far. Others say it's all in the *way* it's done. Fashion straddles the line between art and commerce, and so do its ads. In 2001, a magazine and billboard ad campaign for Yves Saint Laurent featuring a nude Sophie Dahl laid out on her back as if in orgasmic rapture created a firestorm of contro-versy. Some people viewed it as art, like a nude painting or sculpture, while others considered it a shameless ploy for attention. *Vogue* Australia editor Kirstie Clements has nixed ads in the past for being too overtly sexual. "Sex sells *Cosmo,* but not so much *Vogue,*" says Clements. "I've rejected an ad for sex aids, but I have no problem with the Sophie Dahl YSL ads. I think they're very chic. Sexy for us has to be chic and sexy. A sexy-looking Gisele sells, yes. But a girl in bondage, no. Depends on your product."

Sex isn't the only trick in the book. Today, premeditated weird-ness has just as much pull as a gratuitous glimpse of flesh. In 2000, menswear label Daniel Christian's fall ad campaign showed only the face of a wrinkly old woman with the message "buy a Daniel Christian shirt or pair of jeans and the bag comes free." Who *wouldn't* want to buy a pair of jeans after seeing that? "These ads also work because there's so much word of mouth and so many articles about them in the newspa-pers and other media," says Arthur Asa Berger, author of *Ads, Fads and Consumer Culture.* "If you can create an ad that gets talked about in tele-vision news shows and written about in newspapers, you're getting a lot of free publicity . . . for the brand." One of the revolutionaries in this seemingly illogical method of advertising was Benetton, whose ads in the eighties and nineties ranged from the harmless (two smiling children) to the provocative (a duck covered in crude oil) to the controversial (death row inmates). Oliviero Toscani, who photographed the confrontational ads and was dropped shortly after the death row campaign, always maintained that it wasn't *his* duty to sell the clothes—it was the company's. Oh, Oliviero, how we miss you.

2

How We Got Here: From Bear Hides to Bumsters

Dorothy wondered why the animals living in Foxville did not wear just their own hairy skins as wild foxes do; when she mentioned it to King Dox he said they clothed themselves because they were civilized.

"But you were born without clothes," she observed, "and you don't seem to me to need them."

"So were human beings born without clothes," he replied, "and until they became civilized they wore only their natural skins. But to become civilized means to dress as elaborately and prettily as possible, and to make a show of your clothes so your neighbors will envy you, and for that reason both civilized foxes and civilized humans spend most of their time dressing themselves."

"I don't," declared the shaggy man.

"That is true," said the King, looking at him carefully, "but perhaps you are not civilized."

—*L. Frank Baum,* The Road to Oz

The history of mankind has included atrocities that we today can look back upon and wish had never occurred—the Inquisition, the Salem witch trials, *Swept Away*. But at least there's a silver lining—these past mistakes can act as a lasting reminder of things we should never let happen again. When it comes to fashion, however, logic seems to flow in reverse. History shows us how ridiculous fashion can be, yet instead of learning from those blunders, we're destined to repeat the same unsightly trends (just how many times do clogs have to come back before they die?). Plenty of lessons from yesteryear could convince us to distance ourselves from fashion. But instead of backing off, we've become ever more engrossed in it. How have we gotten to this point? The answer can best be summed up by considering the following four eras of fashion.

BEAR HIDES: THE ERA OF NECESSITY

Ages after the primordial ooze began to form into the first signs of human life, in the days of the Neanderthals, our gnarly knuckled predecessors concerned themselves with survival, and little else. Compared to modern humans (give or take a few hirsute chaps recently spotted sunning in Speedos on South Beach), *Homo neanderthalensis* was short, stocky, and scruffy—an exterior suitable for reducing heat loss in harsh Ice Age conditions. The elements showed him no mercy. The Neanderthal, an avid carnivore living between 40,000 and 100,000 years ago, often perished in infancy or early adulthood, rarely making it past his early thirties. Life was rough. It would have been a miracle for him to reach the age of twenty without breaking at least one bone; archaeologists have found remains of children as young as four years old showing signs of broken—and healed—bones, implying that Neanderthal tribes had practiced some sort of primitive first aid.

In many ways, the Neanderthal has developed an undeserved reputation. He wasn't the halfwit he's often made out to be. "They had bigger brain sizes than us, persisted through long cold periods in Europe, made complicated tools, buried many of their dead in cave cemeteries—which all suggest they were no less intelligent than us," says David Frayer, Ph.D., professor of anthropology at the University of Kansas. The Neanderthal was at least sharp-witted enough to fashion tools and weapons from stone to kill big game like the bear, mammoth, horse, deer, and woolly rhino. Then one day some fifty thousand years ago, or so the theory goes, after observing how furry creatures managed to keep warm in cold temperatures, he had a flash of ingenuity: kill one of the furry animals and wear its coat. Archaeologists have surmised from dental evidence that primitive man may have chewed the fat off hides to create a sort of rudimentary leather, a practice repeated by latter-day Eskimos. He draped the crudely cut pelt over his shoulders like a cape, instantly shielding his vulnerable flesh not only from the winter chill but also from animal bites, burns, cuts, rough terrain, and any other nasties that came his way. On this day, Neanderthals stumbled upon the concept of clothing.

The Neanderthal wasn't the first of our early ancestors to discover clothing—researchers believe that people scattered across the globe had already concocted their own versions of attire years before—but due to the lack of communication with anyone outside the immediate vicinity, the Neanderthal was left to his own devices when it came to inventing wearables for himself. But the original seeds of clothing likely were sown long before. "The brains of hominids by 200,000 years ago were fully capable of a wide range of complex thought and planning, including the production of serviceable, if inelegant, clothing," says J. M. Adovasio, Ph.D., director of the Mercyhurst Archaeological Institute in Erie, Pennsylvania. "I have no doubt that the populations that manufactured these items certainly had the capability of using sinew or perhaps even plant fiber to stitch hides together to manufacture rudimentary clothing . . . people were doing much more than simply tying pelts to their bodies in an untanned and untreated state." Adovasio believes that the Neanderthal's predecessor, *Homo erectus*, was actually capable of creating clothing from a simple pattern and then stitching it along the edges. "I don't believe they were necessarily manufacturing fully tailored clothing," he says. "But by the same token, they had stone tools and presumably wooden tools [to create stitches]."

For Neanderthals and those who came before them, clothing was a functional contrivance. Wear a hide; last through the winter. Don't wear a hide; risk perishing from the cold. Cover your sensitive parts with an animal skin and avoid a nasty plant rash. Fail to cover up and suffer the itchy red bumps that crop up. The Neanderthal wasn't yet obsessed with what we think of today as fashion. Although it appears that the desire to look beautiful started earlier than we might think.

Anthropologists have discovered evidence—from stone figurines as well as cave drawings—of hairstyles, complex clothing, jewelry, and other adornments dating back as far as 27,000 years ago, signaling the beginning of dress as something other than purely functional. Back then, says Adovasio, beautifying oneself was done largely to fit in with a certain group. "It was a device of population identity," he says. "It was also, no doubt, something that enhanced the physical appearance of both males and females in a way [that would serve] to attract a mate." Isn't it nice to know that our Stone Age counterparts had some of the same fashion motivations we still do today?

BUSTLES: THE ERA OF SOCIAL DISTINCTION

The poor Victorian Fashion Victim—to dress fashionably in the mid-1800s required not only the financial means to afford the most elegant gowns but also the physical might to hold them up. The lady often needed several helpers to maneuver her into her outfit, which could weigh up to twenty-five pounds. Her daily getup typically consisted of embroidered underwear, stockings, a lace-up bodice or corset, layers upon layers of itchy petticoats, a dress, and a jacket, as well as bonnet, fur, boots, shawl, parasol, muff, jewelry, and whatever other accoutrements she could layer on.

In 1856 (coincidentally, the same year the first-ever remains of our friend the Neanderthal were discovered in Germany), the cage crinoline was first introduced. Made from a series of round or elliptical metal hoops strung together and covered with cotton, the restrictive cage—although it may not sound like an instrument of convenience by today's standards—was cheered by women because it meant they could rid themselves of those heavy, starched petticoats they'd been wearing for years. The metal contraption kept a woman's skirt belled out so as not to touch her legs and reveal any impious outlines of the flesh, and it also created the illusion of an hourglass figure—the oft-painful goal to which nearly every woman aspired at the time. It was an early example of how fashion could charm us into being uncomfortable for the sake of style.

The cage crinoline's popularity took off, and not just among upper-class women. In later years, it would be recognized by many historians as the first fashion article to be mass produced. According to *The History of Underclothes*, in 1859 a steel factory produced wire for half a million crinolines each week. Cages could be bought relatively cheaply, for about 50¢ to $2, according to *Peterson's* magazine. Thus the style was not restricted to the elite—working-class women and girls also wore the conical skirts but with fewer frou-frou touches. To separate themselves from the grubby masses, upper-class women poured on the pretension. In Victorian society, comfort was déclassé; discomfort symbolized wealth and status. The impracticality of an outfit conveyed a strong message about a woman: she didn't work, and she didn't *need* to work. Cage crinolines for privileged women expanded to ridiculous proportions: the hoops, some measuring up to eighteen feet in circumference, made it nearly impossible for the wearer to fit through a doorway, let alone sit down or walk without assistance. She required additional seating room at parties to accommodate her skirt, and needed to practice extreme caution when passing by candles and fire grates, since the skirt might easily brush up against a flame and create an embarrassing, if not deadly, predicament. An August 1864 article in *The Alexandra* magazine stated, "Since hoops came into fashion, cases of injury and death from the burning of clothes have been more common and much attention has been lately directed to them." In one documented case from 1863, twenty-five hundred people died at a church in Chile when the crinoline of one devotee caught fire after coming in contact with a candle.

Florence Nightingale was one of the first women to do away with the bulky crinoline, and was universally looked upon as eccentric for it. In her *Notes on Nursing*, the legendary nurse remarked, "Fortunate it is if their skirts do not catch fire and if the nurse does not give herself up a sacrifice together with her patient, to be burnt in her own petticoats. I wish the Registrar General would tell us the exact number of deaths by burning occasioned by this absurd and hideous custom." It wasn't as if there weren't alternatives to those dangerous, uncomfortable styles. In

1850, Amanda Bloomer created the ultra-practical (but ultra-ugly) tunic
and pantaloon "Bloomer" costume, but it only drew ridicule and seemed
to prove the inherent ugliness of comfort. The outfit, introduced by
feminists as a protest against hoops and the burdensome weight of undergarments, consisted of a full jacket with baggy Turkish-style pants,
gathered by elastic bands at the ankle, under a voluminous skirt falling
slightly below the knee. It flopped. Women everywhere continued to
suffer the restrictive hoop skirts for the sake of taste and style.

In the latter part of the nineteenth century the crinoline gave way
to the bustle. Also called the crinolette or pannier, the small cage sup-
ported the back of the skirt without requiring the full hoop. Many fashion historians credit Charles Frederick Worth, the English tailor in
Paris who founded the first haute couture house, the House of Worth,
with introducing the bustle in 1868, but variations had actually come
and gone since the fourteenth century, being called everything from a
bum roll to a cork rump to a pouf. The bustle trickled down from the
elite to middle-class women, who began making their own at home
from pads, springs, ruffles, wires, or curved boning. Women's magazines of the time touted the "skirt enhancer" as a must-have item. A
snippet from *Peterson's* in September 1873 revealed that the best bustle
"should be long and narrow, and consist of twelve steel springs encased
in muslin and kept in place with elastic bands." A. T. Stewart, who
opened one of America's first department stores, imported and sold a
Parisian pannier gown for $250, although it was suggested that black
silk copies could be made for $125, according to *New York Fashion*.

The bustle outfit, although smaller, was no less a hassle than the
old cage crinoline. In fact, fashion historian Caroline Rennolds Mil-
bank calls the bustle-backed dress—composed of a closely-fitted
bodice, boned lining or corset, and elaborately draped skirt—the "most
restrictive of all nineteenth-century styles." A woman would have to
push it to one side and balance on one cheek if she wanted to sit down.
Inventors did attempt to ease women's discomfort; in 1887, actress
Lillie Langtry lent her name to a bustle that folded up when the wearer
sat down (the humble beginnings of the celebrity clothing line).

Just as the cage crinoline had been embellished to flaunt a
woman's status, the bustle could also be covered with ornate bows,

beading, and ribbons to reflect one's social standing in this "age of wretched excess," as Laurel Wilson, Ph.D., curator of the Missouri Historic Costume and Textile Collection, refers to it. "The way that the upper class stood out then was the same way they stand out today—better design, better tailoring and dressmaking, better materials," she says. At that time, and still today, dressing was unabashedly about impressing others. It was conspicuous consumption at its worst.

By the early twentieth century, signs of the cumbersome bustle had begun to vanish, and then disappeared completely when women began wearing the sacklike dresses of the Flapper Era, and the fashionable body shape shifted from hourglass to floorboard (although the padded rump did make a small comeback in the 1980s thanks to rowdy British designer Vivienne Westwood, who caused quite a stir with her nouveau-bustle, a highly exaggerated pad on the backs of skirts and pants that made twiggish catwalk models look as if they had stuffed two volleyballs into their panties). Historians attribute the disappearance of the bustle and other highly restrictive garments to the "democratization" of fashion, a movement that leveled the playing field between the classes, brought about in large part by ready-to-wear, which brings us to . . .

BROOKS BROTHERS: THE ERA OF READY-TO-WEAR

Henry Sands Brooks was Gatsby long before F. Scott Fitzgerald's famous character appeared on the scene in the twentieth century. The elegant former grocer and son of a well-to-do Connecticut physician had been so widely admired for his dapper English threads that he began special-ordering suits from England for friends and acquaintances. On April 7, 1818, he opened H. & D. H. Brooks & Co., a clothing store in the seaport district of lower Manhattan, near Wall Street at the corner of Catharine and Cherry Streets. At the time, the Big Apple was nothing more than a Little Appleseed—the total population of Manhattan stood at a mere 125,000. James Monroe was president; the steam engine had not yet been developed; the telegraph and the sewing machine were still over twenty-five years away. Nevertheless, H. & D. H. Brooks maintained a remarkable upward momentum, even after its founder died in 1833. Brooks left the store to his four grand-sons, who officially renamed it Brooks Brothers some twenty years later. In its nearly two centuries in existence, the haberdasher established itself as an American classic, and a favorite among presidents, including Abraham Lincoln (honest Abe was assassinated in a Brooks Brothers coat), Theodore Roosevelt, Herbert Hoover, Richard Nixon, and Bill Clinton, and debonair celebrities like Cary Grant, Gary Cooper, and John Barrymore.

In 1845, Brooks Brothers introduced the first ready-to-wear suits to the U.S., and pioneers of the 1849 California Gold Rush flocked to the retailer. The throngs of customers were pleased that they could now buy nice clothes off the rack rather than standing for hours while a tailor fitted them, then waiting for the garment to be made. Of course, ready-to-wear in its infancy wasn't perfect. People who weren't of average proportions still had to get their clothes tailored. But these alterations didn't take nearly as long as it would take to create a custom-made garment. "Ready-to-wear certainly improved the appearance of the lower classes who didn't have the sewing skills or the ability to hire good dressmakers," says Laurel Wilson. But to the upper classes, what was available lacked any semblance of good taste. The mere concept of ready-made clothing disgusted many of the fashion elite. Prêt-à-porter, to them, was the equivalent of paint by numbers—it was a booming mass-market business that lacked any aesthetic value. Early ready-made clothing was referred to as "slops," a term from which the word *sloppy* was derived. "There was a sort of shame in the purchase and wear of such clothing . . . it was at once a reflection upon a man's taste and a supposed indication of his poverty," wrote Claudia Kidwell and Margaret Christman in their 1974 book *Suiting Everyone*.

Before ready-to-wear, practically every home in America was a small clothing factory. Magazines, such as *Godey's Lady's Book* and *Graham's Magazine*, instructed homemakers on how to create clothes. Women spun yarn and wove cloth to make everything from nightshirts and underwear to suits and coats for the family. But various circumstances aligned to propel ready-to-wear's arrival and expansion. In 1832, a 50 percent import duty curtailed the availability of clothing from England, increasing the demands on American industry. Roughly a decade later, the sewing machine made sewing by hand nearly obsolete. By 1850, the U.S. Census counted 4,278 ready-made clothing businesses with 97,000 workers. The Civil War brought with it a voracious need for uniforms, which not only got the American factory system churning but introduced standard body-size measurements to the ready-to-wear industry. Later, the influx of hundreds of thousands of immigrant workers in the 1880s created the perfect labor pool to turn ready-to-wear into a massive industry.

Ready-to-wear brought about the democratization of fashion—clothes became less a symbol of one's wealth and status as more people could afford the most up-to-date looks. As mass production took over, prices dropped and people could afford more clothes. Quality improved throughout the twentieth century as sizing information became more detailed and readily available. Ready-to-wear changed the face of fashion forever, transforming it into big business. By the late 1870s, most men wore suits that came from a factory. Were it not for those first bold steps of Henry Sands Brooks, we might still be making our own clothes or having them custom made by professionals. There would be no malls, no online or catalog shopping. In fact, there would be very little shopping at all. Today, it's easy to take ready-to-wear clothing for granted. Few of us can hem a skirt ourselves let alone sew an entire outfit.

Brooks Brothers remained popular for nearly two centuries with almost no advertising. In 1988, 170 years after Henry Brooks founded his little seaport store, Brooks Brothers was bought by British retailer Marks & Spencer for $750 million. After a few missteps, it was put back on the block in 2001, when it was purchased by Retail Brand Alliance for $225 million. New owner Claudio Del Vecchio said the retailer's mistake under M&S was taking the concept of business casual too far, abandoning its classic suits for khakis and polos—a look that didn't play well with the core customer. "He's still a businessman," Del Vecchio told the *Washington Post*, describing the Brooks Brothers loyalist in 2002. "Some casual things are really not appropriate for the office. There was confusion on the part of the customer as to what was really business casual."

In late 2001, Brooks Brothers introduced its newest innovation: digital tailoring. Now a customer at the retailer's Manhattan location could step into a measuring booth, where he'd be scanned by a strobe light for twelve seconds. A 3-D map of his body would be created and sent to a tailor. About fifteen days later, the finished suit would arrive back at the store. The American pioneer of the ready-to-wear suit had entered the twenty-first century with a bang—and a suit that evoked the exclusivity and eminence of custom clothing, but without the typical six- to eight-week wait.

BUMSTERS: THE ERA OF THE TREND

When Alexander McQueen debuted his headline-grabbing "bumster" trousers in London in 1992, reviews were mixed but relatively positive. The pants hung so comically low on the hips as to offer a peek at the wearer's rear cleavage. "If these jeans were any lower," a McQueen sales rep joked in *Women's Wear Daily,* "you would have to call them chaps." The fashion world's enfant terrible reworked his signature bumsters in subsequent collections—dangling tampon strings from pant crotches in his infamous 1996 Highland Rape collection and stitching them with metallic sequins in giraffe-pattern and wet-look python-pattern in 2000. Each year the Museum of Costume in Bath adds a designer creation to its prestigious modern collection. In 1996, it was the bumster. "I remember sitting through Alexander McQueen's first showing of bumster jeans, and found that aspect of the show quite refreshing," says Shelly Vella of *Cosmopolitan* UK. "Let's face it, through the many decades of fashion we faced, just about every erogenous zone has been dressed—or undressed—in some sort of way. Bums have seen bustles to enhance them, Lycra to sculpt them and then came the bumster to give a little sneaky peek. In a typically witty McQueen way . . . we had the equivalent to 'Builder's Bum' jeans as a high fashion statement. The bumsters, although not mainstream, changed the perception of cutting in jeans manufacture, or mainstream acceptance of it. No matter that every critic didn't adore the bumster, it raised eyebrows—the gold crown for provocative designers like McQueen."

Several years later, designers like Daryl K. and Earl began experimenting with the rise on jeans—the length from the crotch to the top of the front waistband—igniting the popularity of the low-rise jean, a style derivative of seventies hip-huggers. Earl Jeans, a company that former stylist Suzanne Freiwald started after friends kept asking her where she bought her perfectly cut jeans, drove early aficionados to Saks Fifth Avenue, Barney's, and small specialty shops in search of the coveted blues. Paparazzi snapped shots of celebrities like Cameron Diaz wearing the chic style with stilettos, which gave the leg an extra long, lean look. Other designers began to catch on to the trend. When Daniella Clarke, wife of Guns 'n' Roses guitarist Gilby Clarke, started L.A.-based Frankie B. jeans, she added her own touch to the low-rider: Hollywood, sex appeal, and even more celebrity photo ops. When Charlize Theron wore a pair of low-rise Frankie B. jeans to the premiere of *A Perfect Storm* in 2000, the starlet's photo from that event appeared in no less than five major magazines, including *Harper's Bazaar*, *Vogue*, *People*, *The National Enquirer*, and *W*.

Soon, clotheshorses were competing for record lows. Pop singers like Christina Aguilera, Madonna, Beyoncé Knowles (of Destiny's Child), and Britney Spears wore jeans and leather pants so dangerously low and snug while dancing that you worried they'd pop right out or bust a seam (as I saw Jessica Simpson do on not one but *two* awkward occasions). The rise continued to shrink throughout the late 1990s. Perhaps the lowest of the low, the rise on a pair of Frankie B. jeans was rumored to be just three inches (regular-cut Levi's have a rise of ten inches). Print ads for Parasuco showed women's rears peeking over the tops of the jeans like Elizabethan cleavage. Committing a faux pas once made only by pudgy plumbers as they bent over their toolboxes, young women all over the world were baring butt crack in early 2001. That fall, denim brand Lee Cooper in the UK launched Butt Couture, a line of jeans made from lightweight denim designed with a gap between the waistband and the pants to create a peek-a-boo look.

Booty pride became a warped symbol of girl power in the new millennium. After the bottom-baring low-slung jeans that Nikka Costa wore on the cover of her debut album started garnering more attention than the music inside, the singer proclaimed to the *Toronto Sun*, "My pants are very low, mine are lower than anyone else's and I'm damn proud of it . . . if you want to talk about my ass, go right ahead." The rear became ubiquitous—Destiny's Child sang about being "Bootylicious" and Sisqo exalted the rump in his "Thong Song."

Low-riders had migrated to the masses. Levi's latched on toward the tail end of the trend, producing its line of Superlows, which eventually spawned "Too Superlow" jeans and then "Dangerously Low" jeans for women *and* men. Old Navy launched a massive TV ad campaign for its ultra-low-rise jeans, at $26.99, just in time for back to school. As models strutted down a short runway in colored denim, studded, and corduroy hiphuggers, pitchster Molly Sims proclaimed, "They're not just low—they're *ultra* low." Waistlines dropped to ridiculous new lows and butt cleavage became an all-too-familiar sight. Suzanne Freiwald of Earl Jeans compares the outrageously low-rise jeans to the baby tee trend from the early to mid-1990s. "Remember T-shirts used to be cut huge?" she says. "Everyone was wearing, like, a boy's tee in those days. Then someone brought to market the small tee, and some girls started going to stores like Baby Gap and getting shirts made for six-month-olds. Everyone got sick of that one tiny tee, then it became just the small tee again and we still wear that." She foresaw a similar fate for the low-rise jean: a trend improves a style, the trend gets exaggerated, backlash sets in, then it returns to the first trend, without necessarily reverting to the original style: "The three-inch rise is a tiny tee—it's here for a minute then it'll be low-rise again, which is still lower than before."

Grown-ups, who weren't at all taken with the back-crack trend, expressed their confusion. After students at Milwaukee's South Division High School began wearing the extremely low jeans, school staffers found themselves in an odd dress-code position. "With all the training I've had, and all the experience, I never thought I'd have to do booty checks," principal Don Krueger told the *Milwaukee Journal Sentinel* in December 2001.

In its earliest days in the McQueen show, builder's bum seemed far too outrageous for everyday wear, the type of trend that was meant solely for the catwalk, in much the same way as see-through blouses and three-inch miniskirts. Alas, a cheeky trend that had piqued the fashion crowd's interest in the form of the enfant terrible's controversial bumsters soon became a mass-produced product, eventually being worn in a watered-down form by teenage girls in Milwaukee, only to head quickly toward its tacky death, but not before proving that today even the most ridiculous trend can advance to the forefront of fashion.

Over the centuries, clothing styles have gone from functional to elitist to democratic to comically contagious. Today, fashion is all of those things. Our clothes still protect our bodies and preserve our modesty (although we show a lot more skin than in olden days), they still align us with certain social groups (club kid vs. country club kid), and they still act as a symbol of our democratization, since nearly every trend can be followed by anyone. And now, in this day and age of the infectious trend, the bottom line (literally and figuratively in the case of bumsters) reigns supreme. As a result, not only are Fashion Victims constantly on the lookout for The Next Big Thing, but retailers and the media are also constantly touting every item as The Next Big Thing. As a result, fashion doesn't strive to become *better* per se, as perhaps a carmaker might endeavor to create a better-looking, better-running automobile. Instead, companies seem satisfied to dupe the public into thinking that something ugly is beautiful just long enough for them to make a quick buck.

And we fall for it every time. Today, the razzle-dazzle of advertising, media, and celebrities is too much for the Fashion Victim to resist. We know about every trend; we want every new trend. The sad thing is that we don't recognize their absurdity until after they've passed their peak.

Millennia have passed. But still, fashion is the Pied Piper, and we are its mice.

3

Speed Chic

Fashion is made to become unfashionable.

—*Coco Chanel*

For a fleeting moment in 1999, the poncho was fashion's golden child. The slouchy armless sweaters from the seventies first resurfaced in the fall shows of several designers, including Louis Vuitton, Anna Sui, and Ralph Lauren. A handful of perceptive boutique owners cashed in early on, stocking $250-and-up handknits. Chic ladies snatched up the newfangled ponchos and paired them with tapered jeans, leather pants, pencil skirts, and stiletto booties. It didn't matter that the blanketlike wraps severely obstructed one's arm movements—or that when tented beneath several pounds of itchy wool, body heat tends to escalate to ovenlike temperatures. Ponchos, for the moment, looked marvelously cute.

Soon afterward, magazines began hyping the trend; then ponchos filtered into department stores and specialty shops. Clothes makers produced affordable versions, like Free People's black and purple one, which sold for $56 at Nordstrom's. Ponchos quickly arrived in a huge variety of styles: with hoods, tassels, V-necks, fringe, arts-and-craftsy embroidery, doofy pom-poms. Poncho fever was in full swing. Thirtysomethings who'd worn the amorphous pullovers as kids could feel retro yet modern. Stores like Urban Outfitters stocked a selection of ratty secondhand versions, whose endearing griminess proved that they were authentically groovy "Marcia Brady" thrift-store finds, not those soulless *new* items. Benetton carried its soft wool poncho with pom-pom trim for $88, and J. Crew peddled its blanket poncho with a Peruvian-style pattern for $98. Some consumers justified the purchase based on "utility"—ponchos were undoubtedly warm and comfortable. Still, no competent shopper expected the poncho to endure the season. It was a flagrant fad, but a powerful one.

By the time the style hit the masses—and twelve-year-olds in Sheboygan, Wisconsin, had begun wearing the teepee-like knits with flared jeans and chunky platform sneakers—the ladies who had first latched on to the trend would rather have choked on a foie gras croquette than poked their heads through another poncho. The rest of the clothes-buying public followed suit thereafter, and the poncho sank once again into the realm of the horribly uncool. The trend had flashed and burned within the span of less than a season.

SPEED KILLS

We live in an era of Speed Chic. One of the realities of fashion is that we'll fall hard for a new trend, then not only tire of it but begin to despise it. So we're stuck in an endless cycle, trying futilely to hurry up and be cool. To make matters worse, the giant hamster wheel of style continues to accelerate, so today we grow weary of trends much faster than we used to. In the past, fashions stayed in vogue for years, even decades. Now, only a matter of months or weeks after we succumb to a trend, it's already started to look tired, and another trend has taken its place as the must-have item. Most shops don't even wait for the appropriate season anymore. Go to a clothing store in July, and you'll find fall sweaters and jackets on the prominent racks with summer items relegated to the back wall. This ridiculous rate of fashion obsolescence renders us blissfully defenseless to stop it as it whittles away at our paychecks and our good sense.

Speed Chic is the crack cocaine of fashion: cheap, fast, and addictive. The act of consumption provides a temporary high—a fashionable new garment injects its wearer with a euphoric feeling of pride and self-confidence. She stands taller, smiles more, goes home glowing with contentment. Fashion Victims have been known to lose all control, to the point where they don't even blame themselves anymore. In May 2000, former Andersen Consulting employee Elizabeth Randolph Roach pled guilty to embezzling nearly a quarter of a million dollars from her company, where she earned a salary of $150,000 a year. The judge let her off with a light sentence of probation and therapy, declaring that her compulsive shopping problem was the driving force behind the crime. Her condition was so bad, said her lawyer, that it compelled her to accumulate seventy pairs of shoes at one time, shell out $7,000 for a belt buckle, and accrue a $30,000 shopping bill while traveling in London (she was so taken with shopping there that she missed her plane back home).

When a trend appears, we're fully aware that it will disappear, but we buy into it anyway. As a result, we accumulate a glut of clothing destined for the trash, the thrift store, or closet purgatory. Americans spend more than a billion dollars a year organizing their clothing and accessories. And we need to. The average American woman owns thirty pairs of shoes; over 6 percent own more than fifty. A 2001 survey found that she owns nearly forty knit tops. *Men's Health* magazine reports that the average American man owns twenty ties. Another poll put his T-shirt collection at over twenty-five. The excesses of fashion are nothing new for those with money. In his 1870 book *Women of New York*, George Ellington reported that "The elite do not wear the same dress twice . . . It is not unreasonable to suppose that [a wealthy woman] has two new dresses of some sort for every day in the year." But it wasn't until recently that garment gluttony became so universal among average people.

The result? When we're so swept up in following every trend, we never develop our own personal style. One gets the feeling that the trendsetters of yesteryear, like Coco Chanel, Frank Sinatra, and

Jacqueline Kennedy Onassis, were fully aware of how to use clothes as an extension of their personalities. It would be odd to think of Old Blue Eyes in his Rat Pack days wearing cuffed jeans onstage, even though they were in fashion at the time. Instead, most people today are captivated by reinvention. We look to celebrities like Madonna, perhaps the only fortysomething woman who can pull off both Pimp Glam and Heartland Cowboy in the same year. Reinvention *is* Madonna's look. Imitation is ours. Give or take a few rare souls, nearly all of the stars we look up to today as our fashion role models don't even have a clear-cut sense of their own style—just close symbiotic relationships with designers. Scrapping our own eccentricities in favor of fashion monotony can only lead us down a dangerous path—a path where creativity suffers. When we fail to nourish our own personal sense of style and, instead, mechanically follow the current, we put ourselves in danger of forgetting what makes fashion fun in the first place—experimentation and originality.

People in nations less overwhelmed by consumerism certainly don't change their style of dress quite so frequently. The difference is even evident within parts of the *same* country. Some villagers in the Italian countryside have been wearing the same styles for decades, while their counterparts in modish Milan transform their appearance every day. How odd that our taste in clothes changes so frequently while our preferences in other areas remain constant. Our favored type of partner rarely wavers (if you like tall, dark, and handsome, it's unlikely you'll drool over Mr. Short and Pasty). Taste in food is tough to change (a pickle hater would probably not respond to even the most highly prized gourmet pickle). Taste in artwork and movies can be a lifelong predilection. So why are we so fickle when it comes to fashion? In order to figure out Speed Chic, it's important to understand its vital component—the trend.

THE TREND MACHINE

Trends are the fuel in fashion's engine. Without the cycle of cool and uncool, we'd feel no need to replenish our wardrobes until our clothes began to split at the seams. Our closets would consist of only a few sensible outfits: one for cold weather, one for hot, and one for those days in between, plus a few alternates in case we didn't feel like doing laundry. Without trends, fashion would never have grown to be a multitrillion-dollar industry. Retail as we know it would cease to exist.

A basic tenet of fashion is its inevitable obsolescence: most clothes we buy today won't be the clothes we wear a year from now, a season from now, even a month or week from now in some cases. "Everything can be fashionable for a minute—that's the fun element of the fashion business," says Kirstie Clements, editor of *Vogue* Australia. Nowadays, anything can be a trend. We talk about which body shapes are fashionable each season (curvy, boyish, waif). Trends encompass everything from precise fads (Indian bindis, turquoise jewelry) to broader trends (thinner ties, shorter swimming trunks, tapered pants). Even following *trends* can be a trend. An August 2001 study by Euro RSCG Worldwide, the fifth-largest advertising agency in the world, declared, "Trends are out." Among young consumers, the study said, trendy items like body glitter and aviator sunglasses were being replaced by more classic styles like pearls and Audrey Hepburn slides. But now, isn't that a trend in itself?

Although we typically associate trendiness with teenage girls, it's not just one particular type of person that's drawn to the instant gratification of fast fashion. All of us—even those who think they're immune—are influenced by trends, whether it's through the socially acceptable fatness of a tie, width of a lapel, snugness of a T-shirt, or color scheme and fabrics that happen to be on the market (brown and orange polyester in the 1970s, for example). They may not be blatantly faddish neon ankle socks and bubble skirts or male nail polish, but they're trends nonetheless. "People who are shy and don't want to stand out are forced to go along with changes in fashion, or else they'll look different and attract attention that they don't want," says Arthur Asa Berger, author of *Ads, Fads and Consumer Culture*. "Those who like attention keep on the cutting edge of fashion so they'll be noticed."

Although we all participate in the ebb and flow of styles, we also recognize the absurdity of doing so. There's a certain shame that goes along with trendiness. Most of us would be insulted if someone called us "trendy," as if the label implies a sort of flakiness and weak-mindedness. In fact, we consider people who are overly trendy to be out of their minds. Even the words we use to describe trends imply insanity: miniskirt *mania*, the *craze* in shoes, armbands are all the *rage*, military *madness*. So the Fashion Victim maintains a love-hate relationship with the trend. Fashion's perpetual reinvention of itself is an essential part of what makes us love it (and hate it). Trends make dressing fun (and frustrating). They open our eyes to new styles (and impel us to buy things we don't need). Following trends helps us to feel a sense of belonging (and mindless conformity).

Contributing to this maddening situation, nearly every trend that has crashed and burned through the ages has followed a certain pattern. A quick lesson in the life of a trend:

BIRTH: A trend is born when it trickles down from the drawing board of a fashion designer or trickles up from the streets. And it makes its grand debut on the catwalk to great fanfare. It's always quite a marvel during the biannual fashion shows how so many designers appear to be operating on the same wavelength. But most trends are quite predictable, since a trend will inevitably be followed by a backlash. If skinny stilettos are in, next will come thick wedge heels. Tight pants will be followed by looser cuts. White will be this season's black. Long will be this season's short.

Sometimes a trend is driven by the textile suppliers. One might think there's some serious copying going on if, say, Prada, Gucci, Donna Karan, and Calvin Klein all do polka dots in their spring collections. But it's much more innocuous than that. "It all starts with the textile market," says Fern Mallis, executive director of 7th on Sixth, the producers of New York Fashion Week. "If you shop at textile fairs, which is where all the designers go to get everything that they're doing, all of a sudden you walk through miles of booths and all you're seeing is printed fabrics. Yeah, then prints are in. All of a sudden, leather is available because the mills are making it more available and there are leather suppliers and they're doing interesting things with leather, so all of a sudden everyone's got perforated in their collection. It's not because one designer copied another designer—they were all shopping from the same places." Of course, this not only reminds us how frighteningly homogeneous the clothing market is, but also that fashion is a business first and foremost. Many designers aren't led by some romantic notion of creative vision, but rather adjust their creations to use textiles that are abundant (in other words: cheap).

ADOLESCENCE: When a trend first shows itself to the public, it often enters a rebellious stage. Like a teenager with a blue mohawk, it may not please everyone at first. Consumers experience a knee-jerk reaction to any style that strays too far from the norm, but given enough exposure, they'll warm up to it. The first time many people saw those Prada sneakers—the smooshed bowling ones with dozens of clear rubber cleats spiking out from the soles—they wrinkled their noses, certain that they would never wear such a weird-looking style. The next season, nearly every midlevel shoe store, including Nine West and Kenneth Cole, was carrying its own lower-priced version, and the same people who had recoiled in disgust were now scooping up the bumpy sneakers with zeal.

MATURITY: After a trend reaches its peak, it starts its quick descent toward retirement. By this point, it has lost touch with youth and is no longer seen as cool. It's reached mass popularity and only has one direction to go—down. As philosopher Georg Simmel once wrote: "Economists talk about a 'bandwagon effect' when a product is sold more because of simple imitation. But there is also a 'reverse bandwagon effect,' when a 'snobbish' consumer stops buying a product because too many others are buying it." We witness the reverse bandwagon in pop music (indie bands are tagged "sellouts" the second they hit the pop charts). We see it in nightclubs (a club can only stay hot so long as it keeps out the uncool masses). And we see it in fashion (the second a trend hits the mall, it's as good as dead).

DEATH: Sadly, the trend must come to an end. Its time has simply come. But its nosedive into obsolescence is also accelerated by its tendency to become clownish and exaggerated with age. In 1999, zebra, pony, python, and leopard prints graced the runways of such designers as Dolce & Gabbana, Alberta Ferretti, and Gucci. The look—wild, yet clean and chic—quickly caught on. By 2000, animal prints had trickled down to the masses, not in the understated manner in which they had started, but rather as something that resembled a drag queen's nightmare. "I bought a skin-tight pair of dark brown faux-croc pants early in the season before I realized how prolific they would become," says Joanna, a thirty-year-old licensing executive in New York City. "They looked good but seemed cheesy after I started seeing so much bad faux croc everywhere." Trend followers donned fuzzy zebra cowboy hats, stretch jeans with leopard print, faux pony armbands dyed turquoise. If ever there was a signal for a trend's demise, it had arrived.

The trend's life cycle has remained roughly the same for centuries. Why, then, did it suddenly speed up?

HOW TRENDS ARE ACCELERATED

The Fashion Victim's hunger for new trends is not the only engine that keeps the wheels of Speed Chic turning. As costly as it can be to consumers, the constant turnover of new styles is essential to the business of fashion. It's in the apparel industry's best interest to preserve the continuous churning of trends—a style's shortened shelf life ensures that retailers will always have a steady stream of shoppers, as long as they don't fall behind the trends. It's this intentional pushing—in tandem with the convergence of certain timely social trends—that has created Speed Chic's dangerously manic cycle.

A SIGN OF THE TIMES

Our impatience with fashion trends is fueled by our ever-shortening attention spans. Today, the pace of life itself is fast. The speeding data of the Information Age has warped our sense of time. Buying gas with a credit card is too time consuming (now we can pay with the wave of a jazzed-up keychain at the pump). Minute-long news segments are too much of a snooze (major news networks stream live, Web-inspired information feeds along the bottom of the screen for the time deprived). Even toasting a Pop Tart takes too long (now instructions on the back of the box tell you how to microwave it in three seconds). We pass laws to increase speed limits. We invent products to shave off even more time: quick-dry nail polish, drive-through service, ATMs, overnight mail, express trains, "8 Minute Abs," faster-acting drugs and cleaning products. With everything around us moving so quickly, it's clear that change in fashion couldn't continue at a snail's pace. Fashion may have sped up, but so has nearly everything else around us.

COMMUNICATION

In Ses Salinas, a small fishing village on the idyllic Spanish island of Mallorca, it's still entirely possible to exist without a means of communication to the outside world. No TV. No phone. No fax. No e-mail. Not even snail mail. To find a computer capable of sending e-mail, you must drive thirty miles to the nearest tourist district. In the early evening, when the sun is just starting to fade, the men in the village sit and talk for hours on fold-out chairs at their front doorsteps, dressed in guayaberas, those lightweight button-downs with two rows of embroidery stitched down the front. Every now and then, a woman will emerge from one of the boxy stone houses in a shapeless white house-dress to sweep off the dusty entryway or to stretch her legs.

Spain has produced its share of esteemed fashion designers, including Manuel Fernandez and Cristobal Balenciaga. But in Ses Salinas, with its limited connection to the world beyond its borders, the prevailing fashion is the discernible *lack* of fashion. When fashion editors in all corners of the world were hailing sporty chic as the hot new look, residents of Ses Salinas didn't rush out to buy juiced-up sneakers and hooded sweatshirts. They didn't even know these trends existed.

In Ses Salinas, I learned an important lesson: When you don't know what you're missing, you don't miss it.

This is a point lost on most of us, most of the time. With today's high-tech communications, fashion trends are broadcast into our homes instantaneously. "With increased media and communication, consumers are able to see what is on the runway while it is practically still on the runway," says Deborah Christiansen, Ph.D., a professor of apparel and merchandising at Indiana University. When Donatella Versace includes a puckered turquoise minidress in her spring collection, it's now possible for police officer Faith Nadel in Tampa, Florida, to see it at the same time that Jennifer Lopez lays eyes on it as it comes toward her down the catwalk in Milan. It used to be that most of us wouldn't see new designs until they surfaced in magazines or in stores four to six months after they were unveiled on the runway. Now that this time frame has shortened, we see it sooner, so we want it sooner. Designers, manufacturers, retailers, and, ultimately, consumers have been forced to keep up.

It's not only the promptness with which we see trends that has fostered Speed Chic, but also the general rush-rush state of the media. We are children of MTV and the Internet. "Society is conditioned to the instant gratification mentality," says Christiansen. "The Internet and e-mail have made all media and other forms of communication become 'instant' and they've fostered the 'quick response' desire in all of us." Watch an old black-and-white movie and you'll recognize just how rapid-fire most big-budget Hollywood plots have become today. TV editors appear to chop film up for an audience of ADD sufferers, and we've adapted. Imagine watching the cast of *Survivor* or some other reality show for an actual twenty-four-hour day with no edits, just hours upon hours of people sleeping, twiddling their thumbs, sitting. Producers and directors have even added flashy camera angles and edits to awards shows and concerts aired on TV to give them more of a music-video feel. This attitude has seeped into our feelings about fashion.

It's easy to forget that today's communications and entertainment media are relatively young inventions. "In the fifties, we had three television networks, several movie studios, and only a handful of national magazines," says Rodney Runyan, Ph.D., associate professor and chairman of the fashion marketing and merchandising program at Northwood University in Midland, Michigan. "In the past twenty years, we've added dozens of television networks, dozens of independent movie studios, thousands of movie screens, dozens of national magazines, and now the Internet. Technology has increased the frequency and level of exposure to fashion, as well as compressed the time period from inception to exposure."

The result: we're absolutely saturated with fashion information. "Attention spans for trends are about five minutes long at this point," says Elizabeth Kiester, fashion director of *YM* magazine and former market director at *Jane*. "I try to explain to our nineteen-year-old interns that when I started in this business—it was before the explosion of cable TV, before *Marie Claire* and *Jane* and *Lucky* and *Nylon* and *Detour* and *Flaunt* and *In Style*, before *Bazaar* got young and hip, before the Internet and Style.com and satellite TV shows and MTV and *Fashion File*. We are so inundated with information now." Consumers are bombarded with images nearly everywhere they look. "You've seen every trend a billion times before it's even at your local Macy's," says Kiester. "The celebs are wearing next season's stuff on this season's red carpet, and those pics are in *People, In Style, Us* and on every network. Ugh, you want to puke, you can't look at camouflage for one more second, and it's not even at the Gap yet. And then the design houses are trying to keep up, pumping this stuff out, clamoring for the trend, and it's at Old Navy and Barney's at the exact same time. So fashionistas and people on a budget can both have cropped camo pants simultaneously, and the next thing you know is that everyone walking down the street looks exactly the same. It's exhausting."

The high-speed dissemination of trends on TV and on the Internet also throws a monkey wrench into the timeline of fashion. "If there's any negative effect of the shows being televised it's that so much seasonal information is put out into the public before consumers would actually be buying it—for example, summer clothes showing in September," says Fern Mallis, of 7th on Sixth. "You have some very savvy consumers who are, like the industry, ready for the next thing. It's causing stores to be [stocking clothes] earlier and earlier." In the past, when a trend was shown on the catwalk in February—in the collections for the following fall—it might not have been seen by consumers for another three to five months. But eager shoppers who can now check out footage from the shows may clamor for the new trend long before that, creating a plum opportunity for quick knockoff artists to rake in the loot while the original designer is stuck with an already outmoded trend by the time her design hits the stores months later. That's the irony of fashion: we want to look like everyone else, but only if they're cooler than us. Some high-end designers have attempted to combat the damage knockoffs have done to their business with greater customization—their last-ditch effort to make expensive purchases mean something again. In July 2002, Gucci introduced a line of made-to-order handbags, selling for $1,500 to $15,000, that customers could customize by color, size, leather, or monogram.

In 1999, 7th on Sixth decided to move the New York Fashion Week shows up six weeks earlier than usual to get a jump on competitors in other countries. Designers claimed that the earlier opening put them ahead of fashion houses in Europe, leaving more time for production and delivery, and less chance of being accused of copying. It also meant items would turn up on the Fashion Victim's wish list that much sooner, and the fashion schedule would be screwed up that much more.

PROSPERITY

The Quiet Power Automatic Tie Rack holds seventy-two ties. The motorized contraption—made by Sharper Image Design, and priced at $59.95—rotates left or right with the flick of a switch, spinning and illuminating all six-dozen neckties on the rack in a mere ten seconds. The entire compact design takes up just 5 1/4 inches of horizontal closet space. A fabulous space-saving invention, indeed. But the question remains: Does any man really need to own seventy-two ties?

Speed Chic thrives because enough consumers can afford to keep squandering their dollars on short-lived trends. Spending on fashion tends to be correlated with financial resources. If we didn't have disposable income, we wouldn't be able to shop. Our country's prosperity—encompassing even those of us who aren't truly wealthy, per se—allows us to be lifelong consumers. That's markedly different from the reality faced by many people in developing countries, who struggle to afford food, let alone one necktie. While surveys indicate that the average American today spends a smaller percentage of his or her income on clothing than people did in previous decades—due in great part to the trend toward more casual dress both at work and outside it—we're still buying a lot of clothes, partly because our prosperity has allowed us to stockpile Speed Chic items. And while the average American spends just under $2,000 on clothes each year, the trend-happy Fashion Victim typically spends far more. Survey data is misleading; it's dragged down drastically by the people who don't buy much clothing at all. For example, while Sylvia in Palm Beach may lay out thousands of dollars per month on designer duds, Smitty in Iowa may only spend $50 per year on work boots and two pairs of overalls. Voilà—the statistics plummet.

When we keep up with fashion trends, displaying our financial ability to buy new clothes on a constant basis, we convey something about our bank accounts and, essentially, our level of success. It's human nature: the have-nots will always want to be the haves. The frustrating part about Speed Chic, however, is that *everyone* can be a have-not. Even the wealthiest fashionista feels a twinge of competitiveness when she sees someone wearing an outfit cuter than hers. She's pushed to spend even more money, to drain her bank account even further, to drive herself doubly into debt. Clothes, like luxury cars and big houses, are an outward symbol of our prosperity. And, due to our competitive nature, we use our clothes to compare ourselves with those around us. As Barry Schwartz, author of *The Costs of Living*, says, we're not only trying to keep up with the Joneses, we're now trying to surpass them. We become more prosperous, and so do our neighbors. We continually raise the bar; they follow and elevate the standard once again, and we have no other choice but to see and surpass.

To make matters worse, we're now not only trying to keep up with the Joneses . . . we're trying to keep up with the Catherine Zeta-Joneses. We no longer look just at our neighbors, co-workers, and friends as measuring sticks of our own success; we compare ourselves to people with unreachably high social standing and levels of wealth. The Fashion Victim is pushed to spend by everyone she sees, which, today, includes those glamorous millionaires in Hollywood. But it's a dead end, says Gary Cross, author of *Time and Money: The Making of Consumer Culture*. "Keeping up with the Joneses . . . gives individuals ways of expressing themselves, but doesn't necessarily lead to real conversation with others or self-knowledge," he says. We're chasing unattainable satisfaction.

Today, about 3.5 million U.S. households are worth $1 million or more. In 1975, there were 350,000 millionaire households (only a third of the increase can be attributed to inflation, according to Tom Stanley, author of *The Millionaire Next Door*). For the most part, Americans are a wealthy bunch. Yet we're a nation of poor savers. According to Juliet Schor, author of *The Overspent American*, our national savings rate has plummeted. The average American household currently saves only 3.5 percent of its disposable income, about half the rate of fifteen years ago. "The French, Germans, Japanese, and Italians save roughly three times what Americans do, and the British and Dutch more than twice," says Schor. "Even Indian and Chinese households, most of which are dirt poor, manage to save about a quarter of their paltry yearly incomes." Not surprisingly, Americans also make up the biggest slice of the pie when it comes to spending on status luxury goods, haute couture, and high-end prêt-à-porter: the U.S. consumes 25 percent of such goods; Japan, 15 percent; the rest of Asia, 17 percent; France, 16 percent; and the rest of Europe, 18 percent. Other areas of the world combined snatch up only 9 percent.

The average American carries nearly $6,000 in credit-card debt month to month. But the Fashion Victim, thanks to her profligate spending habits, is at risk of carrying much more. Every time we buy the must-have item, we drive ourselves further into debt. This not only adds to our stress levels—requiring us to spend even more money on "retail therapy"—it also steers us into a relentless cycle of overwork. As Schwartz asserts in *The Costs of Living*, people could live happier lives if they consumed less, which would allow them to remove some of the pressures of *making* money. When we get caught up in the cycle of Speed Chic, we don't allow ourselves to truly enjoy life because we're so busy trying to get paid enough to maintain our increasingly expensive lifestyles. For instance, a marketing assistant with a studio apartment, bus pass, and H&M wardrobe can squeeze by on an entry-level salary. When she gets a promotion and a raise two years later, her expenses also mount—she moves into a one-bedroom apartment, leases a Honda Accord, and upgrades to a French Connection wardrobe. Years down the line, when she's making many times what she had earned early in her career, the cost of everyday life will have risen even more—a mortgage, BMW, and closet full of Chloé. She works longer hours than she used to, brings work home on weekends, carries more credit-card debt than ever before. Her attraction to fashion and other forms of consumption prevents her from taking restful vacations. It impairs her relationships because she spends so much time at work. It even indirectly ravages her health when nerve-wracking job and financial worries give her high blood pressure.

"Some people might work less, or take breaks between jobs, or not take a more time-killing job if they weren't such slaves to their possessions," says Cross. "The fashion consumption that dominates so much American spending is problematic because it distorts choices for using affluence. Fashion is a very expensive way of expressing oneself and clothing oneself, and it takes away resources from other things: time for less consumption-oriented leisure, and money for collective culture, such as the arts, recreation, meeting the needs of others, care for the environment, and so on."

In addition to leaving us with an empty feeling, the spiral of personal debt is precarious, to say the least. "The pattern of 'spend now pay later' has put the average family in serious debt," says credit expert Kristi Feathers. "If shoppers would get in the habit of allowing themselves to browse for items but not purchase until the next day, they would either not return for the purchase or buy relatively less. It's an impulse situation." By the time she was twenty, Feathers herself had three major credit cards and seven department-store cards. Over time, she accumulated over $25,000 in debt, which took her six years to pay off—after she had incurred about $9,000 in additional interest and fees. One of her biggest mistakes had been getting suckered into applying for store credit cards, which Feathers says are dangerous for several reasons: "1) They charge enormous interest rates, which ends in the consumer paying way more for the same product that they could purchase with cash, and 2) they approve almost anyone," she says. "Once a person is in debt for at least $3,000, it will usually take them four years to pay it down. Add additional cards to the mix and you have a serious bankruptcy possibility."

The Fashion Victim is willing to put up with some financial pain to experience some fashion pleasure. At a certain point, however, the scales will begin to tip, and the economic anguish will become too much to bear. Feathers wouldn't attempt to suggest that anyone stop buying clothes altogether—just be more judicious about your decisions and lay off the credit cards. "Stop charging immediately, take inventory of your overall credit-card debt, and begin a debt termination plan that includes targeting the debts one at a time to maximize payoff power. And continue this regimen until the debt is gone," she says. "In the meantime, pay cash or *don't* buy it."

MARKETING

Savvy marketers know that in the world of trends, everything new is beautiful and everything old is ugly (up until the point when it becomes beautiful in a retro way years later), so many clothiers have taken the opportunity to play on our fears of appearing passé, while promoting the prestige of novelty. "It makes sense from a business standpoint," says Rodney Runyan, of Northwood University. "If we make denim jeans to last three years, what will we sell until they wear out? We must constantly create new styles, and create a need in the customer to purchase the new style." Planned obsolescence usually comes in two varieties: implied or overt. The nature of fashion itself says that a style will one day be outmoded—that's implied. A store that stocks a new line of goods every month is *implying* that customers will be out of style if they don't buy these new items. Other methods of planned obsolescence are more direct. In his 1997 book *The Conquest of Cool*, Thomas Frank describes an ad for J & F Suits that ran in *GQ* in 1965 and 1966 under the headline "Do you still put your pants on over your shoes?" followed by the copy, "Don't admit it if you do. You shouldn't be able to. Any suit that calls itself new should have tapered pants so narrow you have to put your shoes on last." The desired effect: sensitive readers would deem themselves social losers if they didn't buy one of these new suits. It's a prime example of how companies use Speed Chic to their advantage. Hype the hot new thing while phasing out the old. Get the customers to come back and spend more.

Today, nearly every pitch to get you to buy clothes plays the obsolescence game in one way or another, often by highlighting a style's newness. The word "new" is a staple of Madison Avenue. In the September 2001 *Vogue,* a Ralph Lauren ad touted "A New Kind of Glamour" while Donna Karan proclaimed, "Explore a New World of Luxury." Ads and catalogs flaunt the availability of new products. Even if we never set foot in a mall or store, we'd still be aware of the existence of new trends because companies wave them in front of us on TV, in magazines, at bus stops, along highways, on the Internet. Advertisers attempt to make consumers feel like they're missing out on some grand new trend. Slogans like Old Navy's "You gotta get this look" imply that we're missing out if we don't jump on the bandwagon. When companies advertise major sales, they're effectively publicizing the end of a trend: older styles are listed as sale items, and even *older* styles are promoted as clearance items.

The media also feed into planned obsolescence. Designers reveal their new creations before they hit the stores, and in turn, magazines and trendspotters hype the styles on their "in" and "out" lists. Apparently, there's not room for two trends to hold the spotlight at the same time. Military is in, plaid is out. Indian is in, Oriental is out. Little thought goes into planning the "in" and "out" lists beyond observing what's new. (How big a faux pas would it be for a magazine to put fringe on their "in" list two seasons in a row!) Hosts of TV talk shows and morning programs hype the latest looks—what's hot for the high-powered executive this fall, what's hot for the summer beach wedding, what'll be hot at the Aspen ski lodge this winter. What all this suggests is not only that these new looks have arrived but that the old ones have been officially declared obsolete. All this manipulation by marketers and media should leave a bad taste in the mouths of Fashion Victims. But instead of feeling tricked, we merely follow along.

VARIETY

Clothes are like jelly beans: some of the flavors (jalapeño?) are nause-ating, but we're still happy they exist. As a society of Fashion Victims, we've grown accustomed to variety (at the 2000 MTV Movie Awards, host Sarah Jessica Parker went through fifteen outfit changes). And we raise an eyebrow when there's a lack of it (most of us would notice if a co-worker wore the same outfit twice in one week). Not only does Speed Chic increase our demand for greater variety, its "more more more" mentality is also a direct result of it. The sheer overabundance of clothing that's manufactured today makes it possible for us to fill our closets with a massive array of time-sensitive styles.

In their book on retail, *A Stitch in Time,* Harvard professor Frederick Abernathy and his colleagues state that American con-sumers in 1995 purchased 28.7 outerwear garments (all coats, jackets, shirts, dresses, blouses, sweaters, trousers, slacks, and shorts) per person; in China, the estimated number of such garments purchased was only two per person. After World War II, most men's shirts came in one style—classic white. Today, in addition to the old standby, guys load up on blue, white/blue weave, end on end, 100 percent cotton oxford, pinpoint oxford, twill, poplin, broadcloth, linen, silk, voile, and non-iron. They're patterned in Tattersall, gingham, houndstooth, iridescent, windowpane, graph check, pencil stripe. Collars are either narrow spread, wide spread, extreme spread, English spread, button-down, curved, eyelet, pointed, tab, pin, or Ainsley, with a double, but-ton, barrel, round, angle, or French cuff. There's even endless variety when it comes to pocket styling: classic V, square, pleated, buttoned, inverted pleat with button, pleated diamond. We have a summer hand-bag for day, a summer handbag for night. We even have an assortment of workout clothes (heaven forbid our fellow exercisers see us wearing the same style of shorts two days in a row).

Today, there are over forty-five thousand shopping centers in the U.S. Stores stock racks upon racks of new garments, in a variety of col-ors, prints, sizes. They rotate their merchandise in the store windows and front displays so it appears as though another shipment has just arrived off the truck. With this apparently wide assortment, it's tougher for the consumer to resist. Imagine having a single clothing store in your hometown that only restocked every six months—you probably wouldn't be rushing back several times a month. It used to be that apparel retailers offered only four lines a year: spring, summer, fall, and winter. "Now stores get a new delivery every two weeks," says Jane Werner, associate professor of fashion-merchandising management for the Fashion Institute of Technology.

The retail system today churns trends with unprecedented efficiency. At one time, retailers would be saddled with a surplus of unwanted goods if they couldn't sell all their merchandise, a fact that no doubt caused many shop owners to keep their selection to a minimum. Today, the risk involved in ordering a wide variety of garments has lessened because leftovers can be sold elsewhere. "In the past, it would've really hit a company hard if they introduced a style that didn't make it," says Indiana University's Deborah Christiansen. "But now they can adjust product immediately and send the unused portion to TJ Maxx, Marshall's, or Filene's. The sales, markdowns, and closeouts are just part of the business plan." Outlet stores have also experienced a surge in popularity in recent years, making it possible for retailers to unload the season's surplus within their own discount stores. As these old styles are sold, they make room for a new variety of soon-to-be-unwanted items.

Still, even with all of this supposed variety, there's a surprising lack of different styles at any one time. But we operate under the illusion of personal style. Stores promote their clothes as the ingredients; we use those ingredients to create our own looks. They give us the paint; we create the painting. In 1988, the Gap ran a successful series of ads entitled "Individuals of Style," featuring celebrities like Kim Basinger and Dizzie Gillespie wearing Gap basics paired with more expensive garments—the campaign showed that even the most humdrum clothes could be twisted into interesting outfits.

Street anthropologist Ted Polhemus, author of *Street Style* and *Style Surfing,* believes we live in a "Supermarket of Style," browsing and combining different styles of dress. The ingredients that we have to choose from, he says, came from different periods of history—the punk's leather jacket, the prep's argyle sweater, the mod's pencil pants, the hippie's gauzy skirts. Theoretically, the Supermarket of Style would leave us with limitless combinations. We'd pick from this style one day, another the next, mixing and matching two or three looks. In reality, the ingredients that are available to shoppers on any given day are far more limited, since nearly every store sells the same styles at the same time. Fashion buyers anticipate what the season's trends will be after recognizing major directional changes in designers' collections, then stock their stores accordingly. So, right from the get-go, it's common for many stores to carry the same styles. And after a trend has been proven successful by one retailer, others inevitably follow. What we're left with is a throng of stores carrying identical looks. So, for example, when capri pants are in fashion, you can buy them at the Gap, Benetton, Armani, DKNY, and any number of other stores. When striped rugby shirts are in, consumers aren't limited to one label—they can pick one up at any number of shops. Everyone isn't wearing the exact same shirt, but they look nearly indistinguishable.

THE SPEED OF MANUFACTURING

The wide variety of Speed Chic items is only achievable thanks to technology and the lightning-fast pace of production in the global economy. "The manufacturing process has been sped up due to quick-response technologies, which allow manufacturers and retailers to respond to consumer demands more quickly," explains Christiansen. Quick-response has changed the face of retailing. At the Zara store on 59th Street in Manhattan, for instance, a store manager can input data about what's selling and what's not into a computer. This information travels through an intranet and ends up at a factory in Spain. If shoppers in New York have been complaining about button-fly, the factory can add zippers. If a brown belt hasn't been touched, the factory can change the color to black. If meteorologists are predicting a chilly season, the factory can add a lining to a jacket. Zara, widely regarded as a marvel of modern manufacturing, is renowned for its speed—an item of clothing can go from concept to cash register in just five weeks, compared to a nine-month lead time for many other

stores. Zara stores receive new shipments of stock at an incredible bi-
monthly rate.

A large number of retail giants, including The Limited,
Abercrombie & Fitch, Levi Strauss, Ann Taylor, Guess?, and Reebok,
use a similar quick-response technique but don't operate the system
themselves. Instead, they turn to sourcing companies like Hong
Kong's Li & Fung. The high-tech firm acts as the middleman between
the retailers and a fine-tuned network of more than seventy-five
hundred suppliers in thirty-seven countries. As with Zara, Li & Fung's
clients feed information into an intranet to change the color, size,
and style of their garment orders *as they are being made*. So, no more
turning out three thousand pairs of plaid pants, only to discover a
week later that people are avoiding plaid like the plague. Instead, the
retailer changes the pattern to, say, pinstripes, and off the adjustments
go to the factory in Taiwan.

Manufacturing clothes offshore has traditionally been hampered
by longer turnaround times, but free-trade agreements like the 807
Program of the Caribbean Basin Initiative (CBI) have allowed U.S.
importers and retailers to make goods in nearby Caribbean countries
for far less than they could in the U.S., but with almost equal delivery
time. "The prices are a little higher than in the Orient, but this is more
than offset by the turnaround time," says Rodney Runyan.

Even companies that specialize in basics have been forced to keep
up with Speed Chic. "The demands for freshness and newness have
created a challenging manufacturing environment," says Duane
Hammer, vice president of planning and inventory control at Sara Lee,
which manufactures Hanes and other activewear lines through a network of factories in five countries. "The core products that were part of
our basic stable were once sold year after year with only minor changes.
In today's market our product offerings completely change over every
year. The product line changes developed and sold for the current year
may never be produced again. Something new will take their place."

The speed of manufacturing has helped not only designers but
also copycats, who can get their versions of trends into stores more
quickly. A knockoff artist can see clips from the catwalk and, the very

same day, send plans to a factory in Cambodia, which can begin churning out copies, quickening the pace of Speed Chic even more. Lesser quality often means faster production—after all, one hasty machine stitch is faster than a careful handsewn one. As a result, there's typically a wealth of Speed Chic lookalikes at every price range. Mass-market trend king The Limited erected its own airplane runway at its home base in Columbus, Ohio, to ensure that textiles arrive at the earliest possible date. Cheap chic chain H&M has become so proficient at reinterpreting trends at low prices that it can get a trend from sketch to store in six weeks, long before the original designers' versions are even available for sale in stores. Today, if you want it fast, you can get it. And designers pay the price, having their creations stolen time and again.

FALLING PRICES

We may enjoy prosperity, but we're also suckers for a good buy. Speed Chic is so pervasive because such a wide range of people can afford to participate in it. In April 2002, Asda, Britain's third-largest grocer, launched a womenswear collection aimed directly at Speed Chic. The store's "fast fashion" aimed to cut the factory-to-store time lag from eighteen weeks to seven and refresh the range every month. Back in the early days of haute couture, before technology removed many of the roadblocks to copying, only the wealthy could afford to wear the season's trends. Today, there are few trends that can't be reinterpreted in a less expensive form. A $25,000 diamond-studded dress can be mass-produced with cheap crystals. An $80,000 chinchilla jacket can be turned out as a $55 faux-fur jacket. Stores like H&M, Bebe, Old Navy, XOXO, and Spanish retailer Mango, among others, interpret hot trends at superlow prices. "The concept of our entire society being about faster, quicker, speedier, but cheaper to please has driven product into a state of trendiness that's unmatched in history," says Deborah Christiansen. "That also means it's of increasingly lower quality, which isn't of concern to your typical American shopper, because they know they won't have the product long anyway."

If we're going to remain in the cycle of Speed Chic, it feels a whole lot less naughty if the clothes are cheap. If you can't justify spending $90 for a designer shirt you know will be passé next month, you can buy one from H&M for a fraction of the price and a fraction of the guilt. "I would *never* buy a $500 purse for myself," says Trinity, a twenty-eight- year-old salesperson in Knoxville, Tennessee. "It's not because I don't have money. I earn a good living, as does my husband—over $200,000 a year between the two of us. I just refuse to spend a lot on trendy stuff." Still, a refusal to pay high-end prices doesn't mean we're buying fewer clothes. "I get sick of clothes pretty easily and want new stuff often," says Trinity. "It's my way of justifying shopping more frequently."

Sure, cheap trends make fashion more democratic, allowing a greater number of people to share in the fun rather than restricting a style solely to the wealthy. But ultimately, a fast, cheap knockoff only accelerates that style's eventual demise, since the stylish people who started the trend will abandon it once it becomes too pervasive. In July 2001, Yves Saint Laurent's coveted $2,500 purple silk peasant blouses sold out in days at the New York boutique, leaving wealthy admirers no other choice than to put their names on a lengthy waiting list until October. By that time, other, more mass-market retailers had already knocked off the style, rendering the original YSL version markedly less desirable in the eyes of those early purchasers. By the beginning of 2002, nearly every major women's fashion magazine declared the peasant blouse a must-have for the spring season, and the off-the-shoulder knockoffs could be found for about 1 percent of the price of YSL's purple silk one. At this point would anyone put their name on a waiting list for a $2,500 blouse?

Although quality has improved, mass-market Speed Chic clothes are inexpensive, generally speaking, because they're cheaply made. We accept that. And we treat cheap clothes differently from our high-priced garments, coddling a $250 dress more than a $35 sweater. So our low-priced garb never shakes the aura of being a throwaway item. In high school, I worked as a salesgirl in the women's casual department at Macy's. Even in a store, consumers treat expensive clothes more kindly. Customers would leave unwanted $30 try-ons crumpled on the floor, stepping on them, ripping them, thinking nothing of leaving white deodorant residue on blouses (you don't even want to know what one woman did with a feminine hygiene product one time). But in the designer dress section just across the way, where gowns started at $250 and higher, shoppers were very careful about hanging merchandise back up on hangers after they were done.

We can't help but view these inexpensive garments as somewhat disposable. And dispose we do. Each year, U.S. landfills are stuffed with four million tons of clothing and other textile waste, of which the average American contributes about 67.9 pounds. And that's not counting the heaps of virtually untouched garments that are donated to thrift stores or packed away in the backs of our closets every year. We are bulimic shoppers—while bulimics binge and vomit food, the Fashion Victim binges on shopping sprees, then upchucks the unwanted garments shortly afterward. A pair of pants that originally retailed for several hundred dollars is tossed out like yesterday's trash by its jaded owner. As the Fashion Victim continues to buy into the philosophy that clothes are like Kleenex (one blow, then they go), it's a given that the leftovers will have to go somewhere.

About 95 percent of the clothes we throw out are recyclable. Each year, textile recycling removes 2.5 billion pounds of consumer clothing waste headed for landfills, but that barely makes a dent in the total waste—remember, four million *tons*. Once at the textile recycling plant, clothes are graded and sorted. About 20 percent of these garments become wiping and polishing cloths sold to the government or industries for use in auto garages, furniture finishing, and janitorial supply operations. Almost half are exported to Third World nations. Still, although our clothes can serve a purpose beyond becoming stuffing for yet another landfill, the bulk of them will end up resting underground for thousands of years to come.

Some of us feel guilty wasting food ("Don't you know there are children starving in Africa?"). Similarly, some of us feel guilty throwing away clothes, which is why it's so hard to clean out your closet sometimes. Still, we feel relatively little shame purchasing disposable trends at the pace we do. Twelve dollars spent on a cheap shirt we'll never wear somehow doesn't weigh as heavily on our minds as $12 squandered on a passionfruit martini we order then spill all over the floor (the humanity!).

Perhaps we don't worry so much about clothing waste because there's such an overabundance not only of the finished product but also of the raw materials. We have no qualms about wasting because we have no fear of running out. We feel bad about throwing away perfectly good paper—we're wasting trees. But we still rarely associate clothes with their sources: the poor silkworms that must toil away to make one tie, the now-hairless sheep that produced only part of a cheap sweater, the baby cow that lived a short existence to supply leather for a belt, the petroleum products sucked from the earth then processed to craft a rayon skirt. The Speed Chic process of bringing forth trends and then killing them removes all sense of appreciation for clothes. They're no longer special because they're so ephemeral.

. . .

The greatest injustice of Speed Chic is that under these circumstances, the smartest people on earth can be reduced to the biggest fashion numbskulls. Successful businesspeople can be made to feel like failures when it comes to picking the right suit. A First Lady can be ridiculed for wearing a "frumpy" dress (as Laura Bush was). An Oscar-winning actress can be a laughingstock for choosing the wrong gown. A brilliant professor can be mocked by his students for his eccentric taste in loud jackets. Sometimes, the cheer/jeer meter runs the other way, and otherwise undeserving clotheshorses can rise to the top of this nonsensical pecking order. In 2001, when Victoria "Posh Spice" Beckham appeared on *The Daily Show with Jon Stewart,* she acted like a toffee-nosed snob, shooting down Stewart's attempts to make jokes by telling him he wasn't funny and glaring at him unamused. That year, countless British mags voted Beckham the celebrity with the best style. Congeniality, evidently, counts for nothing in the Miss Fashionable pageant.

No matter how much pleasure we find in shopping for clothes, there's always an underlying frustration that we can't keep up—a steady, low-level feeling of failure from not being able to stay abreast of the rise and fall of trends. The Fashion Victim stands in front of her overflowing closet and screams, "I have nothing to wear!" because whatever she has is never enough. She suffers innumerable Bad Clothes Days when nothing seems to look right, even though the same clothes looked fine just a week ago. Even worse, anxiety that you'll never measure up to some indefinable level of good taste has little to do with how much you actually own or don't own—some of the people with the largest wardrobes are still dissatisfied when they peer into their closets every morning.

What's more, having your confidence trounced by something as inconsequential as fashion is a downer all its own. With so many other important issues to pour our energy into, it's often embarrassing to admit that fashion plays such a pivotal role in affecting our moods. We hate to think that we're so shallow as to allow our appearance to affect us so deeply. We don't want to care what other people think of the sweater we wear to a party, but we do . . . and we're mortified that choosing that sweater required as much painstaking contemplation as it did. Before I attended my first fashion show, I spent an embarrassing two hours pacing in front of my closet trying to assemble an outfit with the appropriate mix of nonchalance and deliberate cuteness. I was so worried I wouldn't fit in among the fashion crowd that I drove myself to the brink of tears over a silly outfit.

In the fashion world, money obviously plays a role in who's well-dressed and who's not. Certainly, a millionaire who can afford custom-made suits and handcrafted loafers might easily have fewer Bad Clothes Days than the entry-level worker who stocks his closet at discount stores. But to a greater extent, the modern-day haves and have-nots are divided by their willingness to play the fashion game. Bill Gates, the wealthiest man in the world, could afford to outdress any style maven, but he's clearly not overly concerned with fashion. Likewise, there are some cool kids on tight budgets out there who manage to whip up the most stunning outfits with nothing but a burlap sack and some thread. Also, greater wealth often brings higher expectations. A socialite can't show up to a gala in a $200 dress (or at least let anyone *know* it was $200). Her what-to-wear anxiety is no less nerve-wracking than that of the struggling actress who's forced to pair $15 items from H&M and Target when she goes on auditions.

Self-esteem is tied quite directly to fashion. Psychologists believe that internal sense of worth plays a large role in compulsive shopping. True shopping addiction affects 2 to 8 percent of American adults, and a majority of those affected are women, says James Goudie, a consumer psychologist at Britain's Northumbria University. Shopaholics get a buzz from acquiring new material possessions that sets off a never-ending cycle. "They get caught in the vicious circle of shopping, accompanied by a mental buzz, followed by guilt and depression and/or anxiety because of what they've done, which is paradoxically relieved by shopping again, and so on and so on," says Goudie. Many mental-health experts now classify shopaholism as a type of obsessive-compulsive disorder, a condition that goes beyond the run-of-the-mill enjoyment of shopping that most of us experience. In 2000, researchers at Stanford University studied the effect of the antidepressant Celexa on compulsive shoppers, a study criticized by some cynics who refuse to accept shopping addiction as a psychological disorder. According to the believers, though, waving clothes in front of a shopaholic is like waving a vodka bottle in front of an alcoholic. The accessibility and attractiveness of fashion trends can trigger bouts of unbridled shopping.

Speed Chic does have some redeeming qualities. To the Fashion Victim, keeping up with trends is a hobby. It can be a diversion, an enjoyment. Just as sports fans monitor their favorite teams' stats, Fashion Victims keep an eye on their favorite designers. Just as the amateur investor watches the stock market, the Fashion Victim observes fluctuations in style. Just as the baseball card collector spends a large percentage of his weekly paycheck on a coveted card, the Fashion Victim splurges on a sought-after outfit. Surely, one could argue that there are bigger wastes of money than clothes, such as alcohol, drugs, or cigarettes, since you don't get to keep those things once they've passed through your body. (Oh, and there's the fact that they can kill you. In all my research, I wasn't able to find a single case in which clothes shopping killed a person.)

That being said, Speed Chic has an amazing ability to cloud our

judgment—it's only months and years later that we recognize the
ridiculousness of the trends we once fell for. We're often so mesmerized by a style's novelty that we don't realize how truly ugly it is (how
else can you explain stirrup pants?). As an experiment, I tried to look
at new clothes through reality-tinted glasses while browsing Girlshop,
one of my favorite shopping websites. At the time, punky slashed
T-shirts had just made a comeback, and several designers were selling
their hacked-up tops, ornamented with graffiti, ribbons, and other
embellishments, on the site for up to several hundred dollars. In
Fashion La-La Land, the shirts were attractive because the flashy
slashed look had made its way onto models and celebrities; in reality,
they were outrageously overpriced T-shirts that I realized I would
loathe within a month. Today, I put clothes through what I call the Test
of the Sixes. See a trend for what it is: Think about what it will look like
to you six weeks from now, six months from now, six *years* from now.
If the garment has the potential to make you look back at photos six
years from now and howl, "What was I thinking?" that's normal; six
months from now, think long and hard about how much you really
want it; six weeks from now, then it's failed the test. You'd be surprised by your ability to see right through unattractive trends once you
peel away those deceptive layers of novelty and marketing. Speed Chic
is built on items that are designed to fail; their brief popularity lies
solely in their newness. Open your eyes to that fact, and shopping
becomes an entirely different experience.

As logic would suggest, there has to come a point when Speed
Chic will start to slow. Otherwise, trends would eventually accelerate to
the point where they would change on a daily and even hourly basis.
Unless there's some marvelous space-age invention that can churn out
new clothes in the time it takes to toast a bagel, I can't imagine that
anyone will be participating in that type of Speed Chic. As Elizabeth
Rhodes, Ph.D., director of the school of fashion design and merchandising at Kent State University, predicts, the general pace of life will
lose a little steam, which will bring with it a slowdown in fashion
trends. "I do find that people are becoming increasingly tired of having to constantly adapt to new things—how many different upgrades of
Microsoft Office must I learn, for example?" she says. "Some desire

seems to be present to slow the pace and smell the roses—which I've actually seen more in young people than in old." In an ideal world, says Rhodes, we'd learn to advance where advancement was needed, and not just change for the sake of change alone. "We may return to more classic looks and more enduring forms for the sake of comfort and familiarity," she says. But even then, we'll never revert to a time when trends disappear. Although TV shows and movies set in the future often portray a society that embraces uniformity in dress (am I the only one who would cry outerspace mutiny if we all had to wear those *Star Trek* unitards?), it's unlikely that we'll see flashy trends disappear in our lifetimes.

4

McFashion

Seventy-five percent of American men own a pair of Dockers khakis.

Sedona, Arizona, is the color of a heated oven coil. The sun tints most cities brick-orange in those seconds right after it peeks out over the horizon. But Sedona remains the same chili-powder hue 24/7, even in winter, when there's the odd chance a few flakes of snow or frost will sugarcoat the red rocks. Within these weirdly wonderful environs stands a familiar sight: the Gap. In fact, there are two. There is a Gap in nearby Flagstaff Mall and an off-price Gap warehouse in Sedona's Oak Creek Outlets, where Dee Estrella, a website manager (and nurse, by training) is shopping to buy a gift for her two-year-old grandson's birthday. She picks up two outfits and a baseball cap—a steal at under $20.

Across the globe in Berkshire, England, a county that lies in the valley of the middle Thames, you don't have to search hard to find relics of a rich history. Royalty from the tenth century onward are buried here, including King Henry I and his wives Matilda and Adeliza, Prince John

of Cornwall, and Princess Constance of York. The Uffington White
Horse, a 130-foot-tall line drawing carved into the chalk of the White
Horse Hill, has stood watch over the region since the Iron Age. Within
Berkshire's borders lies Windsor Castle and the famous boys' school,
Eton College, endowed by Henry VI. Also in and around Berkshire's
historic boundaries lie eight Gap stores. Michelle March Bank, an
eighteen-year-old student, works at the one in Maidenhead as a part-
time salesgirl. She buys a new Gap garment every day that she goes to
work, since she gets everything half price with her employee discount.
Today, it's a pink cotton halter top for £9.

In Vancouver, British Columbia, with its odd juxtaposition of snow-
capped mountains and cityscapes, you can see the world's thinnest
office building. Built in 1913, the Sam Kee Building, on the corner of
West Pender and Carrall streets in the city's Chinatown, is only six feet
wide. The area boasts over 180 city parks and a bald eagle population
larger than any other in the world. The greater Vancouver area plays
host to thirty Gap stores. On this beautiful day, surgical assistant
Rachel Adam is shelling out Can$160 at her local Gap for a pair of low-
rise khakis for herself, plus black cargo pants and dark denim jeans
for her husband.

In Okayama, Japan, a prefecture facing the Seto Inland Sea, you'll find
the sixteenth-century Okayama Castle, often referred to by locals as
"Crow Castle" because of its black exterior. The fifth and sixth floors
have an observation deck overlooking Korakuen Garden, a picturesque
oasis with beautifully shaped ponds and waterfalls originally laid out
in 1686 for the warlord Ikeda. The area is known for its Bizen ware
pottery, a dark, unglazed earthenware that has roots dating back a
thousand years. If you're not in the market for timeless artwork, you
can step into the Gap or GapKids in Okayama as Jiro Shiba, a thirty-
one-year-old English teacher, is doing today. He picks up two striped
T-shirts for 1,300 yen apiece.

. . .

In every corner of the world, the Gap is the same. Walking into the Gap on the historic tree-lined Champs Elysée in Paris is like walking into the Gap in Miami's hulking new Dolphin Mall: pale modular shelves with meticulously folded shirts resting on top, well-groomed sales staff manning their work zones, compartments filled with orderly stacks of jeans and khakis, impulse items like Gap fragrance and candles at the cash wrap—even the smell of the stores seems to be the same. Despite a well-publicized drop in its sales and stock price in 2001–2002, there are still about thirty-five Gap stores in New York City alone, not to mention the dozen or so stand-alone GapKids and babyGap locations. One summer, two Japanese girls stopped me on the sidewalk as I was walking in Times Square. "Excuse me, where's the Gap?" one of them asked, as if she were asking directions to Carnegie Hall, the Empire State Building, or some other landmark. I pointed to all four corners—there was literally a Gap store within a few blocks to the north, east, south, and west of us.

EXTRA CHEESE, PLEASE

We are consumers of McFashion.

In our "I want it now" world, fashion has begun to resemble fast food: fast, disposable, easy, unintimidating, entertaining, and largely homogeneous. Just as McDonald's had taken over the globe, dishing out their uniform and consistent burgers and fries, mass-market clothing retailers like the Gap have succeeded in spreading predictability in fashion. Just as we can enter a McDonald's in Dallas and order the same meal as we can in Munich, we can enter a Gap store in both cities and buy the same shirt. Just as McDonald's golden arches have become an all-too-familiar symbol, so too has the Gap's simple blue sign. Just as McDonald's owes a great part of its success to marketing, the Gap's greatest strength has always been its ability to make no-frills clothes seem like must-haves. In June 1998, the Gap one-upped the McDonald's drive-through window, introducing Gap-to-go, a clothing delivery service for busy New Yorkers. Shoppers simply select the item, color, and size from a menu, then fax or call in their order. Orders can be delivered the same day to any location in Manhattan. And for those on an extremely tight deadline: one-hour rush delivery.

McFashion is certainly not limited to the Gap, but it is epitomized by the chain. "Gap clothes are great for not being noticed," says Jason, a twenty-one-year-old student at the University of Pennsylvania. "I have to commend their truth in advertising, though, since when they say, 'Everybody in Khakis' or 'Everybody in Vests' it happens within a week." The Gap, founded as a single store by San Franciscans Donald and Doris Fisher in 1969, has blossomed into a corporation that includes Gap, Old Navy, and Banana Republic. Over the course of several decades, it rose to the ranks of the number-one clothing retailer in the world, with revenues topping $11.6 billion. The Gap, like McDonald's, has spread swiftly across the U.S. and around the world in a relatively short time. Its aggressive expansionist policies stem from a corporate philosophy known as "clustering," explains Louis Nevaer, author of the unauthorized 2001 exposé *Into—and out of—the Gap*. (The company's top execs were so miffed about the book, says Nevaer, that they prohibited managers from reading it.) "Clustering became very popular in the early 1990s," he says. "The idea is simple: open lots of stores near each other. This has the effect of putting pressure on competitors. When they close up, you can then dominate an area. Because Gap has so much money, it's been able to open more and more stores—increasing sales overall." Despite the company's slump in 2001–2002, it has continued to spread, opening more than 600 new stores in 2001—bringing its total number of stores to about 4,150. And while it did cautiously scale back expansion plans for 2002—to about 7 percent store growth instead of the previously promised 17 percent— it still kept multiplying, with plans to open as many as 280 new stores in 2002. However, projected business looked so bleak in the beginning of 2002 that the retailer did not expect to open any new stores in 2003, according to the *Washington Post*.

There's no shortage of McFashion retailers. Walk into any two Structure, Limited, or Aeropostale stores and you'll be struck by déjà vu—you've been there, seen that. Nearly every major retail chain today represents McFashion. The Gap is to H&M what McDonald's is to Burger King—both establishments may not carry the exact same items on their menus, but they convey essentially the same message: consistency. The elegant trilevel Ann Taylor store on Boston's Newbury Street carries the same workwear shells, dresses, slacks, and blouses as the one in Salt Lake City's Fashion Place shopping center. Urban Outfitters, which to some kids appears to sell clothes that scream individualism, actually sells the same standardized message as the Gap: wear our clothes and you'll fit in. But instead of khakis and plain sweaters, it sells trendy studded belts, downtown-cool muscle tees printed with messages like "Self Service," big-ass tinted shades, black canvas hipsters, and chunky cotton hoodies at every retail location across the country.

WHY McFASHION?

The Fashion Victim has a love-hate relationship with McFashion. McFashion is bland and downmarket, but it's also affordable and abundant. McFashion lets us fit in with certain social groups, but sometimes to the point at which our individuality disappears. McFashion is a diversion, but one that drains our wallets over time and leaves us little to hold on to in the long run.

Although we may often feel like victims of mass hypnosis, McFashion isn't some inexplicable phenomenon that sweeps over us. Its popularity is rooted in instant gratification—it offers on-the-spot relief for all our fashion cravings. What are the attributes behind McFashion's appeal? Surprise, surprise: they're the same qualities that have made fast food a global powerhouse.

McFASHION IS FAST

The key ingredient in any successful fast food joint, and in any winning clothier today, is speed. As we've seen with Speed Chic, the acceleration of trends and the impatience of shoppers have become integral to the industry's success. Before the proliferation of ready-to-wear in the mid-1800s, women were saddled with the responsibility for producing their entire family's clothes, which meant time-consuming hand-sewing before machines came along to do that chore. Today, the invasion of shopping malls, chain retailers, discount stores, department stores, and boutiques into nearly every nook and cranny of the world has made it possible to run out and buy a new item of clothing within minutes, a pace that fits well with our hyperkinetic twenty-first-century lifestyle. The downside to all this speed, however, is that it strips away any purported speck of value from a garment—we forget to care about things when they pass by us too quickly. As a result, a McFashion garment is to a specialty garment what a Big Mac is to a five-course dinner—unsatisfying, commonplace, and utterly forgettable.

McFashion works because the overall wait time—from entrance to purchase—is minimal, aside from the minutes lost waiting for a fitting room or spent killing time in line at the cash register. Pick it, pay for it, put it on. You can even buy cheap yet fashionable clothes in some supermarkets in Britain, while you're picking up a pint of milk. Asda supermarkets—the third-largest chain in the UK, purchased by Wal-Mart Stores Inc. in 1990—sells George tank tops, as well as shorts and other convenient items that shoppers can pick up out of necessity or at a whim.

The driving force behind McFashion's quickness is its predictability. Sit down at a new restaurant and you'll have to spend a few minutes reading the menu—the specials of the day, unfamiliar appetizers, interesting entrees and desserts. Walk into a McDonald's and you already know what you're going to get. The same goes for most chain clothing stores. Walk into a Wet Seal store and you don't have to spend any time acclimating to the vibe; you already know you'll find trendy tops, jeans, dresses, and accessories. Customers of Ann Taylor won't stroll into that store anytime soon to find baggy jeans and studded belts amid their tidy offerings. Even the layout of the same store in different locations is predictable. Once you've been to one Victoria's Secret store, you can walk into any other store location and recognize how it's set up—sexy silk teddies and negligees up front, panties fanned out on tables in the center, bras hanging in the back, and additional sizes folded in drawers underneath—there are no minutes lost finding your bearings.

Still, McFashion never wants to be *too* quick. A fast-food restaurant wants you to order as quickly as possible—it's unlikely you'll order more food just because you stand in front of the cashier longer. Clothing re-tailers, however, want you to take your time browsing; they know that those tempting impulse items at the cash wrap and those reduced-price items so alluringly displayed under the big "Sale" sign will draw more of your dollars the longer you linger. According to Paco Underhill, author of *Why We Buy,* "Somewhere between 60 and 70 percent of what we buy, we had no intention of buying." To the Fashion Victim, there's still a sense of joy to be relished in the act of shopping—we enjoy looking around, trying on clothes, feeling fabrics. Even e-tailers like Bluefly, Girlshop, Purple Skirt, and the many websites of brick-and-mortar stores don't completely remove the browsing aspect from shopping. They've begun to realize that consumers may want to see a pair of loafers from a side angle or head on, magnified or on a model, in the various colors they come in, or set side by side with other items on the website that they could put with the shoes to create a complete look. So while some McDonald's restaurants have experimented with a "sixty seconds or your meal is free" policy in the past, it's doubtful that French Connection or Benetton will ever strive for the same quick in-and-out pace.

McFASHION IS EASY

You would be hard-pressed to find two items at Banana Republic that don't match. During fall, the olive corduroy slacks could be paired with any number of options: the washed-out burgundy turtleneck, the auburn button-down, the chocolate two-button velvet blazer. The gray flat-front dress pants could be coupled with the carrot-colored long-sleeved V neck or the purple cashmere sweater. For spring, the twill pant in Sunset Coral goes with the sleeveless polo in Blue Marlin just as well as it does with the heathered cotton tee in Sesame. Even the most fashion-illiterate can march into a Banana Republic and find an outfit that's socially acceptable. With McFashion, there is no thinking required—everything is preconceptualized and prearranged. Sizes are neatly categorized for you; pieces that go together are displayed side by side; salespeople appear at your fitting-room door to offer items that complement your picks.

Stores that allow consumers to expend as little energy as possible are the winners in today's retail landscape. Shoppers are lazy, and only getting lazier. Part of enjoying the ease of McFashion is feeling pampered. Since clothes sold in chain retail stores aren't essentially that different (when denim skirts came back into fashion in 2001, nearly every store sold them), retailers have to differentiate themselves by doling out "extras." Spend more than a hundred dollars during any weekend during the holidays at Banana Republic's main branch in San Francisco, and the store will provide you with a lift home. At two of the retailer's flagship stores in California and New York, you can check your cell phone with the concierge at the front of the store for a quick battery recharge while you shop. You can also give your PalmPilot to a shop assistant who will upload a map of the store into it. And at Polaris Fashion Place in Columbus, Ohio, shoppers can drop their cars off at one location and pick it up at any other mall exit.

The numerous conduits for shopping make for easy buying. Consumers can peruse the J. Crew catalog, then either order by phone, waltz into the store to make their picks, or check them out online. The advent of e-tailing was supposed to make clothes shopping even easier: log onto a website from home, browse or search for clothes, input your credit-card number, receive your purchase at your doorstep. As it turned out, the Internet failed to make a significant dent in sales at brick-and-mortar stores as quickly as some analysts suspected it would. Instead, it proved that there's still something alluring about walking into a store and seeing the goods in person. For example, as much as teenage girls love Delia's online shop and catalog, they still can't get enough of shopping at the mall. Young shoppers still craved the in-store experience. But all was not lost. Delia's realized it could respond to all of these desires—it created several brick-and-mortar stores. Now, it could give its customers an even easier option: order by mail, phone, computer, or now, at the store.

McFASHION IS CAREFULLY PLANNED

These days, shopping for clothes is very much a manufactured experience. Retailers know that consumers are an impatient bunch and that in-store hassles can turn away valuable dollars. Consequently, they fritter away millions of dollars to conceive new strategies for getting consumers to stay longer and spend more. Every aspect of the shopping experience has been brainstormed on and mulled over by executives at company headquarters so that surprisingly little is left to chance. Shoppers may feel like they're simply browsing, but they're really being led.

Clothes and accessories stored in "dump bins" suggest a good buy. Items displayed in a glass case imply luxury. In department stores, things we really need are most often placed on the upper floors while impulse buys like perfume and accessories are located on the ground floor. Step into the store, and a whiff of its trademark scent will hit you. Its music conveys a message not only about the store but also about you—its target customer (is it bass-pumping techno? classical? hip-hop?). MP3.com can send digital music to retailers, who select songs that meet their store's demographic profile or set a mood. It can also update a store's playlist within twenty-four hours, allowing a retailer to play upbeat music on a rainy day or inject ads for slow-moving products. Many retailers, like Victoria's Secret, have even begun selling their own ambient CDs, so you can feel like you're in the girly pink lingerie store every day.

McFashion retailers customarily hire certain types of salespeople to work in their stores. Abercrombie & Fitch, for example, is notorious for hiring only cool, good-looking kids. A 1999 *Newsweek* article reported that store managers visit fraternities and sororities to recruit attractive "brand representatives," who work as few as five hours a week. Selling skills are not required—the job is to look good wearing A&F and have fun. Urban Outfitters commonly hires cool downtown kids with dreads or cheek piercings or sleeve tattoos. The look of employees is standardized. At Victoria's Secret, the strict company dress code dictates that staffers' outfits be 95 percent black. The lingerie store's six-page code contains such rules as "Only two rings per hand are acceptable" and "Fingernails should have a natural appearance both in color and in length (no longer than three-quarters of an inch from base of cuticle)."

Luring customers one time is good; getting them to return is great. In the same way that fast-food coupons and contests draw customers into restaurants, special hooks and promotions keep shoppers coming back to clothing stores. Pay for your purchase with your store credit card, like the GapCard or Old Navy's credit card (which comes in three color choices: Divine Lime, Power Shopper Orange, and True Blue) and receive rebates in the mail. With trusty discount coupon in hand, the self-respecting Fashion Victim can't help but return to the store another day.

McFASHION IS WELL MARKETED

In a 1992 "What's hot among kids" survey conducted by the Leo Burnett Company, about 90 percent of teens said Gap clothes were cool. Just a year later that figure dropped to 75 percent, and by 1995 it plummeted to 66 percent. Although Gap clothes had never been particularly exciting, the brand had somehow garnered the reputation of being unbearably boring. The retailer needed a shot in the arm . . . fast. It got just that in 1998 when it launched "Khakis Swing," an ad campaign so cool it even managed to make swing dancing trendy for a brief moment. Gap's cool rating soared again. It wasn't that the company's designers had suddenly come upon a fantastic new piece of apparel that every consumer would want that season; it was selling basic khakis to a customer base that already owned plenty of the casual pants. The driving force behind Gap's revival was marketing. Khakis hadn't suddenly become a trend. The Gap *made* them a trend.

Retail clothing chains distinguish themselves in great part through marketing, just as McDonald's, Burger King, Carl's, Wendy's, Jack in the Box, and the multitude of fast-food restaurants do. The power of marketing is such that the "best" products don't necessarily win. "Fashion is a kind of collective behavior," says Arthur Asa Berger, author of *Ads, Fads and Consumer Culture.* "What people buy, when they buy certain brands, is tied to attitudes about themselves, the fantasy an advertisement creates, and what's hot at a given moment in time." For example, in the early days of the soda-pop wars, Pepsi consistently beat Coke in taste tests. But quick-thinking marketers put free Cokes into the hands of troops in World War II, and the cola in the curvy glass bottle became an American classic, propelling it past its competition. Then Coke's cool rating slipped in the 1980s, and Pepsi began to gain ground. It wasn't that the taste of the drinks had changed at all—it was just that Pepsi had embarked on a better marketing strategy: focus on the younger generation. Nike and Reebok have fought a similar war for dominance in recent decades. Nike is currently winning, but it's conceivable that the tide could turn with one triumphant marketing push.

The brands we wear speak volumes about us, and companies know that we know. "[A label] represents how people think of themselves, what their life is actually like, and what they'd like it to be like," says Emily Cinader Woods, chairman and cofounder of J. Crew. "A great brand is relatable to a person and also aspirational—there has to be both." But what does it say about our culture when we can be taken in by marketing over style, when it's not the clothes that matter, but rather the image that the brand represents?

Advertising and marketing attract bodies to stores—and that's more than half the battle. Once shoppers are physically in the store, it's not that difficult to get them to buy something. American Eagle Outfitters, for example, was once perceived to be a brand for mature, outdoorsy types, until it repositioned itself in its ad campaigns as the more affordable Abercrombie & Fitch and hooked up with the WB Network to clothe the young cast of *Dawson's Creek* in 1999. These smart promotions made American Eagle cool among kids, enticed them into the store, and persuaded them to spend their parents' hard-earned dollars. That year, the retailer was named *Fortune* magazine's sixteenth-fastest growing company.

Marketers can work their magic on nearly any product. Take Banana Republic. How did a clothing company that started out selling safari wear end up selling corporate casual clothes? Founded in 1978 in Marin County, California, as a catalog company, Banana Republic became known for its mosquito netting, grass ceilings, and travel trunks, and the Jeep parked in the window of every store. Gap Inc. bought the chain in 1983 and took it nationwide. In the late eighties,

Banana Republic CEO Jeanne Jackson shoveled $150 million into marketing to achieve one of the most surprising transformations in the retail world, rendering the old safari store both unrecognizable and infinitely more popular. The retailer's new ownership had realized the limits of the safari theme—basic clothes that were slightly more upscale than Gap's would surely sell better than safari hats and khaki jackets covered with multiple pockets ostensibly meant for holding bullets, knives, and whatever other tools one might find handy in the African bush. The drastic transformation seemed like a long shot almost on par with Frederick's of Hollywood abandoning sexy lingerie to sell only baggy flannel jammies. But it proved that a clever marketing plan—with enough funds behind it—could convert even the most skeptical Fashion Victim.

McFASHION IS UNINTIMIDATING

Originality is scary. Average people who stick their necks out and dabble in the unusual (unlike a few untouchable celebrities and fashion insiders) are customarily viewed as freaks. People, on the whole, want to stand out just enough so they can feel like individuals, but not so much that they're looked upon as weirdos. The line between stylish and screwball is a fine one. So we have to be careful not to overstep the boundaries of what's considered socially acceptable. "There's a sense of community and belonging in shopping at a widely accepted outlet store," says anti-consumerism activist Packard Jennings. "It's an insecure kind of belonging. These stores have an entire fashion sensibility; no matter what clothing you purchase it is guaranteed to match the other clothing from the store. You're assured by their label that you won't be mocked for your fashion selections—even if you're wearing a fleece vest."

With McFashion, the key is maintaining familiarity. Clothes are either risk-free basics or, if they do stray from vanilla, they adhere strictly to whatever's hot at the time. "Gap is relatively risk free and affordable," says Brennan, a twenty-four-year-old architect in Los Angeles. "There isn't much special about them. A store like Diesel, on the other hand, is way more expensive and more 'fashionable' but not available for every consumer, because it's so expensive and because its style is more limited than Gap."

It's not only the clothes that feel safe, but also the experience of shopping itself. Eating at a ritzy restaurant like Le Cirque 2000 not only requires loose enough purse strings to afford the four-star French meal, it also involves a certain knowledge of table manners, appropriate attire, and demeanor. Eating at McDonald's requires only a pocket full of change. In the same vein, shopping at a chi-chi boutique requires a certain level of sophistication. It can be scary: the too-cool salespeople glare at you, the clothes don't fit, the sizes are sometimes done by measurements, so it can be embarrassing if you don't know whether you're a 28 or a 36. In "better" boutiques, impeccable clothes are often arranged sparsely on hanging racks, leaving anxious novice consumers feeling as if they had walked into a store filled with porcelain figurines teetering on glass shelves—touching the clothes, let alone trying them on, seems too precarious to even attempt. When shopping at a McFashion store, on the other hand, it doesn't matter how cool you are. Chain retailers carry a wide array of sizes, they encourage shoppers to touch the clothes, they invite even the greenest of fashion rookies in with open arms.

Today, any shopper frightened by the world of high fashion can now access it in digestible doses. The glamorous designer world and the gauche mass-market world have collided, making it possible for consumers to believe they're engaging in high style at their local mall. Hanging on the storefront of Express are window-sized posters of well-known jet-setting models like James King and Karolina Kurkova strutting the catwalk. In an issue of *Vogue* you'll see a six-page ad for Nine West starring supermodel Carmen Kass. Turn a few pages, and she's in a twelve-page editorial fashion spread. Gisele Bündchen is the face (and body) of Dolce & Gabbana . . . and also of mall mainstay Victoria's Secret. Chain stores have married high and low fashion, further pushing cheap chic into the spotlight: the late legendary fashion writer Carrie Donovan mugging for Old Navy commercials, Sharon Stone wearing a Gap mock turtleneck to the Oscars, fashion darling Chloë Sevigny posing for H&M. When Old Navy dropped Donovan in favor of chirpy Molly Sims, a Victoria's Secret model and host of MTV's

House of Style, for its campaigns, their ads became less quirky (where had Magic, the dog, gone?) and more fashion-focused, with models in mock catwalk shows. Nearly every fashion magazine now includes a mix of high and low fashion. The March 2002 issue of *Elle* included an ad for Target featuring two Mossimo dresses: one for $21.99, the other for $19.99. Toward the back of the issue was an H&M ad featuring leggy supermodel Nadja Auermann in $29 jeans and a $9 wrap blouse. Oddly enough, the cheap chic ads didn't seem out of place amid the $2,840 Louis Vuitton suede dress with python cord, $5,500 embroidered cotton blouse by Ralph Lauren, and $12,585 embroidered gown by Valentino featured in the fashion layouts.

It's not only mass-market retailers who are trying to ingratiate themselves with the fashion industry. Designers now also strive to establish high-low relationships. In March 1998, Randolph Duke was the most talked-about designer after he outfitted Minnie Driver in a stunning red gown for the Oscars. Today, he sells an exclusive line of dresses on the downmarket Home Shopping Network. Anyone who has been too intimidated to shop for a designer label at a snooty boutique can now dial up and have a dress delivered to their doorstep.

McFASHION IS ENTERTAINING

As the sun rises and sets in Bloomington, Minnesota, more than twenty thousand ladybugs flutter about in the Mall of America. Crews released the legions of cutesy insects into the mall's seven-acre amusement park, Camp Snoopy, as a natural means of pest control in the indoor garden. The undertaking was the product of creativity: some imaginative employee had evidently been thinking outside the box. And here, at America's most visited destination (around forty-two million visitors each year—that's more than Disney World, Graceland, and the Grand Canyon combined), creativity counts for extra brownie points.

The Mall, a pristine 4.2-million-square-foot fortress located fifteen minutes from downtown Minneapolis, is not only a marvel of enormity but also a symbol of where McFashion has brought us. The

Mall's management loves its massiveness, boasting in press materials,
"If a shopper spent 10 minutes browsing at every store it would take
them more than 86 hours to complete their visit to Mall of America."
With all that leasable space, though, it's somewhat surprising that its
big draw isn't some grand selection of unique stores. In fact, the shops
are the typical mall offerings: Limited, Gap, Victoria's Secret,
Structure, Casual Corner, Ann Taylor. Its true selling point is entertainment—too many attractions to list. Among them: a twenty-six-ride
amusement park with Ferris wheel and roller coaster, bowling alley,
shark tank, eight nightclubs, eighteen-hole mini–golf course, a college
campus, and twenty-seven fast-food restaurants. It even has its own
chapel, where more than twenty-five hundred couples have been married since opening day. By the end of 2010, the Mall will complete a
billion-dollar Phase II expansion, which will add hotels, offices, con-
dos, a spa and fitness center, business conference centers, theaters,
and a high-end specialty retailing district, expanding the behemoth to
a whopping 9.7 million square feet.

Although two of McFashion's basic principles are its quickness
and ease, most consumers don't just buy clothes; they *shop* for them.
Buying is deliberate; shopping is aimless. Buying is work; shopping is
leisure. Buying is boring; shopping is entertaining. If shopping is a
religion, the Fashion Victim, particularly in the States, is a devout disciple. The U.S. already has more than forty-two thousand malls, where
nearly two-thirds of America's retail trade takes place. Although most
of us complain that there aren't enough hours in the day to take care
of what we need to, we still take an average of three or four clothes-
shopping trips per month. According to Harvard professor Juliet
Schor, Americans spend three to four times as many hours per year
shopping as Western Europeans. We do spend slightly less time
per visit than we used to—about an average of seventy-three minutes,
down from ninety minutes in 1984. But quicker shopping doesn't
mean we're buying less. Between 1995 and 1997, the average mall customer's spending rose 13 percent, to $67 dollars per visit, according to
the International Council of Shopping Centers.

We're crazy for shopping, and twelve states rank malls among their top three tourist attractions. Between 1972 and 1992, the annual rate of new shopping-center construction outpaced the growth in population and potential consumers, according to Frederick Abernathy and his colleagues in the book *A Stitch in Time*. The number of independent department stores declined dramatically in the 1980s, but specialty shops blossomed. In 1964, there was enough retail space in the U.S. to give each person 5.3 square feet all to themselves. By 1996, it had risen to 19 square feet per person—that's enough space to build a comfortable studio apartment in New York. In comparison, per capita retail space in Mexico is estimated at 0.3 square feet.

With so much competition for consumers' dollars, vendors need to make themselves stand out. Entertaining malls—those with games, rides, shows, and other attractions—have left smaller, "non-entertaining" ones in the dust. Retail prognosticators estimate that during the next decade somewhere on the order of eighty-six-hundred malls, more than a billion square feet of leasable space, will go bankrupt or be adapted for another use. Mall developers worry that the time spent shopping will continue to wane, and have been forced to think of different ways to attract people, pouring billions of dollars into attractions to set themselves apart from the thousands of competing shopping centers. As a result, there are two types of new malls that have popped up around the country in the past three decades: the pseudo-luxe fashion center and the mega mall.

The pseudo-luxe fashion center caters to the bourgeois adult. It has a puffed-up name—like the Arboretum at Great Hills, Towne West Square, or The Shops at Willow Bend—that avoids the use of the word *mall*, which would conceivably suggest a lack of sophistication. Common areas are filled with mahogany coffee tables, burgundy rugs, and dark leather couches, the type of decor you might expect at a posh private club. Even the tenants are different, usually described in publicity material as "fine shops" or "better stores." In addition to the mall mainstays like the Gap and Banana Republic, there are stores like Gucci, Burberry, and Prada, anchored by swankier department stores like Saks Fifth Avenue and Neiman Marcus. The pseudo-luxe fashion center has a few "better" restaurants and cafés scattered throughout, but rarely a formal food court (the scent of Panda Express wafting in front of the Louis Vuitton store would surely turn off some customers).

The mega mall, on the other hand, panders to children—the young and the old ones. Common areas look like the bedrooms of spoiled rich kids: bright splashes of color, big letters, giant playthings hanging from towering ceilings, proprietary talking animated characters. Corridors are designed to look like slightly more modern versions of Disney World's Main Street. At Florida's Sawgrass Mills, a giant wooden alligator head greets you at every parking entry. Entryways with names like the Pink Flamingo Entrance and Yellow Toucan Entrance broadcast multilingual greetings. Walk inside, through the lively corridors with thousands of colorful banners festooning the ceiling, and eat at the Hurricane Food Court. You can dine at a theme restaurant with the whole family, catch a film, sit down and watch a cooking demonstration, attend a baseball card show, or get the autograph of one of your favorite soap-opera stars. At the mega mall, the catchphrase is: shoppertainment.

The concept of so-called shoppertainment, years in the making, didn't truly come into its own until the early 1980s. In 1981, Canada's West Edmonton Mall opened with more than eight hundred stores and a hotel, amusement park, miniature-golf course, church, a water park for sunbathing and surfing, a zoo, and a 438-foot-long lake. After witnessing the success of this soon-to-be rival, Mills Corporation, a mall developer based in Arlington, Virginia, set out to spread shoppertainment around the U.S. "We see ourselves more as a Disney-type venture than a mall," Mark J. Rivers, executive vice president at Mills, told *Businessweek* in 1999. The concept of mixing shopping and attractions has been further fueled by several studies, including a 1996 survey conducted for direct-mail company Metromail, which found that 34 percent of shoppers said they are driven more by emotional factors such as fun and excitement than by "logical" factors such as price, quality, and convenience.

The mega mall is conceived as a biosphere, a self-contained metropolis where we could conceivably survive cooped up for the rest of our lives. It is our town square, our church, our theater, our general store, our saloon, our cobbler, our tailor, our park, our zoo. Even the lingo has changed: Shoppers are now "guests," shopping is an "experience," and malls are "entertainment centers." The shoppertainment idea has spread all over the world, from Korea's Lotte World, which has a shopping mall, deluxe hotel, folklore center, indoor theme park, and sports center to Japan's Torius Mega Mall, the country's first American-style mall, opened in 1999 with an amusement park, karaoke bar, petting zoo, and bathhouse. Its developer, Torius, Inc., plans to open ten more mega malls throughout Japan by 2010.

Sometimes, it's not even necessary for people to use the mall's exciting bells and whistles—it's enough that they just *know* about them. The Mall at Short Hills once offered helicopter rides to bring people from New York City to its New Jersey locale. "Actually, nobody ever really rode in it," says Rosemary McCormick, president of the Shop America Alliance, a national consortium of shopping malls and retailers who market themselves as tourist attractions, and former marketing director for the Mall of America. "It was a PR gimmick but it was a great PR gimmick. The media loved it in New York City."

In some cases, attractions aren't added solely for the purpose of entertaining shoppers. Many shoppertainment malls have become massive billboards for companies. Corporate sponsorship is not only acceptable, it's highly encouraged. American sports fans rolled their eyes as stadium after stadium was renamed to promote some company: Staples Arena, Bank One Ballpark, Qualcomm Stadium, PacBell Park. Inside the malls you'll see plenty of similar corporate canoodling, from the Mall of America's Pringles Snack Stacks Showdown to the General Mills Cereal Adventure with the Cheerios Play Park and Cocoa Puffs Chocolate Canyon. In 2000, credit card company Discover Financial Services bought the naming rights to Sugarloaf Mills, a 1.3-million-square-foot outlet mall in Gwinnett County, Georgia, to rename the center Discover Mills. The unprecedented naming-rights deal is unlikely to be the last of its kind.

The amusement park/McDonald's Playland feel of many malls has also seeped into the stores themselves, with retailers realizing that they too can set themselves apart by offering touches of fun. The Old Navy flagship store in San Francisco features a DJ booth, mechanized mannequins, and a giant television playing Old Navy ads. In-store DJs spin bass-heavy house and techno at some Diesel stores. The one in the Mall of America has its own sit-down deli, Torpedo Joes. Even the luxury market is getting in on the fun. Prada's 24,500-square-foot flagship store, opened in December 2001 in Manhattan's SoHo district, includes a towering auditorium where shoppers can sit on long wooden steps with their well-groomed terriers, high-resolution TV screens in the fitting rooms to replace mirrors, and touch-screen computers that allow shoppers to search the store's inventory. Dressing rooms have sheets of liquid-crystal glass that become opaque or transparent at the push of a button. It may not be a Ferris wheel, but it's amusing nonetheless.

Rents at shoppertainment malls are generally higher, but the retail dog and pony show pays off. Clothing sales in this type of environment are simply more successful. For instance, the average store at the highly entertaining Mall of America takes in about $540 per square foot annually, compared to the national average of $341 per square foot. Good for business: yes. Good for the overall state of fashion: no. When it comes down to it, the whole concept of shoppertainment is a sad commentary on what McFashion has done—the clothes themselves are so lackluster that their surroundings have to be jazzed up to make them look appetizing to the public. But it works. It gets people into the mall and, as a result, into the stores. Today, when people make lists of their favorite hobbies, many, disturbingly, include shopping. McFashion has helped make the act of browsing and buying a national pastime. And the retailers reap the rewards.

McFASHION IS DISPOSABLE

Upon entering the H&M store on Manhattan's Fifth Avenue, you can clearly view a four-story slice of the retail mecca. If you step back and watch the activity within the 35,000-square-foot giant, it resembles what one would assume goes on inside an ant colony: hundreds of tiny bodies scurrying about, moving along aisles and up channels, carrying objects from place to place. On the morning of the store's grand opening in spring 2000, curious shoppers lined up around the block. In the first thirteen minutes, over two thousand shoppers had rushed in. An editor I worked with at the time was there for the opening weekend. "How was it?" everyone inquired at the office the next day, as if she'd just returned home from the film festival in Cannes. "It was pretty good—I got this skirt for $5.99," she said, twirling to show her knee-length red-and-white gingham miniskirt. Two years later, the H&M hype has hardly fizzled. On a normal Saturday afternoon, it's still not uncommon to see shoppers waiting over twenty minutes just to get to the fitting room. Today, Manhattanites spend over $500,000 a day there. By the end of 2003, the Swedish retailer plans to have eighty-five stores in the U.S., in addition to its nearly eight hundred other locations around the world.

H&M (short for Hennes & Mauritz) has been a retail powerhouse in Europe since 1947. Today, the $3.9 billion Swedish chain sells about 400 million articles of hip, trendy, supercheap clothes a year. The company employs a team of seventy in-house designers who keep a close watch on trends. They have McFashion down to a science, utilizing a well-oiled network of sixteen hundred suppliers throughout Europe and Asia, making it possible for them to jump on a particularly hot item and get it into their stores around the globe within a few weeks. The key to H&M, more than its inviting interior and its cool print ads featuring celebrities, is its ability to keep consumers from feeling guilty about wearing an item once or twice then never again. As J. Crew's Emily Cinader Woods puts it, "You're buying it for three months." In some cases, even less.

"It's hard not to get sucked into the idea that fashion is disposable, thanks to all the inexpensive knockoff chains like H&M, Delia's, and Aldo," says Elizabeth Kiester, fashion director of YM. McFashion chains like H&M thrive because they're cheap. Although the end of the twentieth century ushered in a new era of luxury in which Louis Vuitton, Christian Dior, and Manolo Blahnik became household names, a growing number of people today spend their money buying a lot of inexpensive clothes, mixed in with a few pricier items.

No one expects to find the highest-quality merchandise when they shop at the mall. More likely, they're surprised when they find something that is well made. We've filled our closets and wardrobes with cheaply made clothes, fully aware that we won't wear these clothes next year. If every trend were prohibitively expensive, the trend cycle would sputter out. But today, any new style can usually be found somewhere for under $30, and easily found for under $50. Can't afford a $750 Prada bowling bag? Buy an imitation at H&M for under $20. Can't shell out $500 for Jimmy Choo sling-backs? Snag a similar pair at Nine West for $40.

Disposable clothes are the wave of the future. Between 1995 and 1999, sales of George, the line of cheap clothing that sells in Great Britain's Asda supermarkets, surged from $399.7 million to $941.7 million. And Marks & Spencer, Britain's number-one retailer, tops the basics market there with men's suits for under $150 and women's pants for under $25. In Japan, 480-store Uniqlo, owned by Fast Retailing Company, has become a powerhouse, offering well-crafted basics like denim jackets for $25, half as much as its rivals.

In the late 1990s, numerous writers declared that cheap chic was posing a threat to the design world: consumers were becoming less interested in spending big bucks on high fashion, they said, since there were so many inexpensive alternatives. In the past quarter-century, high-fashion houses have had to cater to the middle-of-the-road "career wear" market, or else have all their business taken away by sketch-happy knockoff artists. Today, designers' lower-priced lines like DKNY, CK, Polo, Moschino Cheap & Chic, Armani Exchange, and Miu Miu (although by no means cheap to the average consumer) are not only big moneymakers but also help to publicize illustrious fashion names to people who wouldn't normally be able to afford bona fide luxury goods.

Although fashion lovers greatly value wealth, they also appreciate a bargain. It used to be that outlet malls catered to a segment of society that cared more about rock-bottom prices than about fashion. The factory-outlet mall of old, often visible from the highway during long car trips, typically consisted of a few lame shops, like some store that would sell tacky towels, an athletic footwear warehouse, and always, for some reason, a store that sold dishes, like Mikasa or Pfaltzgraff. But with the advent of the premium outlet mall, perfected by Chelsea Premium Outlets based in Roseland, New Jersey, which owns twenty-six centers, including two in Japan, retailers' unsold merchandise has become hot stuff. Sales at outlet malls have risen to about $20 billion per year, up from $12 billion in 1995. At Chelsea-owned Woodbury Commons in upstate New York, shoppers come from hours away to buy Banana Republic, Club Monaco, and Armani Exchange merchandise that had been selling in full-price stores sometimes just weeks earlier. The concept of the outlet has metamorphosed from tacky to cool.

Cheap chic is nothing new. What's new is that the stigma associated with it has diminished. Today, cheap chic stores hold varying levels of cachet: a $4 tank top from H&M is considered far more fashionable than its near-identical counterpart from Wal-Mart. Likewise, a clearance-rack denim jacket from the premium outlet mall is preferable to a full-priced one from JC Penney. Part of the reason consumers are more open to cheap chic is that they've actually seen it looking good at some point. An increasing number of fashion magazines have started showing clothing from stores like Gap and H&M in their fashion spreads, either mixing them in with more expensive designer clothes or showing them in the context that affordable clothes can indeed look good (well, at least on a professional model with impeccable lighting and styling). And in the late 1990s, a major women's magazine sent supermodel Heidi Klum on a mission: go to Kmart and create a cute outfit within a certain budget. Klum took the paltry sum she'd been allotted and assembled a striking ensemble, which included a child's terry-cloth bathrobe that she tied around her torso to create a chic wrap top. Of course, this was no sparkling endorsement of Kmart's clothes, since Klum, who had earned the nickname "The Body" in the media, could've wandered into the automotive section of the store and no doubt looked ravishing in a dress constructed of car mats and an oil funnel hat.

Discount superstores have gotten a boost in fashion credibility with the help of Target. During a fashion show for six hundred members of the fashion media and other industry pros, Target VP for special events John Remington proclaimed, "We are on a mission to democratize style and fashion. We want our guests to know that they can bring style and fashion into their everyday lives!" In recent years, the store, founded in 1961, assembled an armada of stylish folks—Phillippe

Starck, Todd Oldham, Mossimo Gianulli—to design exclusive lines for them. In July 1999, Target teamed up with the Council of Fashion Designers of America (CFDA), an elite group of two hundred top fashion designers, to hold a contest. The two winners of the Target/CFDA initiative would win design jobs at Target. The relationship culminated in a fashion show of the store's fall offerings displayed before seven hundred journalists, designers, and other fashion insiders. In December 2001, the company gained street cred, inking a deal with Ecko Unlimited to manufacture and sell Physical Science, a trend-inspired sportswear line for young men and boys, exclusively in all Target stores.

Today, it's getting tougher to tell cheap chic and expensive chic apart. On New York's Metro Channel, fashion commentator Robert Verdi films a recurring segment he calls "Where'd ya get that?" in which he asks people on the street to talk about their outfits. During the spring 2002 Fashion Week in New York, he stood outside the main tent at Bryant Park and stopped a few people. One girl recognized him and said playfully, "Hey, where'd ya get that?" Seizing the opportunity for a funny bit—and the chance to talk about his own clothes—Verdi played along.

"Where'd you get that coat?" the girl inquired.

"Where do you think I got it?" Verdi replied.

The girl blurted out, "H&M."

Actually, the coat was Burberry . . . over a thousand dollars more expensive than anything sold at H&M. Similarly, in a feature for *Marie Claire* in the late 1990s, a writer showed people photos of five women and asked them to guess which one was wearing the priciest outfit. The women wearing the most expensive designer threads looked no better than the ones dressed in clothes from cheap mass-market stores. No one wants to throw down a thousand dollars for an Armani coat only to find out that everyone thinks they bought it from Old Navy. But today, as low-priced brands get more adept at emulating designer styles, disposable fashion doesn't necessarily have to *look* cheap.

THE PROBLEM WITH McFASHION

Just as too much McDonald's gradually puts a choke hold on our arteries, too much McFashion progressively narrows our channels of creativity and individuality. And our unhealthy consumption of it has begun to take its toll.

THE BLAHS

A few years ago, I showed up at a holiday party thrown by my boy-friend's company wearing the same spaghetti-strapped dress as his co-worker's girlfriend. "I like your dress," I joked with her as she walked by. She, it appeared, did not appreciate the hilarity in the situation. Several people commented on our inadvertent Olsen-twins moment that night. With the seemingly endless variety of clothes available, how could this happen?

Although it would appear that we have vast options, we're rarely open to all of them. Similar people shop at similar places: I and my holiday doppelganger both apparently shopped at Emporio Armani. The bulk of our clothing purchases are made in the same stores over and over again; rather than venturing out to experience new retailers, we stick with our tried and true. McFashion's formula is proven and successful, which makes it easy for those chain retailers to muscle out more local stores. Where once the retail landscape might have been dotted with interesting individually owned boutiques, it's now inundated with the same stores, state after state and country after country. It's McFashion's homogeneity that makes it desirable to many people in the first place. Humans inherently want to fit in. "In many ways, while people want to be individuals they also desire a high degree of conformity and group acceptance," says Elizabeth Rhodes of Kent State University. "The larger chains have offered this cookie-cutter look. The merchandise is the same the world over, and the consumer can count on brands that offer consistent sizing and a certain quality of performance with which they are familiar."

But it's that same initially attractive uniformity that will continue to eat away at us. The consistency has bred a scary level of homogeneity. In the U.S., 75 percent of men own a pair of Dockers khakis. One in five women's shoes is sold by Nine West. Wal-Mart, the world's biggest retailer, sells 19 million pairs of women's jeans a year, and an average of 19,634 pairs of shoes an hour. Eighty percent of Americans own at least one pair of Levi's jeans. The grand openings of big chain retailers draw bigger crowds than some sporting events and concerts. When new mass-market stores are unveiled, thousands of eager shoppers make the pilgrimage to check out the wholly clichéd offerings. When Old Navy introduced its Chicago store in 1998, more than ten thousand people lined up hours before the doors opened. We wait with bated breath to buy the same clothes everyone else is wearing.

The Fashion Victim is willing to endure a little boredom in order to feel safe. Remember, McFashion is unintimidating. Venturing beyond one's comfort zone is scary. "The two critical mercantile discoveries of the twentieth century were the need to conform and the need for consistency," says Joseph, a twenty-nine-year-old computer engineer in Cambridge, Massachusetts. "This is why a McDonald's in China looks, feels, and tastes exactly like one in Manhattan—that clientele *wants* a consistent experience. No wonderful local cuisine, but by the same token, no nasty surprises. It's the same with clothing."

But what we're beginning to forget is that it's these surprises, nasty or not, that make clothes something beyond the superficial: an actual expression of one's personality. When more consumers begin to buy only the same handful of mass-market brands, the smaller, individually owned labels that sell more original clothes will eventually fade away from lack of business. McFashion stores will have effectively pushed originality out of our closets. Eventually, we'll forget that our clothes can serve as a creative extension of ourselves. And we will be a society of outrageously boring dressers.

McFashion, like McDonald's, has come to symbolize America. In an April 1998 essay, *New York Times* writer Lisa Napoli described her surprise when friends visiting from Paris wanted to make the Gap the first stop on their New York shopping tour: "They didn't want some funky, original Gotham boutique, where they could find something unique to the city. They wanted what they perceived—rightly—as a slice of America."

KNOCKOFFS

McFashion has not only made knockoffs profitable, it's made them an entire industry more lucrative than innovative fashion design itself. Copying is harmful to the overall process of creating *and* detrimental to a designer's bottom line. After all, fewer customers will buy an original full-priced garment if they can buy a similar one for half the price. But this pattern isn't without consequences. As fashion houses lose money due to copycats, they'll eventually produce fewer original clothes, either because they'll go out of business or they'll have less money to generate as many pieces in a collection. And with even less innovation put out into the marketplace, we'll gradually move closer to a time when McFashion chains have crushed any semblance of distinctiveness that was once available.

Copying has been around for many years. In fact, it had been ingrained in the fabric of the industry since its early days. In the first half of the twentieth century, American clothes makers paid fees to French fashion houses like Christian Dior for the rights to copy their designs. Today, designers aren't privy to such kickbacks. Even though McFashion knockoffs are a predictable step in the fashion cycle, they're still a thorn in designers' sides. A.B.S., a successful California-based company that reinterprets designer and celebrity dresses at low prices, operates on a ninety-day turnaround, meaning A.B.S. versions of runway styles appear in stores at the same time as the designer originals. In a 1996 profile, Miuccia Prada expressed her frustration at the knockoff market. "We are experiencing an incredible attack from people who want to know what we are doing," she said. "They hang around our fabric mills, they want to see our prototypes—it's really becoming unbearable." Designers have had to take drastic steps to protect their work. Nicole Miller copyrights each of the prints she designs, and the firm has successfully filed more than fifteen hundred infringement cases since 1986 related to firms that copy the designs.

Yoriko Powell, who worked as a shoe designer for Kenneth Cole for several years, witnessed the process firsthand. "In general, not only at Kenneth Cole, if you're in the Italian shoe industry, it's not difficult to see the new trends," says Powell, who now designs her own line of ladies' shoes and bags. Copying isn't taboo. "Sometimes, we see some prototypes of well-known brand shoes and we have opportunities to copy them if we want to," she says. "For example, [in summer 2001] I see what some high-fashion brands are making for summer 2002 . . . mostly the concept, so not the exact styles, but you can get some ideas as to what kind of feeling we will see next year." Catwalk copying can be frustrating for high-end designers, who toil away at their creations, only to be trumped by imitators. "Many of the Italian factories make copies of those runway show shoes very quickly and we can get ideas from them," says Powell. "So, sometimes, the copies of those runway show shoes can be in the stores at the same time as the originals."

When McFashion retailers copy designers' creations, they dilute them, transforming them into weaker, cheaper, usually less attractive versions. Fashion, as a whole, suffers, because by the time The Hot Trend is seen by the mass public, it's far less attractive than when it started out, like Yves Saint Laurent's purple peasant shirts—knocked off in a variety of less attractive colors, fabrics, and styles. These unsightly remakes not only mar the image of styles that could have at one point been considered beautiful but also accelerate a style's demise (which is, as we have seen, part of Speed Chic).

In the fashion industry, there are two types of copying: knockoffs and counterfeits. At least in a legal sense, there's a big difference between the two. Knockoffs may look very similar to a designer product but are produced under a different—legal—brand name. Counterfeit products, on the other hand, which brandish a fake brand label, are illegal. What has made the practice of counterfeiting even thornier is that it's become increasingly acceptable to consumers. When once a shopper would have felt ripped off by a fake, she now feels somewhat empowered to be spending fewer dollars for a replica. "I live for Kate Spade fakes, especially if they have the Kate Spade tag sewn on the outside, not just glued on," says Erica, a twenty-six-year-old publicist in Brooklyn, New York. "I'm too rough on my purse to actually spend $400 on one, but I love her clean designs. For me, it's not about the label. I never try to pass it off as the real thing." Others, like Rosa, a twenty-six-year-old office manager from Chicago, are torn between their desire for cheap imitations and their belief that it's wrong. "I bought a pair of sunglasses from a flea market for $20; the lady said they were original Oakley," she says. "The truth is: I think that it's unfair that there are knockoffs out there. I think it's unfair to the original designer. As far as the people who sell these products, I think they should be careful selling them so they don't get caught by the law."

Counterfeit handbags and clothes sold on websites and street corners are a multibillion-dollar problem, but just as troubling to many designers are the less blatant imitations. Even the most venerated brands in the world aren't immune to accusations of copying. In February 2001, Gucci was ordered to pay one million francs to Parisian men's shoe maker Berluti for allegedly copying two styles—a 1930s-style spat with a metal side buckle and perforated embellishment and a moccasin with tassels and a dotted ridge across the top. Gucci spokespeople scoffed at the idea that styles of shoes—especially *men's* shoes—could be claimed as unique inventions. "There are a limited number of things you can do to decorate men's shoes," the company's legal counsel, Allan Tuttle, told the *Wall Street Journal*. "There is nothing unique about these shoes." In April 2002, editors at fashion website Hintmag.com unearthed evidence that Balenciaga wonderboy Nicolas Ghesquière had copied a patchwork vest originally created by a little-known designer from San Francisco named Kaisik Wong in 1973. The story sparked controversy, and most people expected Ghesquière to be embarrassed for having been found out, but instead he unabashedly owned up to it, saying that *everyone* uses past designs for inspiration. And it's true. History is nearly every designer's greatest muse. But where should the line be drawn between inspiration and downright copying? Shouldn't there be a distinction made when 95 percent of the garment resembles the original, versus only 5 percent?

Years ago, Donna Karan foresaw the flourishing knockoff industry as the death of designers. In many ways, she was right. Much in the same way that musicians have complained about music-sharing websites like Napster stealing their songs, designers complain about knockoff artists ripping their designs off, and essentially stealing money directly from their pockets. And it's not just designers that suffer. When labels lose business, consumers ultimately suffer. If a design house can't make a profit, it will consider other strategies to make money. The obvious solution? Raise prices.

As much as it may infuriate them, many fashion insiders agree it's a waste of time, energy, and money to fight the natural course of imitation. "Coco Chanel said she would worry when people stopped copying her and, more recently, [Karl] Lagerfeld said the same thing," says Bernadine Morris, a fashion writer whose illustrious résumé includes a thirty-year stint as senior fashion writer at the *New York Times*. "There's little they can do about it. Copying has long been part of the business. With so many pictures and TV, it's hard to control."

LOSS OF CULTURE

McFashion contributes to a sort of artificial existence we live today. As our homogenized culture spreads across the world like processed cheese, mass-market stores have begun to vanquish the colorful local styles in other countries, too. "With the exception of Third World countries, when I travel all over the world shopping starts to look the same," says Elizabeth Rhodes. "No longer am I tempted to purchase clothing because it's new or exciting or different. Shopping is boring and predictable. I can go to an unknown mall or shopping area and, with a high degree of accuracy, predict where the stores are located and what will be in them."

Just as the arrival of yet another McDonald's restaurant in a new country triggers moans and groans from some locals, worried that this tasteless facet of American culture will gradually begin to overtake their own, the arrival of yet another McFashion store elicits the same reaction. "Our possibilities of perception are dwindling due to manu-factured experiences throughout our lives," says Akbar Ali Herndon, a cultural analyst who runs a website about vanishing American culture. "The world offers less and less opportunity for an original anything, including clothing. But I think the loss still eats at us. We worship con-sumption and replication while retailers like the Gap benefit."

Our dwindling sense of culture isn't entirely retailers' fault—

consumers bear some of the blame. Mass-market retailers stay in business because they make a lot of money. "Stores like Gap, Old Navy, and H&M can only exist today because we're attuned to their offerings," says Herndon. Retailers may make McFashion hard to resist, but it can only survive because we shovel money into it. As with everything in fashion, the Fashion Victim is less a victim of cultural dilution than a willing participant. And, in the end, our loss of cultural integrity is also a product of larger social deterioration. "We live in the cookie-cutter era," says Herndon. "Music is sampled from former hits. Every year, a greater number of films are remakes from the sixties or seventies. Why should our fashion choices be any finer than a remake of *Leave It to Beaver*?"

Within American society, we lose a sense of what other countries are really like because we're exposed to them so much in a manufactured way. Clothing stores at the mall promote an artificial worldliness. Benetton promotes its "United Colors" multi-culti theme. Guess? tries to project its French image, as does Bisou Bisou. Malls themselves suck the local flavor from cities and towns and replace it with a sort of faux culture—the equivalent of feeling worldly because you've visited all eleven "countries" at Epcot Center. At the food court, you can feel international when you choose between the Chinese, Japanese, Mexican, Cajun, Italian, Greek, and French places, where an Au Bon Pain ham and cheese can be passed off as "French" and chicken chow mein is considered Chinese. But they're all Americanized versions of those ethnic cuisines.

Purveyors of McFashion don't seem to understand that when you replace a real thing with something manufactured, it's no longer the "real" thing. Mills infuses each of its malls with a bit of the local flavor—but local flavor that's seemingly gone through the ringer at Disney and Las Vegas. Mall developers are keen on using terms like "avenues" and "courtyards" to invoke a small-town spirit when describing hulking corridors and pristine common areas. Each "neighborhood" at Atlanta's Discover Mills reflects a Georgian theme: A Walk in the Woods, Georgia Style, The Arbors, Georgia Sports Hall of Fame, Georgia Music Hall of Fame, and Atlanta Icons. The food court isn't just where you go to shovel pizza down your gullet, it's a cultural experience: the Towne Square Festival Food Court (the old-world spelling of *Towne* is what makes it *really* special). Florida's Sawgrass Mills's new 300,000-square-foot open-air expansion, The Oasis, was inspired by the South Florida Latin nightclub scene. The decor of Nashville's Opry Mills includes giant cowboy hats and colossal light-up guitars. Malls invoke local spirit the way the Venetian hotel in Las Vegas, with its indoor waterways strewn with gondolas, clouds painted on the ceiling, and immaculate verandas, embodies the real Venice—the colorized, sanitized Cliff's Notes version of a real place.

Developers tear down trees and natural habitats, then attempt to plug the semblance of nature back into the design of their malls. Numerous malls offer petting zoos, massive skylights to let sunlight pour in, gigantic potted trees. The Mall of Georgia features five interior courtyards inspired by the geographic regions of the state—Coastal Region, the Plains, Atlanta, the Piedmont Region, and the Blue Ridge Mountains. The mountain corridor, for instance, is designed to look like a lodge with a pitched wooden roof, quiltlike carpets, and twig furniture. Now you can do everything you used to do outside in the mall. At the Block at Orange in California, kids can zip down the half-pipe at the open-air mall's skatepark. At Biltmore Fashion Park in Phoenix, Arizona, you can buy fresh produce at the farmer's market every Friday. At various malls, you can join a fitness group to hoof it through the air-conditioned corridors in the morning. Spain's Madrid Xanadú, developed by Mills and set to open in spring 2003, boasts a first-of-its-kind indoor Snow Dome that will offer snowboarding, skiing, sledding, and other alpine activities.

It's infinitely sad to see shopping quickly eclipsing other, more rewarding activities (art, reading, volunteering) in popularity. Something is seriously wrong when we'd rather spend three hours at the mall than with friends at the park, and when our main motivation for taking a trip across the country is to visit the hot new destination mall. The act of shopping may offer us temporary respite from our daily worries, but consumerism adds few lasting benefits to our lives.

So, here we are, stuck on the fast track to Dullville. Once we've traded our local culture and beautiful outdoor areas for contrived shopping-center ones, and swapped our interesting regional style of dress for a homogeneous American one, we may finally start to crave those things once again. Let's hope it won't be too late. McDonald's boasts "Billions Served"; McFashion has served nearly as many. And with so many customers hungry for more, it looks like McFashion will, sadly, become an indispensable part of our style diet.

5

Nonstop Fashion Coverage!

Fashion is a relentless obsession. You can never have enough of it.
          —*Brandusa Niro, cofounder,* Fashion Wire Daily

It's 7 P.M. and seats are beginning to fill up in the main tent for the BCBG Max Azria spring 2002 womenswear show at Bryant Park in midtown Manhattan. An eminent squad of editors, including Cindi Leive from *Glamour,* Hal Rubenstein from *In Style,* and Emil Wilbekin from *Vibe* wait patiently with notepads in tow and goody bags at their well-heeled feet. Writers, photographers, publicists, friends, and a smattering of buyers kiss-kiss their seating-chart neighbors, chat about tonight's after-party at Lotus, last night's party at Serena, tomorrow night's party at The Park, and the Ungaro bash last week at the 26th Street Armory (did anyone see the entire Hilton clan—Mom, Dad, and the infamous sisters—all decked out in Ungaro garb? *Quelle coincidence, non?*).

On the main floor of the tent, which is flanked by bleachers like a high school auditorium, the ticking of shutters and sparkle of flash-bulbs has attracted more than a few curious eyeballs. Two TV stars are mugging for a few dozen photographers. Audience members whisper, "Who *is* that?" The actresses—one from *Saturday Night Live* and another from one of the *Law & Order* spin-offs—are the kind of stars who are recognizable by sight, if not by name, certainly not in the same league as the Gwyneth Paltrows and Nicole Kidmans most paparazzi trample each other over. Regardless, tonight they're royalty. Despite the blinding flash of cameras, the actresses gladly maintain their most photogenic poses—slightly turned to one side (their best side, of course) with photo-ready smiles (it's all in the eyes!)—for a good thirty minutes and answer the questions du jour: "Who are you wearing tonight?" "What do you like about BCBG?"

Famed photographer Patrick McMullan, who has shot nearly every celebrity fashionista that has ever graced the New York party scene, arrives stylishly late and receives an ebullient hug from at least one member of each clique he approaches on the floor. Meanwhile, Michelle Behennah is making her rounds wielding a microphone, and trailed by a cameraman, to find the celebrities and recognizable editors. Behennah, a model who's best known for her photos in the *Sports Illustrated* swimsuit issue as well as her print work in fashion glossies, is filming interviews for the Style Network, the new off-shoot of E!, which has planned twenty-four-hour coverage of Fashion Week. Elsa Klensch she is not. The British beauty may not be a trained journalist or "fashion expert," but she's comfortable in the fashion world and, more important, she looks great on camera.

At 7:50, just shy of an hour late (as is fairly customary), the lights dim and deep bass sounds begin to thump through the speakers. A procession of gorgeous young things in angelic silk slips and skinny suede pants parades down the runway. Ten minutes later, it's over. The models take their final walk, Mr. Azria emerges for his congratulatory bow, attendees clap, then the whole room scrambles for the exit. My friend Lisa, an entertainment editor and fashion show newbie, went with me to the show. She summarized the experience well: "That's *it*?" We had spent fifty minutes engrossed in the fashion show circus and ten minutes looking at clothes. Thus the first lesson in today's fashion coverage:

It's not about the clothes.

. . .

Up until about fifteen years ago, fashion, for the most part, was predominantly about clothes. Catwalk shows weren't televised; they were more straightforward affairs attended by magazine editors, newspaper writers, and store buyers. The season's styles could be seen in time-honored fashion warhorses like *Women's Wear Daily, Vogue,* and *Harper's Bazaar,* but rarely, if ever, in entertainment magazines and general-interest publications. Oh, how things have changed. Today, the worlds of fashion, media, and entertainment have collided, creating a mutually beneficial Big Bang of art, commerce, and theatrics, and saturating our daily lives with images of (and stealthy advertisements for) fashion.

Ever wonder why our society is so obsessed with style? We're soaking in it. "Nobody needs to buy all these things, but with the influx of fashion on websites—Style.com, for example, where you can see every look that walked down the runway, fashion on TV, fashion columns in newspapers, and all the fashion magazines—you get to feel that you must buy into all the trends each season, or else you'll be out of it," says Marilyn Kirschner, editor-in-chief of *The Look On-Line* and former senior market editor of *Harper's Bazaar.*

Traditional advertising is expensive, and as more companies vie for the same conventional ad space, its effect becomes less potent. A one-page ad in a major magazine like *Vogue* can cost over $100,000 (typical one-pagers run about $80,000). A thirty-second TV spot on a major network during prime time can run you anywhere from $150,000 to a whopping $2 million during big events like the Super Bowl, and that's not counting the costs of producing the actual commercial. To circumvent some of the expense, companies have brainstormed for alternative methods of promoting themselves, realizing that showing their wares in a variety of different arenas can be a beneficial supplement to their conventional campaigns. "Many TV shows seem to have become long advertisements—the trend is just one more example of the increasing commercialization of our culture," says advertising critic Jean Kilbourne, Ph.D., author of *Can't Buy My Love: How Advertising Changes the Way We Think and Feel.* Fashion plays such a large, often subliminal role in modern media and entertainment that the lines have been blurred between what is advertising and what is not. Designers and producers make deals ("I'll outfit your cast in return for an on-screen credit"). Celebrities have become walking billboards (fashion houses offer them loaner and freebie outfits in hopes that the stars will be photographed wearing them). Certain slick publications coo over the genius of their advertisers' collections, muddying the so-called separation of church and state. Even serious news media have become mesmerized with the world of fashion, covering catwalk shows and trends, at times critiquing stars' style, as only the gossip rags once did. No format is sacred. In 2001, Italian jewelry company Bulgari commissioned a novel by British author Faye Weldon. *The Bulgari Connection* contained just under a dozen mentions of the brand and its products, marking the debut of paid product placement in fiction. What could be next? *Harry Potter and the Sorcerer's Cartier Stone?*

Promoting one's business through outlets other than print ads, TV commercials, and billboards has become increasingly prevalent as companies recognize that it's necessary to do so in order to keep up with their competitors. Fashion has always straddled the line between art and commerce, but it's gradually moved closer to commerce over the past several decades. This leaves many designers to grapple with the predicament of how to balance the artistic expression of fashion with the cutthroat realities of business. It's not enough to design a gorgeous collection; it also has to sell. "Part of the reason Yves Saint Laurent claimed he was retiring was the whole corporate thing: 'What's the bottom line? Are we going to make money?' " says fashion photographer Randy Brooks. "I think there were more designers in the past who looked at fashion as art. Now, there are more companies in control, and the bottom line is the dollar versus the art."

Innovative promotional deals are popping up all over. In 2001, Dolce & Gabbana outfitted 'N Sync and Dido for their tours, then wardrobed Aussie pop star Kylie Minogue in 2002. Halston provided clothes for Mariah Carey's latest tour. Tommy Hilfiger sponsored Britney Spears's 1999 summer tour, which hit fifty major cities in North America. During the tour, Hilfiger also ran in-store retail promotions with sweepstakes and radio promotions, and Britney made personal appearances at Tommy Jeans outlets. In February 2002, *GQ* magazine announced it was opening a trendy lounge in Hollywood and would open a similar one in Manhattan. It took over L.A.'s famed Sunset Room, renaming it the GQ Lounge. On the renovating agenda was a full redecoration of the place to reflect the tone of the magazine and incorporate products sold by twenty-two *GQ* advertisers—like grooming products by Paul Mitchell in the men's room and the Corum Cocktail, named after the watchmaker, at the bar—into the decor. Even the walls at the glam lounge are subtle advertisements, with photos of models wearing Calvin Klein clothes and decorations featuring a new Klein logo.

The smothering approach to fashion promotion works. Even people who don't consider themselves slaves to fashion can't help but be influenced by styles they're bombarded with on a daily basis—from the Versace glasses they see in a video to the Hugo Boss suit they see on their local news. The Fashion Victim wants what she sees. She longs for an Hermès handbag after seeing one on *Sex and the City*. She fancies Burberry after spotting Kate Moss in paparazzi shots wearing the clothier's trademark plaid. She wears a knockoff of Cate Blanchett's Oscar gown to a holiday party. Consumers are being sold to at every turn. The danger comes when they don't realize that they're receiving a pitch from outlets that are presumed to be impartial . . . or simply don't want to notice.

CUT ON THE BIAS

The new crossbreed formed by fashion's merger with media and entertainment has created an environment with plenty of backslapping but little constructive criticism. "I believe there's very little fashion journalism," says Robin Givhan, fashion editor of the *Washington Post* and former associate editor at *Vogue*. "There's plenty of coverage of fashion shows, models, product launches, trends, and celebrities, but there are few publications that apply journalistic standards of fairness and accountability to the coverage of the fashion industry." The problem with fashion media is that there's no system of checks and balances, no critical eye, no scrutinizing body. Reporters, whom we would expect to maintain at least some semblance of journalistic integrity, sometimes fall victim to promoting clothes rather than reporting on them. "The industry seems rather uncritical of itself," says Barbara M. Freeman, Ph.D., associate professor of journalism at Carleton University in Ottawa, Ontario.

Unlike impromptu reviews by filmgoers as they exit the theater—when it's not uncommon to hear "It sucked" or "Thumbs down"—it's rare to hear a fashion show attendee giving a bluntly honest opinion on camera of what he or she has just seen (which is odd, considering the amount of catty criticism that Fashion Victims bestow on clothing styles in the privacy of their own living rooms). There's a time-honored formula for attendance, as with live theater: even if you weren't wowed by the show, don't diss it publicly. Fashion, since it holds the tricky distinction of being both art and commerce, leaves some journalists scratching their heads about just how to review it. Like an art critic, a fashion writer can analyze a designer's technical skill, innovation, or bravery. But whether or not someone will truly enjoy a painting or a garment is subjective.

Some fashion insiders, like Stig Harder, publisher of the online fashion magazine *Lumière* and Internet portal *Fashion Net*, don't think it's a fashion writer's job to criticize in the first place. "To be honest, fashion really isn't important enough of a subject to warrant deep, objective analysis," he says. "More important is to report on the collections editors like and then pretty much ignore the rest—if a designer had a bad season, the lack of good press will encourage him or her to do a better job next time. The fact is that many designers don't have a lot of money, and sharp criticism in the press is potentially lethal to their businesses. I've seen this happening many times. So our approach has always been to look at the collections with a healthy amount of good humor. There really is no need to be so serious." But as a commercial product, like a car or a computer software package, shouldn't fashion be treated with more forthright, exploratory criticism? Absolutely, says Freeman: "Whether it's art or commerce, it should be open to criticism, both positive and negative." The way companies and industries improve is by receiving and pleasantly accepting astute constructive criticism.

And it's not just the clothes themselves that lack evaluation—no one turns a critical eye on the industry or on fashion as a whole. Fashion reporters fail to delve into the shady ethics and practices of some of the apparel companies. They let the public's mindless adherence to fashion trends and the ridiculous prices of luxury goods pass under their noses without comment. The entire institution of fashion is ripe for review, yet so few take the opportunity. Criticism exists, but only on a modest level. People have no qualms about playing fashion police in the privacy of their homes when judging individual outfits that they find repulsive. Yet when it comes to passing negative judgment on fashion itself, they shy away.

The potential for bias exists in the fashion media just as it did in radio in the days of payola. It's no secret within the industry that editors receive many luxurious "no strings attached" gifts from designers. Granted, gift giving isn't always bribery. Much in the same way that providing celebrities with freebies helps promote products, bestowing lavish goody bags on top fashion editors and on-air reporters can also help create buzz about a brand. These are the visible fashion authorities, after all. A highly regarded editor seen carrying a designer's latest bag will have a domino effect on imitators. Publishing companies set rather vague rules, stating that gifts are acceptable unless they're extravagant. Certainly, it is possible for one's judgment to remain intact. But, the mere implication that a gift could wield some pull toward featuring a particular designer over another is worrisome. After all, wouldn't suspicion be cast on a political reporter who accepted a gift from a senator, or a restaurant reviewer who accepted a lovely present from a chef? "I would be fired if I accepted the kinds of gifts and perks that magazine editors regularly accept—period," says Givhan of the policy at the *Washington Post*. "If it's not available to the public, then I have no business accepting it. Basically, that rule applies to anything of significant value. Believe me, I have my share of lipsticks and T-shirts. I've sent back many a handbag or sweater. Sometimes, it's painful. But in the end, you feel much freer in what you write."

The lovey-dovey relationship between the media and fashion businesses creates a dangerous situation in which a few supposedly impartial media outlets pitch products. Some major magazines have been known to purposely ignore the proper separation between editorial and advertising, giving preference and sometimes extra coverage to advertisers—the people who pay *their* bills. A fashion editor I used to work with was notorious around the office for trying to plug advertisers into editorial features. It's no wonder that designers want to convince editors to show their products in their feature pages—it's free advertising that's endorsed by the fashion experts at the publication. "People have said to me that being mentioned in *In Style* is like having a license to print money," says *People*'s Martha Nelson. One time, Nelson recalls, the magazine showed a handbag by a fledgling designer in a wedding story. "The designer wrote me a letter that said, 'If you see the tears on this page they are the tears of happiness that I'm feeling because of the huge response that I've gotten,' " says Nelson. "The bag was about $250, and she had gotten 2,000 orders. Do the math for a small business and think about someone making these in her spare room."

Much of the fashion media's lack of criticism seems to stem from its financial dependence on the industry it covers. Catwalk shows are held on an invitation-only basis. Designers are free to invite (or not invite) whomever they please. Reporters need to tread lightly: offend a designer and you could end up in the back, in standing-room-only seating, or even worse, not get invited at all. Criticism is unwelcome in the fashion business, and reporters may not be invited back if a designer's collection is unfavorably reviewed. It's happened before. After Carrie Donovan of the *New York Times* wrote that Karl Lagerfeld's collections tanked, the designer banned her from his front row. Similarly, Alexander McQueen banned *London Sunday Times* fashion editor Colin McDowell from his spring 2000 Givenchy show for insulting his work. And in 2001, LVMH banned acclaimed *International Herald Tribune* fashion editor Suzy Menkes from its shows due to a negative review of John Galliano's show for Christian Dior, topped off with the headline "Dior's Aggression Misses the New Romantic Beat." LVMH lifted the ban forty-eight hours later. The medium that must tiptoe most lightly is television. Top fashion writers can afford to be more critical in their articles because their livelihood depends less on access to the designers; they don't need on-camera interviews.

Journos also have to be careful not to offend because they'll run the risk of incurring the wrath of the seating-chart organizer. What a scandal it would be if a top writer wasn't invited or was seated unfairly. "I've certainly had my share of designers and publicists unhappy with something I've written—I've had them give me a bad seat because of it," says Givhan. "I've had conversations with them about stories they haven't been pleased with. But ultimately, I think even the most sensitive designer understands that a compliment given gratuitously isn't as valuable as the one given based on merit. Besides, journalists manage to cover secretive institutions like the Pentagon. A good reporter should be able to deal with a grumpy designer. We don't need to be friends, just professionals."

SATURATED WITH STYLE

It might be excusable if only one form of media had its hand in fashion's cookie jar. Au contraire. On a day-to-day basis, the cushy new hybrid of fashion, media, and entertainment comes at us from every angle.

TV

Belkys Nerey has been called "the queen of fun news." One of her duties at WSVN, a Fox affiliate in Miami, is to film a weekly two-minute segment called "Fashion Forward" about "what's in, where you can get it, and who's got what." Each week, she picks a different trend—flag fashion, boots, Greek chic—then talks to local merchants about where viewers can pick up these items. She admits she's no fashion expert, but rather relies on secondhand sources. "I must confess I'm one of those people who reads *Vogue, Bazaar, In Style, Vanity Fair, Marie Claire*," she says. "So I know what's in style, and it's usually in my closet. But I also work with large stores and small boutiques to try and find out what they have in stock the day I need to shoot." Segments like "Fashion Forward" have become commonplace on local news networks around the country. Akin to ending a broadcast with a sixty-second "puppy rescued from drainpipe" segment, feel-good fashion stories are mixed in with the news lineup to help cushion the audience's reaction to the day's standard fare of bank robberies, dead bodies, and sexual predators. Along with their daily updates on neighborhood crimes, accidents, and city council skirmishes, viewers can tune in and get a helpful fashion tip. "The news we put on TV can't be all bad," says Nerey. "Viewers need a mix of other stuff, not to mention that for some viewers, that half hour or hour of news they get a day may be their only exposure to information. They may not read the paper or subscribe to any magazines, so that one source had better have it all."

Fashion has taken over the airwaves—on news programs, on music videos, on sitcoms, dramas, soap operas, even on cooking shows ("Bobby Flay's wardrobe provided by . . ."). The average American watches three hours and forty-six minutes of TV each day. By age sixty-five, we will have spent nearly nine years of our lives glued to the tube. While every TV show, except for public access or PBS, is about commerce in some way due to commercial breaks, fashion programs in particular are inherently about the big sell. Although the buy-buy-buy pitch isn't quite as blatant as on the Home Shopping Network or in an infomercial, the underlying theme of consumerism in fashion programming isn't difficult to see. Clothes featured on shows like E!'s *Fashion Emergency*, for instance, are not only shown on-air but also credited up the wazoo. As makeover subjects schlep in and out of the dressing room, brand names and prices flash across the bottom of the screen. At some point in the program, one of the resident fashion experts, like Leon Hall or Brenda Cooper, will inevitably proclaim something like, "Now, Janine, doesn't Escada just make *the* loveliest jackets?"

You can't blame the producers and experts for being highly biased toward their gracious fashion sponsors. They'd have no show otherwise. In order to produce a TV show about fashion (on a reasonable budget), you must rely on the generosity of clothing companies and designers. Fashion "experts" aren't customarily paid to appear on these shows, but there's no shortage of takers. Todd Oldham's MacGyver-like do-it-yourself segments on *House of Style* in the early 1990s weren't just charity; designers, like experts in other fields, appear on shows for self-promotion. Likewise, when Old Navy teamed up with MTV for a back-to-school clothes giveaway contest, it wasn't generosity driving the retailer. The promos for the contest featured none other than Molly Sims, who just happened to be working double duty as an Old Navy spokesperson *and* host of *House of Style* and *Mission Makeover* on MTV. On MTV's special, *Fashionably Loud*, models showed off the season's hot looks, set to live music. Alas, the show wasn't just pure entertainment; buying information for the clothes appeared on the channel's website.

The 1980s ushered in the first major fashion-focused TV programs: CNN's *Style with Elsa Klensch*, *Fashion Television*, and MTV's *House of Style*. *Fashion Television* host Jeanne Beker recalls only two TV crews backstage at the shows when her program launched in 1985: hers and CNN's. "Elsa was very no-nonsense—it was about hemlines, shade of beige—unless you really cared about clothes, it probably went over your head," says Beker. "We were the only crew doing in-depth designer profiles and covering parties. Now there are countless crews backstage." The past fifteen years have seen another crop of fashion-centered shows. Some have focused on voyeuristic views of catwalk shows and designers; others have had more of a do-it-yourself angle, including *House of Style*, the *VH1/Vogue Fashion Awards*, *Fashion File*, the Learning Channel's *A Makeover Story*, *Fashionably Loud*, *Mission Makeover*, *Fashion Emergency*, *Style World*, *Model*, *Fashion Classic*, *Model TV*, *Videofashion!*, *The Look for Less*, the offerings on the Style Network, and *Full Frontal Fashion* on New York's Metro Channel, which broadcasts twenty-four-hour coverage of New York Fashion Week. The shows have spanned various demographics, from the diehard fashion fan who craves couture to the average consumer who wants to see more affordable styles. "Fashion has become a real spectator sport," says Beker. And it's not all in vain. Viewers do typically get a little more than entertainment out of the shows. "The people that watch our show—some just watch for T&A—but they're learning by osmosis," says Beker. "People are a lot more fashion conscious. Look at men: finally men are starting to shop for themselves. That was unheard of in the eighties."

In addition to programs devoted entirely to fashion, makeover madness began to saturate talk shows and other general-interest programs in the 1990s. Viewers clamored to see "Geek to Chic" and "Help! My mother dresses like a hoochie" transformations. Everyone wanted to see the plus-sizer learn to dress for her figure, the burly truck driver fixed up to look like an accountant, the teenage goth transformed into a clean-cut Ivy League student. Makeover segments played out as the ultimate Cinderella fantasy (whether the subjects were willing participants or not). The message: You can change your life by changing your clothes. "Women, especially, have a fascination with transformation as a [means] of revenge on those who thought they weren't pretty or special enough," says Joyce Millman, TV editor for Salon.com. "There's a new element to the makeovers you see on *Oprah, Ricki Lake, The View*, and other shows—the makeover is not presented as merely a cosmetic change, but a spiritual transformation, a way to become a new person inside by becoming a new person outside." Just as Hollywood—with its numerous Cinderella remakes like *She's All That, Can't Buy Me Love, Pretty Woman, Miss Congeniality, The Princess Diaries*, and *She's Out of Control*—tells moviegoers that geeks, tomboys, and hookers can become attractive members of society with a little makeup and a costume change, television was telling us we could all do the same.

Fashion increasingly cozied up to the world of TV. Oprah showed viewers how to part with clutter in their closets. Fashion editors chattered on about three-button versus two-button jackets on morning shows. Stylists demonstrated how to snip and sew an outdated piece of clothing from last season into something acceptable (a zebra-print skirt becomes a charming throw pillow!). MTV gave viewers a peek at how pop stars like Britney Spears and Pink shop for their daring awards-show outfits. Television audiences were being showered with positive fashion messages from many different angles.

Of course, fashion criticism does exist on TV, but it's of the brutal, rather than analytical, sort. In Hollywood, Joan and Melissa Rivers's catty Oscar fashion analysis became so popular that the duo became red-carpet fixtures at every major awards show, including the Golden Globes, the Emmys, the People's Choice Awards, the Grammys—they even hit the Riviera to critique what stars were wearing at Cannes. The commentary can get cruel. At the 2002 Golden Globes,

Rivers took a look at Sela Ward's peculiar red Valentino gown with bows tied at the front and asked the actress, "Who are you representing? Kmart?" As a comedian, Joan Rivers can get away with far greater insults than a TV fashion reporter would be able to, and the network (E!) can place the culpability on her shoulders—don't get mad at us, it's *her*. Celebrity mag *Us Weekly* employs a similar tactic in its popular "Fashion Police" feature. It allows comedians, radio deejays, and other personalities to verbally rip apart the most heinous celebrity outfits of the week. The magazine publishes hilariously mean comments about stars' clothing choices, while brilliantly transferring accountability to the independent panel of judges.

Today, the preshow fashion coverage of awards shows is nearly as important as the actual event. For those who don't get enough of the fashions on the Rivers's two-hour pre-Oscar coverage on E!, they can switch over to ABC's thirty-minute "On the Red Carpet," which pulled in a whopping 26 million viewers in 2002. The major-network show included the obligatory fluffy questions, with nominees and other attendees making their way along the crimson conveyor belt, but frankly, it was just a last chance to see what everyone was wearing before they went inside to sit down.

Now even venerated news sources have joined in on the criticism of individuals. In a time when witty news-anchor banter has become de rigueur, an easy topic the day after any awards show is indubitably fashion. The morning after the 2002 Grammy Awards, CNN ran a segment called "CNN Grammy Garb: Hits & Misses," in which its morning anchor and two fashion experts critiqued the red-carpet looks. This would have been understandable had any of the celebrities shown up in a newsworthy Jennifer Lopez–like Versace number, but the red carpet that year remained relatively tame and seemed oddly paired with the morning's other stories about war in Afghanistan and suicide bombings in Israel.

This type of personal ridicule may be entertaining, but it isn't particularly constructive. In this environment of casual cruelty, the people who generally get picked on are those inventive few who follow their own taste rather than that of a high-paid stylist—like Björk for her famous swan gown at the 2001 Oscars. But what kind of message are we sending when people who stick their necks out to look like individuals are mocked for it? It's sad that most onlookers didn't understand that Björk, in her own endearing way, was thumbing her nose at the uniformity of conventional Oscar attire. The industry is so hubristic and impervious that no one seemed to notice. The media and public have become so attuned to what is widely considered beautiful that they immediately reject anything else. We live in a time that favors bland conformity over daring fashion dissidence. The only reason Jennifer Lopez's famous green Grammy gown was forgivable was that it was Versace. Public opinion about that dress could easily have swung the other way. Even Gwyneth Paltrow, who was widely ridiculed for her seemingly see-through, punkish black Alexander McQueen Oscar dress in 2002, was not slammed quite as badly as she could have been since she was wearing a major designer. People were willing to give her the benefit of the doubt—maybe she *meant* to look that way.

But this way of thinking is dangerous. Heaven forbid we scare off all the people who push the envelope. We need them, not because we'll all be wearing swan dresses one day but because their quirkiness is what flavors the fashion of tomorrow. As more of those true originals capitulate, abandoning their idiosyncrasies in exchange for friendlier reviews, the ones who remain will become increasingly fearful of showing their faces. The true originals will die out. And we will all inch closer to the bland—but socially acceptable—middle.

The Runway Report

Catwalk shows and television seem like a match made in media heaven: beautiful people, plenty of skin, flamboyant personalities, extravagant clothes, theatricality, famous audience members. As in Hollywood, everything on the runway is exaggerated, but even more so: the models are taller and thinner than the average woman, tops are indecently transparent (or nonexistent), miniskirts reveal butt cheek, makeup and hair are severe. The sexy, voyeuristic nature of fashion shows certainly has the potential to reel in viewers beyond just the hard-core fashion fans. Bernard Arnault, chairman of LVMH, the world's largest luxury conglomerate, which owns such labels as Louis

Vuitton, Christian Dior, and Givenchy, has said he employs flashy Paris couture shows to promote the image and name of a brand in order to push the real moneymakers—handbags and fragrances. In 2000, he pointed out the example of John Galliano's offbeat spring collections for Dior in *Time Europe*. "His ideas are not meant to be worn, but the ideas descend down to prêt-à-porter and to everything in the line," he said. "And that's what we sell." Fashion on TV relies on ostentation, and a healthy dose of sex appeal. Of the 1.5 million who visited the 1999 Victoria's Secret webcast fashion show in one day, it's doubtful that many were actually looking to stock their panty drawers, but the publicity and brand recognition garnered by the show were priceless. Similarly, when MTV staged its 2002 *Sports Illustrated* Swimsuit Issue fashion show, it may have been called *Fashionably Loud*, but it was more about skin than about fashion. Most viewers may not have watched the show because they were actually in the market for a new white two-piece thong, but having their suits shown on TV was good exposure for the designers nonetheless.

The introduction of television cameras into fashion shows changed the industry enormously. "I don't want to diss TV because it's done amazing things for fashion—it's pushed the envelope," says Beker. "For better or worse, it's caused the fashion show experience to be more fun." Television leveled the playing field for designers who weren't necessarily the premier artistes but who could put on a dazzling show. It was no longer just fashion houses like Christian Dior and Givenchy that were worthy of attention. Now more casual stars of design like Betsey Johnson, Tommy Hilfiger, and Calvin Klein could garner as much (if not more) mass-media attention by staging celebrity-filled, media-friendly shows. Sean "P. Diddy" Combs allegedly spent a million dollars to produce his fall 2001 Sean John show. More impressive than the dramatic sound track, giant video screen, and the clothes themselves was the mob of famous attendees Combs's team assembled—a motley crew of stars including Busta Rhymes, Destiny's Child, Tommy Hilfiger, Combs's lawyer Johnnie Cochran, *Vogue* editor Anna Wintour, and Katie Couric, among others. The show's hefty price tag turned out to be worth every penny. The Style Network ran a special two-hour telecast that was simulcast on E!

to spotlight the show. The two-year-old line saw sales skyrocket to over $100 million that year.

Haute couture designers succumbed to pressure and allowed cameras to broadcast their collections for the first time in 1998. Isabella Rossellini hosted the special telecast, "Paris Fashion Collection," which aired at 9 P.M. Thursday night on ABC and featured highlights of shows from some of the world's most esteemed design houses, including Christian Dior, Alexander McQueen, Christian Lacroix, Valentino, and Gaultier. Television made some designers celebrities in their own right. The camera adored those with TV-friendly personas who produced witty sound bites, like Isaac Mizrahi and Jean-Paul Gaultier.

Originally conceived as a showcase for buyers and select media, the major shows today are packed with a virtual who's who of writers, photographers, socialites, and celebrities. Each year, nearly two thousand members of the media crowd into the tents at Bryant Park to catch a glimpse of the season's new looks. Buyers are no doubt an important component; they're the ones who stock their stores with designers' merchandise. But publicity-savvy designers have realized that it's even more important to create that all-important buzz about a collection. Now most buyers place their orders well in advance of the shows, says Lisa Armstrong, fashion editor for *The Times* in Britain, so the shows are mainly used for publicity. For example, the audience at a 1986 Marc Jacobs show would have been equally split between press and buyers, but today's audience contains about 90 percent media and celebrities, a spokesperson for the designer told the *New York Times* in 2001.

Despite attempts by some programs to delve into somewhat more cerebral topics, such as the history of hemlines as it relates to prosperity, runway coverage on television has never been able to move beyond its shallow stereotype. "When a story can only be three or four minutes, it's too easy to be superficial," says Robin Givhan. "Reporters don't have the air time to do much more than ask the most basic questions." This hurried format leaves time for a few video highlights from each show, ten-second sound bites from designers summing up the new looks, raves from celebrities in the audience, and not much else.

Televising the shows has also transformed fashion, a once-hallowed institution, into a veritable circus at times. It's one thing to add a little entertainment value to a show. Who can blame designers for wanting to keep audiences amused? "Given that fashion shows are really for the benefit of the press, and ultimately the reader, it's totally counterproductive to bore an audience to death by showing them every variation you ever came out with on a jacket," says Armstrong. But there's a fine line between injecting a bit of entertainment value into a show and turning it into a gross display that has very little to do with fashion anymore. The personalities, the scene, and the after-parties can easily become the focal point for invitees. And the shows themselves are sometimes such a spectacle that it's possible to forget that the clothes are the main event. John Galliano's Paris spring/summer haute couture collection in January 2002 was the self-proclaimed Greatest Show on Earth, with harlequins, ribbon-twirling gymnasts, taiko drummers in loincloths, clowns, and a contortionist. In November 1998, Paris-based designer Alphadi staged a $2.5 million show in Niger, a Saharan country where the average person lives on less than fifty cents a day. Models sashayed outdoors against a backdrop of cliffs and sand dunes, as well as turban-clad soldiers and local beggars (it could only have been a more grotesque display had the finale included buckets of money being tossed into a shredder for use as confetti). Oh, and there were clothes, too.

The need for publicity is so strong that sometimes a designer will show a collection on the runway that's completely different from the clothes that will actually be available for sale. "It confuses the public, and it proves that all the designer wants is a cheap photo opportunity," says Armstrong. She cites as an example Stella McCartney's debut collection in 2001 for her eponymous line. When much of the press panned it, the reaction of the fashion house was to try to get journalists in to see what was on the racks because it was completely different. "You can't have it both ways—you can't use sensationalist tactics to get your clothes in the newspapers and then complain that the reporting is unrepresentative of the true nature of your work," says Armstrong. "It's hard enough trying to see eighty shows in one week, let alone going along to all the showrooms afterwards. Designers have to decide where their priorities lie—seeking notoriety or building a serious fashion label."

Sitcoms and Dramas

Jami, a thirty-two-year-old manager for a graphic design company in Philadelphia and consummate *Sex and the City* fan, wore a big flower on her lapel for a year until she finally got sick of people calling her "Carrie." The razzing by her friends may have convinced her to drop the flower look, but she says she still enjoys watching the show for inspiration. "Philly is a fairly conservative town and there just aren't a lot of fashion-forward folks taking risks in self-expression," she says. "I like the clothes Carrie wears because I like to see what she can get away with." Jami is such a huge fan of the show, she and her friend Dayna went on the *Sex and the City* tour in New York City. The three-hour, $25 sightseeing tour travels to about thirty sites related to the show and includes trips to Tiffany's to see where Charlotte got her engagement ring; to Onieals, the SoHo bar used as a show location, to sip Cosmos; to Patricia Field's quirky Greenwich Village boutique; and, of course, to the Jimmy Choo and Manolo Blahnik boutiques.

No other show in the history of television has inspired more trends (and more articles about them) than *Sex and the City*. In many ways, fashion is like a fifth character. Since the show debuted on HBO in 1998, fashion writers and editors have been gripped by the power of the show. The network even allows viewers to bid on eBay for clothes and accessories worn on the show, from a Nanette LePore rainbow-striped sundress to a Baccarat crystal ring worn by Kim Cattrall. The show effectively raised the bar for other shows to become more fashion conscious. But it's not just the four famous friends from *SATC* who have become boob-tube fashion icons. Stars of the small screen have always had some influence on trends. Bob Mackie made Cher and Carol Burnett sparkle on their eponymous shows in the seventies. Likewise, the stars of *Charlie's Angels*, *The Mary Tyler Moore Show*, and *Dynasty* both reflected and affected fashions of their eras. TV sitcoms, dramas, and even news programs have become much more fashion-forward in recent years. Having a product shown on TV is like placing an ad—a very successful ad. When *SATC* leading lady Sarah Jessica Parker toted a wacky horse-head purse on the show, the bag's maker, Beverly Hills designer Timmy Woods, was immediately flooded with a thousand orders. A garment on TV is money in the bank. Sharon Lee, co-president of youth market research company Look-Look, once said that an episode of *Friends* will inspire thirty thousand calls about where to get Jennifer Aniston's pants.

It's the costume designer's job to convey personality through the characters' clothing. Certain labels can do that. For example, a woman's Louis Vuitton logo-print bucket cap says she's probably into fashion and labels. Similarly, a white thirteen-year-old from the suburbs in head-to-toe FUBU can communicate a message about the character before he even utters a word. Likewise, the outrageously stylized wardrobe on *Sex and the City* makes sense because shopping and love of fashion are part of the characters' personalities.

Now we have seen the advent of personal digital recorders like TiVo, which allow viewers to record live video. Surveys in 2002 showed that 71 percent of TiVo subscribers skip commercials, leaving companies scrambling for new ways to get their advertising messages to viewers. Today they realize that synergy with TV shows can be lucrative. So now, many wardrobe stylists are courted by designers and sometimes strike deals with clothing labels to costume characters. Fashion product placement is part of a larger $1 billion industry whose business it is to put a Pepsi can in the hand of a show's protagonist or an iMac in his office. Striking deals with designers and retailers to parade their clothes on a show saves a producer money and, if it's done correctly, could lead to potential cosponsored promotions. In 1998, a friend gave Emily Cinader Woods, of J. Crew, the script for the pilot episode of *Dawson's Creek*. That year, J. Crew worked with the show's producers to wardrobe the entire cast. As an added tie-in, the stars modeled for the clothier's catalog. The following year, American Eagle Outfitters, which had apparently envied the setup—recognizing that viewers of *Creek* were their ideal target audience—took over the show's wardrobe.

Sometimes clothing companies aren't actively seeking out placement deals—wardrobe stylists will request certain clothes or a brand name will be written into a script because it adds realism, like when Rachel got a job at a fashion house on *Friends* (although to make the jump from coffee-bar waitress to Ralph Lauren exec in such a short span of time *was* stretching the limits of credibility). "On one episode of *Seinfeld*, Kramer was ordering J. Crew chinos in the shower from the catalog," says Cinader Woods. "We don't come after those. They come after us; and we read the script and we say, yeah, amazing, of course. *Just Shoot Me* did an entire episode around Christmastime on a guy named J. Crew. And David Letterman has referenced J. Crew two or three times over the years. We don't go get those, but they've certainly been beneficial."

It's advantageous to inject fashion into shows not only from a ratings standpoint but also from a more straightforward financial one. Sometimes, money can be made directly off a well-dressed star. In the first season of *Buffy, the Vampire Slayer*, wardrobers dressed star Sarah Michelle Gellar like a typical high school girl. Soon after, they dropped the realism in favor of a more fashion-forward look. Fox Consumer Products launched a *Buffy* clothing line in 1998, featuring Buffy's signature tight pants, hoodies, and slip dresses. Similarly, *Friends* costume designer Debra McGuire parlayed her experience on that show into her own line of clothes, which sells at her boutique in Pacific Palisades, California.

Fashion has also hit MTV in a big way. Increasingly fashion-savvy video directors have found many obvious ways to insert designer labels into their work. And it's a mutually beneficial relationship. The artist looks cool; the fashion house gets promoted on TV by the cool-looking artist. Ja Rule frequently wears Burberry in his videos, Jennifer Lopez, Versace. Jay-Z's *Girls, Girls, Girls* video featured two Christian Dior T-shirts: one said, "J'adore Dior," the other had a smiley face with the letters *C* and *D* for eyes. The video debuted shortly after Dior launched a national print ad, with the shirts as its stars. Consumers who missed the ad in *Vogue* would see the shirts every time the video played.

Now placements don't end when the director says, "Cut." The next frontier of product placements? Reruns. In 2001, New Jersey–based Princeton Video Image was negotiating a ten-year deal to embed computer-generated logos and ads into reruns of *Law and Order* when it aired twice a night on TNT. For example, a Kenneth Cole billboard could be added to the background of an outdoor shot, or a logo could be prominently added to a shirt. The possibilities are scary to think about. One day, we could be watching a rerun of *ER* with George Clooney wearing a logo that wasn't originally there or repeats of *Miami Vice* with Don Johnson walking in front of billboards for companies that didn't even exist back then.

The Real World

Fashion product placement is somewhat expected in the fictional world of TV—on sitcoms, soap operas, and dramas—but now, clothing companies have begun to recognize the benefit of placing their clothes in the realm of nonfiction—on news programs, game shows, talk shows, and so-called reality shows. And producers have been happy to oblige. In March 2002, entertainment news show *Extra* ran a fashion segment in which they sent a reporter to try on the season's menswear looks. The show's host, Leeza Gibbons, followed up by informing viewers that the last suit seen in the segment was the "Deal of the Day," and could be found by logging on to the show's website. On MTV's show *Becoming*, in which fans get made over to look like their favorite artists and then re-create one of their videos, the show's producers arrange for the fans to receive a room full of goodies. So at one point in every episode, the lucky recipients are filmed gushing about the gifts: "Oh, these pants are from J. Lo's new line!" "They hooked us up with new Nikes!" On MTV's product-filled *Real World/Road Rules Challenge*, cast members would read aloud messages from their cell phones like "Come wearing your Puma gear."

Hosts and correspondents on news programs and talk shows can be nearly as effective as celebrities at setting trends—they're seen by millions of viewers each day, unlike Hollywood stars who aren't typically in view on a daily basis. On *Today*, Katie Couric mentioned her dainty mules on the air one morning and sparked a barrage of phone calls to Manolo Blahnik stores. Knowing the potential for such publicity, companies have become much more aware of this forum. When the end credits roll on many local news programs and talk shows, you're likely to catch a "Wardrobe provided by . . ." plug. In return for a quick credit, clothiers are more than willing to supply hosts and anchors with free or loaned clothes. From *E! News Live*'s Jules Asner, to the Food Network's *Hot off the Grill* host Bobby Flay, to *VH1 News*'s Rachel Perry—all have their outfits' suppliers plugged when the closing credits roll.

Today, there's only a faint dividing line between advertising and programming. It's a dangerous setup, since it will make it increasingly difficult to know who has an impartial opinion and who is on payroll. Regis Philbin's monochromatic-suit-and-tie look from *Who Wants to Be a Millionaire?* earned him his own clothing line with Van Heusen in 2000. Anytime a man wore the Regis look, he acted as a walking billboard for the show; anytime the show aired, it acted as an ad for the clothes. It's sometimes hard to tell whether a TV personality is being genuine or promoting a product. On a September 2001 episode of *Live with Regis and Kelly*—after his signature look died down and he reverted to wearing other designers' labels—Regis conspicuously fished for compliments on his suit. "Beau Brummel," he pointed out, at which his cohost Kelly Ripa gushed, "It's *very* nice." Whether it was an intentional pitch or not, it was a veiled endorsement seen by over four million people.

FILM

Days after seeing the trailer for Cameron Crowe's 1992 grunge-era flick *Singles,* I went out and bought a pair of black combat boots like the ones Bridget Fonda wore in the movie. I hadn't even seen the film yet. It was the shortest period of time I had ever waited to buy something after seeing it on-screen. After watching *Flashdance* in the eighties, I positioned a cut-up sweatshirt ever-so-nonchalantly off my shoulder. I bought thigh-high stockings after seeing Liv Tyler wear them in *Empire Records.* And in my adolescent Madonna phase, I bought a black mesh top after watching *Desperately Seeking Susan.* But I know I wasn't the only one.

Throughout filmmaking history, costumes have influenced trends, from Audrey Hepburn's little black dress in *Breakfast at*

Tiffany's to Jennifer Grey's pedal pushers and canvas sneakers in *Dirty Dancing. Saturday Night Fever* did more to bring the leisure suit to the masses than Studio 54 ever could have. And Michael Douglas's high-powered look in *Wall Street* made a huge mark on corporate fashion of the time. Designers and clothing companies, fully aware of the influence that the big screen can have on consumers (can't you still picture that red dress Julia Roberts wore in *Pretty Woman*?), are now trying to take full advantage of the medium. When you go to the theater, you could be watching a two-hour commercial.

Having a product featured in a film and associated with a major star can provide invaluable exposure for a clothes maker, says Susan Safier, vice president of product placement for Twentieth Century-Fox, who has brokered many big fashion deals including those with Fendi and Versace in *Bedazzled*, Express in *Never Been Kissed*, and Armani in *Entrapment*. Fashion placements are well planned. It's not in a clothier's best interest to provide garments haphazardly. Designers don't want their clothes to be ridiculed in a film (for example, it's doubtful that Calvin Klein would hand over a pair of shorts if the script called for someone to make fun of them). They choose placements that allow their clothes to be seen by the greatest number of eyes, and by the best possible audience. Most labels wouldn't want to outfit a controversial racist character, for example, for fear of being associated with that type of person. "Chanel won't lend you suits for a teen summer movie—there's no payoff if their target audience won't see it," says Nancy Brous, a fashion stylist in New York City. Companies also look for placements to be as prominent and recognizable as they can be, so they've become all the more obvious. "The bottom line is that no one actually reads all the end credits after a movie, which is where a company is thanked for their participation," says Brous. "So it's better if the product is noticeable and identifiable—some shoe companies have requested that the boxes, with the brand name, be included in a shot somehow, or a shopping bag with a logo be shown."

The deals cooked up between filmmakers and designers don't end at on-screen exposure. In some cases, Safier will negotiate promotions such as giveaways or cosponsored events with companies that provide prominent placements to coincide with the film's theater or home video release date. Getting the support of a star beyond just one movie can be a major coup for a designer. Harrison Ford likes to wear Cerruti in his movies, Pierce Brosnan wants Brioni, Michelle Pfeiffer prefers Armani. Those stars not only request to wear those labels in future films but also wear them to press events. Ermenegildo Zegna provided clothing for Kenneth Branagh in *The Gingerbread Man*, in the March 1998 issue of *GQ*, at the Cannes Film Festival, at the 1997 Academy Awards, on press junkets, and at the premiere of Woody Allen's *Celebrity*. Attaching a big-name designer to a film can create buzz throughout the entire publicity campaign. Take 1996's *Romeo and Juliet* starring Leonardo DiCaprio and Claire Danes. The stars not only wore Prada and Miu Miu in the film but also dressed exclusively in Miuccia Prada's labels while publicizing the movie. "We have a deal with the marketing department for this movie," Danes told a Philadelphia paper that year. "I wear what they give me and I get to wear whatever they give me when I'm not promoting." Tommy Hilfiger exclusively dressed the cast of the 1998 film *The Faculty*, and its stars appeared in the designer's ads.

It's essential that product placements reproduce real-life conditions, adds Ian McQueen, vice president of marketing at ISM Entertainment, a product-placement firm in Los Angeles. "Actual products instead of generics add credibility to the productions, creating more realistic situations. As long as the product placements aren't obnoxious, it's a win-win situation for the studio, corporation, and consumer." Unfortunately, that's not what's happening in some studios. All this wheeling and dealing may be good for the clothing provider, but if done incorrectly, it can harm a film by impairing the costume designer's ability to properly dress the characters to reflect their intended personalities. According to Deborah Nadoolman Landis, an Oscar-nominated costume designer and president of the Costume Designers Guild, it's not filmmakers who are trying to borrow clothes from fashion designers—it's the designers who are pushing their wares on the filmmakers. "There are definitely pressures to exploit the medium," she says. "Fashion designers would love every star to be sporting their clothes at all times." The popular misconception about costume designers is that they are the film world's version of the fashion stylist. "We're not personal shoppers," says Nadoolman Landis. "Our goal is not to make a star look as beautiful as they can be. That's the goal for the runway and the red carpet." In fact, she says, it's usually not in the best interest of a film's director or producer to show designer products. "In most contemporary TV and film, it's counter-intuitive because it's distracting if people recognize the clothes," she says. "Also, if you use a known fashion designer, your film becomes automatically dated. I don't think any director or producer wants that."

Stories about costume designers being pressured to work with certain fashion labels have circulated around Hollywood in recent years. In 2002's *Death to Smoochy*, for example, Edward Norton reportedly wanted to wear Armani. The problem, costume designer Jane Ruhm told *Premiere* magazine, was that his character was a hippie. Norton had Armani make a hemp suit. "There's all this weird negotiating about what they want in return," Ruhm said. "These are neat clothes, and they're fun to have and all," she added, "but I could've made Edward a great suit without having to go through millions of phone calls and negotiations. In the end, I didn't want him to wear those clothes, but . . . Well, he is." Average moviegoers may not notice one or two subtle details. But if these types of deals continue to flourish, there will come a time when they will.

CELEBRITIES

If you were to make a list of the ten most influential trendsetters, chances are good that the list would be dominated by entertainers. No matter what your taste, there's a star to act as your style inspiration. Pop star wannabes can look to Britney Spears while cool fortysomethings can look to someone like Michelle Pfeiffer. Hip-hop stars have become big trendsetters for men, says *GQ* fashion director Marc Berger. "Urban streetwear is the fastest-growing fashion segment," he says. "Rap/hip-hop has fueled an entire clothing industry."

Clothing companies know that hooking up with a celebrity will bring instant buzz. Designers put a lot of energy into getting stars to attend their shows and convincing them to wear their clothes.

Branding experts go to great lengths to figure out which stars will be the best matches. "As cool-hunters the world over can tell you, knowing who or what is going to be the next big thing is no small business," says Debi Hall, fashion branding strategist for JY&A Consulting in London. "The difficulty is pinpointing the name of the moment, catching their wave of success, and riding with it." Take Burberry, for instance. For years, the British brand had been thought of as a stodgy granddad's label. Then a smart redesign of its image and products, and alignment with the right celebrities, helped the company post triple-digit growth. "Getting our bikini on Kate Moss cut the average age of our customers thirty years in one fell swoop," CEO Rose Marie Bravo told *Time* in 2001. The problem with all this is that there's so much money and free stuff and other incentives for celebrities to wear certain labels that they're becoming live-action ads for designers.

If you are a designer, you can make your sales skyrocket by getting your name mentioned in the media in association with a star or having a garment worn by a celebrity. Famous faces attract attention. The average person didn't know who up-and-comer Zac Posen was in early 2002, but when Natalie Portman was photographed for several national magazines wearing one of his dresses to the *Star Wars* premiere, millions of people saw his name.

Fashion's emphasis on celebrities is perhaps most noticeable in the print world. If you flipped through a fashion magazine ten years ago, you'd have to search for celebrities. Today, most magazines devote entire front-of-book sections to star style and flaunt celebrities on their covers. A few holdouts, like *W, Harper's Bazaar, Cosmopolitan,* and *Vogue,* do still have a few covers per year with models on them, but for the most part, celebrities rule. The typical consumer judges a magazine by its cover, so it's vital to newsstand sales that the cover—and its featured face—*sell*. "I remember at one point another editor of a fashion magazine was quoted saying 'I will never put a celebrity on the cover'—those were words which she certainly had to eat," says Martha Nelson, *People* magazine editor and former founding editor of *In Style.*

Actresses and singers are the new fashion models of today. One factor that has fueled designers' interest in using stars as mannequins is celebrity weight loss. Former grunge rocker Courtney Love proved that almost anyone, with enough help, could be transformed into a cover girl. Already-thin stars like Jennifer Aniston and Renée Zellweger became the ultimate clotheshangers at their thinnest. Still not as tall as models, but certainly just as thin, these stars now had the body types that were "meant" to wear these clothes. "To get the free clothes—to get them faster, which is certainly a status point—you have to wear sample size, since that's what's shown on the runway," says Merle Ginsberg, entertainment editor of *W* and *Women's Wear Daily*. "If you're somewhere between a size four and a six, you can borrow the most incredible clothes. You might even get them for free. Unfortunately when you're thinking about extreme high fashion, it does look better on thinner people because it was designed for them."

Until the 1990s, models dominated the magazine industry. True, some top models of the 1970s, such as Lauren Hutton and Rene Russo, were able to parlay their modeling gigs into long-lasting celebrity. But it wasn't until Cindy Crawford, Linda Evangelista, Naomi Campbell, Christy Turlington, and Claudia Schiffer began to reel in salaries in the millions that the true supermodel was born. Unfortunately, the success of supermodels was also their downfall. "Supermodels got a little too hotty, a little too glamorous," says Ginsberg. "We would constantly see them drinking champagne at fabulous parties in Europe, they were going out with rock stars, running around like royalty, and who could relate to that?" Not that we don't see celebrities living it up (Jennifer Aniston is married to Brad Pitt, and Julia Roberts rakes in $20 million per movie—who can relate to *that?*). But still, most celebrities possess a slightly more humble, relatable quality than their five-foot-eleven, 113-pound Amazonian rivals. "I do think that women have a difficult time identifying with models," says Nelson. "Models are generally very young, very tall, and very thin; and most of the population is not very young, very tall, and very thin. The clothes look great on the models—there's no denying that—but people can't identify with them."

Celebrities, on the other hand, bring a different element into the mix—their personal lives. "We follow their life and their life story as well as their romances, their ups and downs; they get in great shape, they get out of shape, they change for a role, they color their hair—their personal narrative makes it much easier to connect with them," says

Nelson. "They are the bearers of our mythology and pop culture *and* they do come in a variety of shapes. They're not like the average woman, but they are closer to the average woman than a model is." Actors and musicians have a story to tell and, usually, a project to sell. Models, for the most part, don't. This added selling point is like catnip to magazine editors for several reasons: 1) they can sell a cover story along with the beautiful photo; 2) they don't have to shell out thousands of dollars to pay their cover star. Nicole Kidman will get the publicity for her upcoming film, and *Harper's Bazaar* gets a free cover girl who, most importantly, draws readers' eyes to their magazine.

Marie Claire has taken the celebrity cover girl to another level. Instead of sticking to the formula celebrity feature, editors at the Hearst magazine cook up high-concept ideas like giving Debra Messing a personality test or challenging Susan Sarandon to complete a set of dares or banishing Gwyneth Paltrow to a deserted island. Readers were drawn to the newstand by the October 1999 issue of *Jane* with a cherubic close-up of Keri Russell with the racy coverline, "I lost it on the closet floor"—and she wasn't talking about one of her contacts. When *Vogue* put Hillary Clinton on its December 1998 cover, it not only transformed the First Lady's image but also helped boost its sales among a different audience with a ten-page feature. The reader gets a saucy celebrity story plus beautiful photos in designer clothes. It's a far more interesting formula than the standard fashion-model fare.

Take a so-so fashion ad, insert a celebrity, and you instantly have something ten times more interesting. Stars are usually more eye-catching than models, like Drew Barrymore for Guess? and Sofia Coppola for Marc Jacobs. Because we know a little about their personalities, we can associate the brand with the person. Skechers broke its young, skater-style mold by casting Matt Dillon and Rob Lowe in ads. A slew of female stars including Mena Suvari, Julianne Moore, and Marisa Tomei did a campaign for Coach. In the nineties, Courtney Love, Madonna, and Jon Bon Jovi did Versace; Bruce and Demi did Donna Karan. In spring 2000, trendy discount chain H&M snagged gritty superstars Chloë Sevigny and Benicio Del Toro for its billboards.

A paid star's support doesn't end at the photo shoot for the ad.

Smart designers know that the right relationship with a celebrity can not only focus eyeballs on their print and TV campaigns, it can also ensure that the star will be clothed in that label at events and in magazines. When Penelope Cruz first arrived on the scene in Hollywood, more people saw her modeling Ralph Lauren at events than had actually seen her in a movie. Some celebrities who have relationships with designers also insist on wearing their clothes on magazine covers. "We understand that when you wind up booking a star who has a long association with a particular designer, chances are, they'll want to wear that designer, and the designer is going to want them to wear that," says Ginsberg.

The power that celebrities possess in the fashion world has grown so great that many more stars are taking advantage of it by launching their own clothing lines (imagine the poor fashion-school grads who toil for years and never get their own lines). The ever-growing list includes hip-hop artists (Wu Tang Clan, Jay-Z, Lil' Kim, P. Diddy), music producers (Jermaine Dupri, Russell Simmons), royalty (Prince Charles), pop stars (Jennifer Lopez, Chris Kirkpatrick of 'N Sync, Kylie Minogue), actors (Jaclyn Smith), TV personalities (Regis Philbin), and models (Kathy Ireland, Emme). And then there's that group of headliners who've achieved some level of notoriety for activities not in the least related to fashion, like former White House intern Monica Lewinsky, who designs a line of handbags, Hollywood madame Heidi Fleiss, and Shoshanna Lonstein, who parlayed some of the fame she earned from dating Jerry Seinfeld into a wildly successful sportswear and swimwear line. In February 2002, Brit soccer star David Beckham inked a £1 million deal with Marks & Spencer to help to design a new line of boys' clothes. It's brilliant marketing. When P. Diddy appears at an awards show, he wears Sean John. He can plug his line on a morning TV appearance on *Good Morning America*, an afternoon appearance on *TRL*, and onstage at a show. He can even give props to Sean John in a song, like he did in 2002's "Trade It All."

When celebrities aren't on a designer's payroll, they're being dolled up as leased mannequins. Designers dole out millions of dollars in free clothes to celebrities, socialites, and editors each year in the hope that they'll be spotted in public wearing the fashions and be photographed. This has created a form of real-life product placement. It's veiled advertising at its finest. The setup suits both parties: A designer gives a celebrity clothes; the celebrity wears them in public; a photographer shoots the celebrity in the designer's clothes; a magazine prints a gorgeous shot of the celebrity with a nice fat credit to the designer; the designer and the celebrity get their free PR; sales at the boutique and the box office go up. After Jennifer Lopez showed up at the 2000 Grammys in that now-infamous barely-there green Versace gown, her image was downloaded from the Grammy website 642,917 times over the following twenty-four hours. Versace was receiving publicity months, even years, later. Likewise, the appearance boosted J. Lo's album sales and ticket sales.

Placing clothes on celebrities is big business. New York PR agency Stylefile collects fees of $3,000 to $5,000 to facilitate the appearance of an A-List celeb in a designer gown. The company's finest moment was luring Courtney Love into a white satin Versace gown at the 1996 Oscars. Love not only got to keep the gown, which was worth thousands of dollars but also managed to scrub her grungy image after only a few minutes on the red carpet. Like Stylefile, L.A.-based PR firm Film Fashion hooks designer clients up with celebrities who wear their clothing or accessories to awards shows, charity events, movie premieres, and other events. President Susan Ashbrook used her experience as director of PR for Richard Tyler to start Film Fashion in 1994, reeling in a whopper of a first client: Ralph Lauren. Now Ashbrook places garments on celebrities for all types of public events. When client Iceberg Jeans sponsored the premiere of the 2001 Ben Stiller movie *Zoolander*, Ashbrook arranged to have up-and-comers Ashley Scott, Ashton Kutcher, Michael Vartan, and Gabrielle Union attend the event wearing Iceberg. "In exchange for their attendance, Iceberg gave them their outfits," says Ashbrook. "I consider this to be a 'bartering' of services, which is how celebrity attendance is usually handled, unless it's someone with superstar status like Jennifer Lopez." Promotional deals can be made around any event, not only the typical Hollywood fare. "Just a few years ago, Escada made Jennifer Lopez's wedding gown in exchange for public relations opportunities," says Ashbrook, who arranged the deal. "The wedding was photographed exclusively for *In Style,* garnering Escada international attention worth millions of advertising dollars."

Getting a new product on a celebrity's body is the holy grail of most fashion designers. When Jordache relaunched in 2001, the jeans maker sent free garments to the likes of Mariah Carey, Rosie O'Donnell (who wore head-to-toe rhinestone Jordache on her show), Christina Aguilera, and Gwen Stefani. Suzanne Freiwald's Earl Jeans started out as a celebrity phenomenon, which helped get the word out about the sexy, skinny jeans. "I don't know how celebrities found out," says Freiwald. "They totally dug us up from under a rock; they'd literally come knocking on my front door. Cindy Crawford came into my old office once. Celebrities used to come over all the time. It became important. We, as a small company, didn't have money to advertise. Her assistant called first and said, 'Cindy wants to come over and get some jeans,' then she showed up at three o'clock on a Tuesday, on the dot. We helped her out." Freiwald now gives and loans what she calls "slightly seconds" to celebrity fans. "Jeans are expensive," she says. "So we're really particular about damages like fat threads. We weed it out as second quality; I and friends and relatives and celebrity friends will get them. I promo a lot of those—just free or cheap."

Just as companies don't dole out clothes for product placements on TV and in films haphazardly, they don't randomly hand out goodies to stars for real-life placements either. There is a loose formula to the freebies. Ashbrook says her clients select which celebrities to target based on the stars' image, the amount of press attention they receive, and their personal reputation. The top three categories include 1) new, young stars—they always try to look good; 2) established stars—they maintain their public image and have recognizable style; and 3) nominees and presenters—they guarantee press coverage. All the strategizing that fashion companies go through to pick the right stars just goes to show how artificial the act of dressing has become in Hollywood. Most celebrities don't choose their clothes; their clothes choose them.

Fashion has forever changed the way events are reported by the media. All of the publicity that designers garner from placing products on celebrities couldn't be possible without the raging paparazzi industry. It's hard to believe, but the whole concept of the fashion paparazzi is somewhat recent. "When we started [in 1993] we couldn't find photographers who were shooting the *clothes*—it was all about the faces," says *People*'s Martha Nelson of her time at *In Style*. "Then we started having to say 'Be sure to give us the full length.' If you go back into archives you get a very different kind of celebrity coverage."

Having celebrities photographed at your fashion show, especially ones wearing your designs, can ensure even more editorial coverage. Designers entice celebrities to events and fashion shows with first-class plane tickets, limos, free clothes, and store credits for thousands of dollars, as well as the possibility of cementing a relationship with said designer. Salma Hayek and stylist Phillip Bloch, invited as guests of Armani one year, were flown to Milan and put up at the luxurious Principe Di Savoia. In 1997, Armani flew Mira Sorvino to shop his Milan runway show. In past seasons in Europe, Chanel bankrolled a Concorde trip for Julianne Moore to fly to Paris for a show. At Australian Fashion Week in 2000, designer Marc Keighery had Macy Gray perform live at his show, wearing his sequined trousers. Local journalists speculated that the photos of that product placement would be well worth the $25,000 it cost him to have her there. British designer Charlie Brown brought in former model Jerry Hall for a fee "in the area of" $100,000 to strut alongside the other models on the catwalk. And at all the shows, Cate Blanchett sat front row, next to *Harper's Bazaar* Australia editor Karin Upton Baker, as its guest editor for Fashion Week.

Securing an A-Lister in the front row can be a major coup. "Designers need celebrities to come to fashion shows, so they want to work directly with celebrities [rather than going through a stylist]," says Bloch. "Once they get in, the celebrity feels pressured, 'What if it doesn't look good but he made it for me'—and I've had that happen. Also, designers want personal contact. 'Come stay at my house in Capri' or 'Oh, come to my fashion show' or 'Can we have a fashion show at your house?' " Well-known non-entertainers can be just as effective, if not more so. Remember glossy-haired Chelsea Clinton sandwiched between Madonna and Gwyneth at Versace's 2002 show? This was a bold move for Donatella Versace, who could have seated P. Diddy or Salma Hayek or any number of other superstars in her place, but made a play for a smarter, younger demographic by choosing the made-over daughter of an ex-president.

The biggest real-life product placement event of the year, of course, is the Academy Awards. The Oscars are watched live on six continents by more than a billion viewers worldwide (73 million in the U.S. alone last year). You can't buy advertising like that. When Sharon Stone accidentally ripped her Valentino gown before the 1996 Oscars and pulled together her own impromptu outfit—a black Gap mock turtleneck, long Valentino skirt, and velvet Armani coat—it made headlines around the world and is *still* talked about to this day. Even an unknown like costume designer Lizzy Gardiner, who made an evening gown out of American Express Gold Cards, can make it into national magazines for her fifteen minutes of fame. Nicolas Cage and Kevin Spacey wore Hush Puppy shoes to the 68th Academy Awards. Published photographs of them flaunting the footwear led to the sale of more than thirty thousand pairs of similar shoes, according to Jeff Lewis, vice president of marketing. "One shot of an Academy Award–winning actor wearing our shoes is worth a dozen Hush Puppy ads," he said. Several years ago, Jimmy Choo designer Sandra Choi said her company put all its marketing money into the Oscars. And thanks to that real-life product placement, it was able to thrive with very little conventional advertising. Designer Pamela Dennis once said, "Having a dress on a celebrity is like placing a $30,000 ad. If a star wears your dress to an event, your sales go up immediately." Dress a star at the Oscars, however, and the financial rewards increase exponentially.

Companies scramble to get the top celebrities to see their clothes. Susan Ashbrook wastes no time offering them her clients' services. The day that nominations are released and presenters are announced, Film Fashion approaches certain celebrities with "look books" on behalf of clients. In order to snare that all-important actress, designers fly into L.A. a week before the Oscars and set up the most expensive flea market in the world. This year, twenty-four fashion companies, including Prada, clamored for suites at the über-chic L'Ermitage in Beverly Hills, where they created glitzy showrooms open only to VIPs and their stylists. "For the Oscars and the [Golden]

Globes, it's ridiculous—in September and October they start hounding," says Phillip Bloch, who's worked with stars like Halle Berry and Salma Hayek for the big night. "Those are people, I think, who don't know what they're doing, and they're just hoping to cash in on something."

Now, there's a new hook. In January 2002, the Diamond Information Center unveiled its *Red Carpet Diamond Collection,* a set of fourteen necklaces, rings, and earrings created by some of the world's top jewelers, including Harry Winston and Tiffany, valued at over $13.5 million. A group of celebrities, such as Jennifer Love Hewitt and Sela Ward, and their stylists got to view the collection at a special Beverly Hills luncheon and select a piece to wear to either the Golden Globes, the Grammys, or the Oscars. For every piece worn by a star to one of these events, a $10,000 donation would be made to the American Foundation for AIDS Research in their name. When Sharon Stone wore a $400,000 eleven-carat ring by the Royal Asscher Diamond Company to the Oscars that year, she wasn't shy about talking about either the charity or the company. And when *Dark Angel* star Jessica Alba wore a ring from the collection to the Golden Globes, she told sound bite–hungry reporters: "M. Fabrikant & Sons is donating $10,000 to amfAR because I wore their ring." Celebrities could feel extravagant and charitable at the same time, while the jewelry makers got a nice international plug. Fashion with a conscience or clever marketing ploy?

Fashion's obsession with Hollywood has not only created a shifty system in which stars' fans are bombarded with camouflaged advertising messages, it has also taken attention away from the clothes themselves. "The celebrity fascination is good because it draws more eyes to the fashion industry, but I think it's bad when designers use a flashy front row as a crutch," says the *Washington Post*'s Robin Givhan. "I find it appalling when writers blather on about who was in the front row and don't even bother to mention that there were a few frocks coming down the runway. For me, the buzz about celebrities is long over. Stars get no coverage unless they do something newsworthy—fling a tofu pie at a model in fur, for example. If someone surprising like Meryl Streep turned up at a Sean John show, I'd mention that and also ask her why she was there. I found it interesting, for instance, that Puffy's lawyers all turned out for his show. George Clooney at Versace? Yawn. Gwyneth Paltrow at Calvin Klein? So what."

London stylist and fashion writer Navaz Batliwalla agrees that celebrities are played out. "I am heartily sick of them and of magazines fawning over them," she says. "To me, people like Jennifer Aniston and Gwyneth Paltrow are just averagely well-dressed, pretty women. They are no more 'beautiful' than the average girl-next-door-who-got-a-makeover, but the media has hyped them into these so-called style icons, which is ridiculous. But through the cult of 'The Celebrity' you get the trickle-down effect. If the celebs tout the Gucci bag of the season, the mags feature it and the public buy it."

Celebrity events have become overly styled—a star would be far less likely to take a chance on an outfit that she personally likes if her stylist gives it the thumbs down. As a result, it's impossible to recognize what anyone's real style is anymore. "Everybody in fashion has had 'helpers,' " says Bernadine Morris, former fashion columnist for the *New York Times*. "Diana Vreeland helped Katharine Graham of the *Washington Post*, [Audrey] Hepburn had Givenchy, [Jackie] Onassis had Halston and others, but the stylist game has reached its peak in the last few years when designers send staffs to Hollywood before [the] Academy Awards and other events. As a result, we really don't know what individual tastes are."

The increased use of helpers, though, has played right into designers' hands. Today's stylists are another medium designers can use to promote their veiled advertising messages. There has always been talk of some stylists who aren't exactly impartial. "Everybody's got their relationships, and certain stylists are very influenced by their designer friends, and want to help them," says Ginsberg. Rumors circulate about those who receive deep discounts if they dress the star in a certain designer. Others are influenced by extravagant gifts, or VIP treatment at fashion shows. "[Gifts are] also a matter of goodwill," says Nancy Brous. "If they give you something, you'll be more likely to consider them when you're styling the next high-profile job." Brous has been allowed to keep clothing that was officially on loan, and designers have requested that she pass along clothing to actors as a gift, in exchange for a photo of the actor wearing the items. "While I've known magazine editors to receive Tiffany clocks, spa visits, and Godiva chocolates from companies, it's more likely for a stylist to receive the company's own products—shoes, clothing, etcetera, in the hopes that the stylist will be seen in the clothing," says Brous.

Gifts are common, but the motives aren't as underhanded as it seems, says Phillip Bloch. "We have a joke: 'No front row, I don't go,' " he says. "It's not a joke, really. There are ninety million fashion shows. If I'm not in a front row, I'm not going to go. I don't have time. If you really want me there, then you need to sit me in the front row." Bloch insists freebies aren't meant to butter up stylists as much as they are to keep them in business. "Designers sometimes fly me to places, but it's not like a prerequisite," he says. "I'm a freelancer; I can't afford to fly myself to Milan to a Versace show. People want to turn it into a mean thing or that I'm a diva. There's an expression, 'The higher the monkey climbs up the tree, the more people talk about his ass.' And I'm definitely a product of that, but you take the good with the bad." (And the man can give a smashingly good sound bite—always a plus in fashion media.)

. . .

With so many forces working together to shovel heavy doses of fashion down our throats, it's no wonder we're hooked. If these entities were teaming up to inspire greater clothing creativity in society, that would be one thing. But for the most part, this shady mélange of advertising, entertainment, and fashion has inspired only one very self-serving outcome: higher profits (and a fresh load of soon-to-be-dumped clothes for the Fashion Victim).

6

The Thin Spin

I've always thought Marilyn Monroe looked fabulous, but I'd kill myself if I was that fat.

—Elizabeth Hurley

One balmy spring afternoon, at the southeast corner of 42nd Street and Sixth Avenue in Manhattan, Carmen Kass was crossing the street, looking anything but pedestrian. Around her buzzed the usual lunchtime crowd of tourists—a roly-poly sea of khaki shorts, tucked-in T-shirts, sneakers, and fanny packs—and midtown workers carrying white paper bags filled with slices of pizza, Starbucks cups, and soft-serve ice cream slowly oozing south. As she waited for the eastbound traffic light to turn green, dressed plainly in dark denim low-riders and a basic black tank top, Carmen radiated. She possessed that mysterious "it" that agents and editors talk about. At a newsstand one block north was that month's issue of *Vogue*, featuring Carmen on the cover wearing a red one-piece Christian Dior swimsuit with artful slashes across the front, glossy ironed hair reflecting the sun, skin thoroughly toasted—the Estonian Breck girl of the new millennium.

Just a year earlier the twenty-two-year-old had been voted Model of the Year at the VH1/*Vogue* Fashion Awards.

On this street corner at the uppermost border of Bryant Park, where Fashion Week is staged twice a year, it isn't too uncommon to see the occasional model or celebrity. The neighborhood is home to the glistening monument to magazinedom where I worked, the Condé Nast building, as well as numerous fashion showrooms, modeling agencies, and shops. New Yorkers, particularly in an area like this one, tend not to get starstruck when they spot a long-limbed beauty they recognize from a billboard or magazine cover. (Tourists are another story—I often wonder if it's a regional thing. A friend, upon arriving home to New York from a business trip to Austin, Texas, once commented, "everyone *stares*," in stark contrast to Manhattanites, who tend to avoid eye contact as if strangers' pupils contained tiny solar eclipses.) But on this day nearly everyone took at least a second to look Carmen up and down.

"Hey, she's that model . . . d'you know who I'm talking about?"

"Oh my god, does she *eat?*"

"[Gasp] I could see her bones."

Carmen's thinness brought out the cattiness in passersby, including me. I told a few friends back at my office at *Mademoiselle* that I'd seen her. "She was *so* skinny. Her upper arm was like my wrist," I said. My co-workers feigned shock. "I wonder if she has an eating disorder," they said. "That is so sad."

Many models come and go through the Condé Nast building on a daily basis, doing "go-sees," visiting friends, meeting with editors. But Carmen was the first supermodel I had stood arm to arm with. Next to her delicate limb, mine looked like one of those giant turkey drumsticks people gnaw on at Disney World. For several months afterward, I became somewhat fixated on arm blub, that bulbous wing of fat along the tricep, the saggy pillow of jelly that continues to wag long after you've waved good-bye. Looking in the mirror, I'd cup the back of my arm and strategize how to tighten it up. On the sidewalk, at work, in bars, I'd notice who had blub, who didn't, who hid it, who showed it. At family gatherings, I'd do visual arm blub inspections of my aunts and older cousins to see what the future had in store for me. I'd scrutinize actresses whose arms looked lean and muscular even when they weren't flexing.

Was my obsession with underarm flab Carmen Kass's fault? Could I blame the supermodel for my harrowing body issues? Had one sight of her wiry body knocked me right into a nosedive toward self-doubt? Shouldn't she have been more responsible and *not* worn that tank top in public?

Such is our blame game with fashion. We point a critical finger at fashion for causing our body-image woes, yet rather than turning our backs on the system, we only descend deeper, abiding even more by fashion's body ideals and buying more clothes to heal our dissatisfaction. Fashion is a business built on vanity. Our constant vacillation between self-love and self-loathing is an essential component of the game: were we ever to stop and love ourselves unconditionally, we would no longer feel the urge to buy clothes; were we ever to abhor ourselves completely, we would abandon all desire to dress nicely. So we ride the roller coaster of body-love and body-hate, and fashion reaps the rewards at every turn.

The debate over whether or not fashion causes negative body image has been a favorite topic of fashion critics, psychologists, feminists, and even the government for decades. Over the years a throng of feminist books, like Susie Orbach's *Fat Is a Feminist Issue* in the seventies and Naomi Wolf's *The Beauty Myth* in 1990, have charged fashion and media with conspiring to make women hate their thighs. Researchers have produced surveys, studies, and reports to expose the industry's sinister plot. Today, a mind-numbing amount of data exists, wagging a finger at fashion for causing negative body image. A sampling:

- A woman between the ages of 18 and 34 has a 1 percent chance of being as thin as a supermodel.
- Nearly 50 percent of all teenage girls in one study said they wanted to lose weight after viewing magazines, when only 29 percent were actually overweight.
- An Australian study of anorexic and bulimic women found that 75 percent believed media images had influenced them.

But the body image issue isn't as simple as fashion's critics have often tried to make it. Even though we're deluged with increasingly disturbing statistics, a remedy for our dissatisfaction has remained exasperatingly elusive. All the research and mass-media arguments are little more than tinder on the fire. The real as-yet-unanswered question we should be pondering is: If we know so much about the link between fashion and body image, why aren't we better off for it?

. . .

The Fashion Victim is unquestionably swayed by the images of beauty propagated by the fashion industry. She (and I refer to her as "she" only because it's a sad reality that this is an overwhelmingly female concern) nibbles on baby carrots for lunch, goes through periods when she'll consume nothing but chicken breasts and cans of albacore tuna packed in water (never oil, heaven forbid), buys Tae Bo tapes, a Pilates Pro, and Ab Roller destined to languish in a closet after a few months, frowns and sucks her tummy in when belly fat peeks out over her jeans. She is willing to sacrifice time, money, happiness, sanity, flour, dairy, sugar, red meat, alcohol, pleasure, anything to be thin. Twenty-seven percent of women would give up three years of *life* to be thinner, according to a 1997 *Psychology Today* survey. Even when she's not "dieting," the Fashion Victim is on a perpetual diet. She never eats exactly what she wants to, instead adopting an unofficial diet she calls "eating in moderation." She hawks over portion sizes, still eats a tiny spoonful of mashed potatoes at a restaurant (so she can insist she's not *really* on one of those unhealthy low-carb diets), skips breakfast to balance out the calories she consumed the night before after eating a second chicken leg for dinner. Her thinness complex often consumes her. The Fashion Victim's insecurities are just low level enough that no one would recommend she seek professional help, but significant enough to weigh on her mind day in and day out. She wonders what Kate Moss and Frankie Rayder eat, how many ab crunches Geri Halliwell and Janet Jackson must do, how many hours she'll have to clock on the treadmill, and how many lunches she'll have to forgo to fit into a smaller size. In a curious way, she's glad she has something to blame for her self-absorption other than herself. She blames fashion for her body image woes but, puzzlingly, remains a loyal follower.

Still, her self-sacrifice leads nowhere more frequently than it leads anywhere. The Fashion Victim's inner dialogue reminds her, "You'll be happy when you've dropped a size," and repeats the message even when she's a size smaller. If the day comes when she can squeeze comfortably into her desired size, will she be content, look lovingly into the mirror, and never view herself as imperfect again? Not likely. Instead, the yardstick will merely be adjusted and a new standard set, forever unachievable in the long run. After all, a person whose goal it is to waste away to a mere nub of a human being, all bones and skin and zero meat, can never be guaranteed happiness.

To confuse us further, the same industry that has convinced us throughout our lives that our bodies aren't good enough begins to pepper its message with positive "love your body" statements, creating a puzzling con game similar to that of antismoking ads paid for by tobacco king Philip Morris. The Thin Spin is built on confusion. The Fashion Victim's intellect tells her she's being silly; her emotions tell her she needs to lose weight. She puts all her hope and energy into losing weight, yet harbors an intense hatred toward the tyranny of thinness.

BODY BITCHFEST

Our relentless body-image mood swing not only wreaks havoc on our self-esteem, it also turns us against each other. The Fashion Victim rarely keeps her vanity to herself, instead allowing it to manifest itself as cattiness toward others who are more "fashionably thin," like poor Carmen Kass. In the mid-1990s, during the height of the waif era, lanky model Jodie Kidd was publicly called a "sick, anorexic giraffe." Mothers pointed at her in disgust as they passed her on the street and blamed her for causing their daughters' eating disorders. She, along with Kate Moss, was named in nearly every anti-waif article written at the time. Today, still modeling at a heavier size ten, Kidd ardently maintains that she never suffered from an eating disorder, and that she was just young and her body hadn't developed yet when she first started modeling. Since then, magazines like *Self* and *Cosmopolitan* have applauded the self-confidence that radiates from Kidd's new size-ten body, publishing features in which the model talks about loving her new curves. She had been considered a *bad* role model when she was thin, but became a *good* role model when she gained weight. The message inherent in this warped thinking was clear. Loving your body when you have meat on your bones is empowering; loving your body when you're ultra-skinny—even if you eat like a lumberjack—is irresponsible. This was surely no way to think either. Fashion has pitted the thin against the average against the fat, and no one can possibly emerge as the winner.

Within the arena of thinness, people don't hold back their barbs. On her personal website condemning fashion's hold on our psyches, writer Kelly Emeren Tynan described a photo used in a fashion spread for *Harper's Bazaar*, of a thin model in a bikini, her head thrown back with a look of bored anguish: "Thank goodness for the model's breast implants—we might otherwise think the picture is from a piece on the horrors of Auschwitz," she wrote. When I looked at the photo, I didn't think the model looked like she had breast implants at all. Tynan made her point, but it was muddied when it turned into a personal attack on the thin woman, rather than on the true culprit—the thin ideal.

The Fashion Victim sneers at skinny girls, partly to bring them down a notch, partly to make herself feel better. When the Victoria's Secret Fashion Show aired on prime-time TV in November 2001, Megan, a twenty-three-year-old research analyst in Arlington, Virginia, ripped its stars apart with her friends. "We watched it for about thirty seconds before the comments started: 'Ew, she's so skinny' and 'She has *no* boobs,' " says Megan. "I think the main reason we do this is to make ourselves feel better about not being as thin as these women. It's easier to deal with the fact that you're not thin if you portray their thinness as unattractive or disgusting."

The Fashion Victim often attempts to tear down what is conventionally considered beautiful but buys into it at the same time. A February 2002 letter to the editor let off a little steam to *W* magazine about a December feature starring Gisele Bündchen: "What sets Gisele apart from all the other models? Her chest! What cover model doesn't have long, thin legs and great skin and hair? In fact, there are prettier models than Gisele but they are flat-chested. Nor is Gisele a gift from God, as the story implies. The next time you write an article about this model call it 'Gisele's Breasts.' Physical attributes shouldn't determine whether a person is better than others. I doubt Gisele can solve a calculus equation or write a brilliant essay. The person who can is a gift from God." But would a mathematician wearing a sparkly bikini get you to pick up the magazine?

FASHION'S FAULT?

Most fashion insiders will even admit that the industry does deserve at least a speck of blame. So the only question that remains today is how *much* blame? Eating disorders—anorexia, bulimia, and the like—are complex conditions with a multitude of possible causes. Could fashion be one of them? Certainly. A fifteen-year-old girl who thumbs through fashion magazines religiously may grow up with a slightly skewed view of what a "normal" body size is. Likewise, a man who only feels content buying skinny Prada pants may be setting himself up for disappointment when he doesn't look the same in them as the svelte runway models. But, as nearly every eating-disorder expert will attest, most people who fall into the trap of excessive dieting are vulnerable to begin with, says Melanie Suhr, Ph.D., a psychiatrist at Baylor College of Medicine. "They don't feel good about themselves anyway, and for them dieting is a way to try to fit in, to make other people like them. So while I think that fashion and our culture contribute to [the problem], it's more than just fashion." A 1999 study of adolescent girls published in the *Journal of Social and Clinical Psychology* backed up that notion, finding that those who already had low self-esteem were the only ones vulnerable to eating disorders and body dissatisfaction after being exposed to thin models in magazines.

Negative body image is also linked to larger social issues. In some cultures, fat is considered a sign of prosperity. In Western culture, we see the opposite—a trim body proves that a person has the time and money to stay slim. Not everyone has the leisure time to devote an hour or two each day to yoga class, outdoor jogs, and weight-lifting sessions at the gym. Fattening foods, like burgers, pizza, and fried chicken, are cheap; healthy foods, like lean cuts of meat, whole grains, and fresh produce, are expensive. Gym memberships, exercise equipment, personal trainers, and workout clothes cost money. We view celebrities who manage to lose ten pounds in eight weeks as superhuman, as if they must possess greater willpower than we do. Simply put, though, they often just have better resources. Our body-image affliction has other societal roots as well. In her 1981 book *The Obsession*, Kim Chernin suggests that women's body issues stem in part from the gender war, observing that "men are drawn to women of childish body and mind because there is something less disturbing about the vulnerability and helplessness of a small child—and something truly disturbing about the body and mind of a mature woman."

Since body dissatisfaction can be blamed on a variety of causes, fashion can always maintain some semblance of innocence. Magazine editors and fashion designers have historically deflected responsibility for it. When the subject is broached, defenses tend to go up like a security wall. As Alexandra Shulman, editor of British *Vogue*, once said, "young women who tend toward anorexia do not get it from magazines, but from feelings of loss of self-worth that are instilled in them long before they are looking at *Vogue*. To them there is little difference between Cindy Crawford and Trish Goff. They are all just thin." Others, like Jeff Burns, account director for Frontier Aviators, one of the leading advertising agencies for the fashion industry, place a majority of blame on mothers and fathers. "The models are not responsible for these kids—these kids have parents," he once told a reporter.

As fashion insiders try to redirect culpability, eating-disorder experts attempt to shift it back. "Of course, the fashion industry isn't responsible for having created our culture—but this doesn't mean that they don't have a responsibility for what they do," says Paul Hamburg, M.D., assistant professor of psychiatry at Harvard Medical School and associate director of the eating disorders program at Massachusetts General Hospital in Boston. For the industry to claim that people who develop eating disorders do so only because they're predisposed to them is ridiculous, says Hamburg. "This is a bit like claiming that since HIV-infected patients are more vulnerable to infection, a fast-food chain bears no responsibility for meat contaminated with Listeria germs."

The link between fashion and body image has sparked such controversy that it has drawn government attention. In June 2000, a month after a report from the British Medical Association warned of the dangers young girls face by being exposed to images of extremely thin models, the Women's Unit of Britain's Labor government held a "Body Summit" with fashion editors, doctors, psychologists, and modeling agents to hash out the issue, but ultimately it resulted in no policy changes. In a 1997 press conference, President Bill Clinton condemned the fashionable "heroin chic" look. In August 1996, a parliamentary committee in New South Wales, Australia, convened to target the "plague of eating disorders among young women" related to the advertising industry, women's magazines, and fashion designers. In addition, some private groups have taken it upon themselves to make a statement about the issue. In 1999, Moda Barcelona, a fashion company in Barcelona responsible for the famous Salon Gaudi show, decided to no longer invite waiflike models onto its catwalk. At the time of the controversial decision, Salon director Paco Flaque said, "If we promote the image of skinny women we are hurting our young people, and I am against that." The Spanish health ministry immediately decried the policy, saying it is not fair to "illegalise" thin people.

In all fairness, it should be said that experts have also tapped into fashion's potential to have a positive effect on self-image. In fact, doctors have found that clothing can actually serve a positive role in treating patients with eating disorders. At several European clinics, including Britain's Priory and France's Centre Arthur in Marseilles University Hospital, psychiatrists use clothes to boost self-esteem, taking patients on shopping trips and letting them try on designer clothes. Theoretically, when the patients see themselves in these fabulous clothes, they get a boost in self-esteem and realize that they're not as unattractive as they feel. (If only retail therapy could be used to treat other afflictions, such as the common cold, pneumonia, or PMS.)

For better or worse, fashion, if we let it, wields a massive power to shape our perceptions of our bodies. How? Let us count the ways:

MAGAZINES

Back in 2001, I edited a workout story at *Mademoiselle* entitled "I Only Have 20 Minutes." Four photos were to accompany the article, which detailed an instructional full-body exercise plan, to illustrate proper form on several of the moves. When the film came in, several days after the shoot, a photo editor brought me the contact sheets. There, on the page, sat a windblown model, seemingly poured into teensy Chrissy-from-*Three's-Company*-style shorts and rainbow leg warmers, her willowy arms looking as if they could barely lift a can of creamed corn, let alone exert any upward force on a dumbbell. I muttered, "Yeesh," knowing that her disproportionately large breasts and "I love exercising!" expression would make her far too contemptible to the average reader. The photos were attractive, but not for a workout story. It ended up being reshot using a different model.

Our dilemma wasn't an isolated event. Women's magazines today strike a delicate balance: support the "any shape is beautiful" message, while showing only thin models (who it's presumed look best in clothes) and instructing readers on how to "get a bikini body in six weeks!" Readers send angry letters to magazines almost every day, complaining about models being irresponsibly thin. They predictably threaten to cancel their subscriptions and to convince their friends to do the same. Editors and publishers take the threats seriously, not necessarily because they care about losing one nutty reader here or there but because they know that being unresponsive to the issue could draw wider criticism.

Most experienced editors know prior to publication when a photo will spur readers to take up angry pens against them; they've become understandably mindful of using models who look too gaunt. When I worked at *CosmoGIRL!* several years ago, nearly every editor, upon seeing the photos that were to run in an upcoming swimsuit feature, shrieked, "Oh my god, those girls are too thin." The crack-house olive-drab lighting and concave poses only made the girls appear more sickly. It was too late to reshoot; everyone knew that some readers wouldn't be happy. So we tried to talk ourselves through it. Was it irresponsible to show such thin models? Not really. Those girls repre-

sented a segment of our readers that had been drastically under-
served—the naturally lanky growing girl. One could even argue that *not*
showing them would be worse. Perhaps hiding skinny models from
public view would lead us down an even more dangerous path, in
which we would become so hypersensitive to thinness—and our own
*un*thinness—that we could no longer even bear to see it.

Fashion magazines have long been among the biggest targets of
eating-disorder studies. And many of the results have been damning.
In a now-classic sample of Stanford undergraduate and graduate students, 68 percent felt worse about their own appearance after looking
through women's magazines. In 1998, a British survey by the Bread for
Life campaign showed that 89 percent of women between eighteen and
twenty-four wanted more "average-sized" models used in magazines.
And more than two-thirds of girls in grades five through twelve said
magazine photos influenced their notion of the ultimate figure,
according to a study published in the March 1999 issue of the journal
Pediatrics. "Women are supporting their nemesis," says Eric Stice,
Ph.D., an assistant professor of psychology at the University of Texas
and lead author of several studies on body image and media. "They're
buying hope or ideas concerning how they can approximate the thin
ideal better—without having to actually eat healthy diets and exercise."

With all of these studies pointing to the public's apparent need
and desire for more "realistic" body shapes, it would seem likely that
magazine publishers would bow to public pressure. But magazine publishers know that survey respondents are more virtuous on paper than
they are at the newsstand. Top editors and publishers know that thinner cover girls sell more issues. "Fashion mags are about fantasy," says
London fashion writer Navaz Batliwalla. "It's about aspiration—wanting what you can't have: a beautiful face, long legs, expensive clothes.
Models are unusual creatures—they have unattainable figures and
facial beauty and for this reason they are a rarity, like rare tropical
birds. They're an exaggeration. I don't see why models get so much
flak for being thin, yet no one complains about their faces. People
always say to magazines 'Why don't you use more fat models?' but they
never say 'Please use uglier girls.' "

What's more troubling than the magazine industry's use of

ultra-thin models and its obsession with thinness is that fashion glossies can't seem to decide which side of the issue they stand on. "Love your body" has become their favorite catchphrase, while photos still communicate the opposite, showing only the very lean, sinewy body type. The last thing magazines want to do is shoot themselves in the foot by admitting that they play a role in creating negative body image, so they do their best to help women break out of that mind-set. But at the same time, they can't ignore that readers do want to lose weight (or, as most magazines now call it, "get fit"), so they're forced to play both sides. The August 2001 coverline of *Glamour* was "Hey, Weight Obsessers! Shut Yourself Up—Here's How." The next month it was "Yes! Be a Fat-Burning Success Story—Without Starving." The article featured answers to questions like "Why am I flabbier than friends who eat and exercise the same amount that I do?" "How do I know how much fat I should lose?" and "Can I spot-reduce the fat from my stomach or butt?" In both issues there appeared a full-page ad for Hydroxycut weight-loss pills with the following quote: "With the weight gone, I now have more energy and feel younger and more beautiful than ever!" from Brandy in Marina del Rey, California. Finding the proper balance can create a difficult line for editors to walk, and a confusing message for readers to take in.

"Most women's magazines have paid lip service to body-image issues, but they continue to feature very thin models in their editorial and ad pages," says Cyndi Tebbel, former editor of the Australian edition of *New Woman* and former editorial coordinator of *Vogue* Australia. "I always remember the attitude at *Vogue*, where if you were featuring someone like an author or artist or any nonmodel type, the art department's first question was always, 'What does she look like?' If the answer was 'well, normal,' the photo would always be the size of a postage stamp, if used at all." Even well-intentioned articles can send a confusing message. The editors of *Bitch*, a feminist magazine with a pop-culture slant, slammed an article that ran in the June/July 1998 issue of *Jane*, which showed a photo of an impossibly skinny model, her hand thrown exasperatingly over her eyes, next to the tag, "Oops . . . I forgot to eat." The accompanying copy seemed to be an empowering statement about body image: "A chubby tummy is sexy and an empty tummy is so not." But the photo, said the *Bitch* editors, proved that an actual chubby tummy clearly wasn't sexy enough to show in the magazine, prompting them to list, among their Ten Things to Hate About *Jane*, "their fake, sanctimonious, look-how-we-encourage-you-not-to-be-obsessive-and-negative-about-your-body tone, combined with models even skinnier than *Vogue*'s . . ."

Many glossies are simply afraid to change their formulas. "[Magazines] are definitely about money, of course—but they're about the *advertisers*' money, not the readers'," says Lisa Miya-Jervis, editor of *Bitch*. "What this adds up to is editors being terrified of taking any risks at all. They have this formula that has worked for years, and they're scared to tinker with it, because it's an unknown." Sometimes, even advertisers aren't supportive of the thin ideal. Some have attempted to show their displeasure with magazines' perpetuation of the thin ideal by hitting them where it hurts most—in the wallet. But it's rarely easy. In 1996, upscale watch maker Omega famously threatened to withdraw its advertising from *Vogue*, complaining that the "skeletal appearance" of women in its fashion pages might help push girls into anorexia. "I thought it was irresponsible for a leading magazine which should be setting an example to select models of anorexic proportions," said Giles Rees, brand manager. Shortly after the threat was made, it was withdrawn, presumably after the company realized that it wasn't wise to piss off an entity as powerful as *Vogue*.

Editors who flout the skinny-model standard run the risk of being cast out. When Cyndi Tebbel was appointed to the top post at *New Woman Australia* in 1996, she ushered in an attitude of gentle feminism—not as mindless as ordinary women's-magazine fare, but not radical enough to frighten readers either. During her eighteen-month reign as editor, Tebbel refused to print diets, and instead concentrated on self-help, relationship issues, and profiles of women who had achieved more than just being photogenic. In 1997, she decided to devote an entire issue to body image and the acceptance of larger sizes, a groundbreaking concept for a woman's magazine at the time. Plus-size model Emme appeared on the cover, surrounded by the headlines "Why body image is a national obsession," "Why we're risking our health to be thin," and "How to love your body: our cover girl Emme leads the way." While deciding on the coverlines for the issue, Tebbel suggested the strap "Fat Is Back" to the magazine's advertising sales team. "They were horrified, and said that *New Woman* would be known as 'the fat girls' magazine,' " she recalls. "I thought that was rather alarmist, but toned it down to The Big Issue."

Circulation figures for The Big Issue neither rose nor fell; a heavier model on the cover didn't help, but it didn't hurt. Judging by reader mail, however, the issue was a smashing success. Grateful letters poured in. But cheers weren't heard all around. Soon after the issue hit newsstands, a major cosmetics advertiser pulled its business from the magazine. Their reason? The Big Issue didn't present a very "glamorous image." (Tebbel has never revealed the name of the company, just that it was a multinational French corporation.) After encountering several creative differences with the publishers, both directly and indirectly related to The Big Issue, Tebbel stepped down. As a result of the controversy, various women's groups, radio programs, and TV shows invited her to speak about the issue. *New Woman*'s publishers and advertisers appeared often to offer their side of the story, which one cosmetics marketer summed up as "Nobody wants to buy a lipstick being modeled on a big, fat frumpy woman," recalls Tebbel.

Similarly, Liz Jones, former editor of British *Marie Claire* was criticized by fellow media figures for becoming too obsessed with body image. Jones, a recovering anorexic who had subsisted on fewer than six hundred calories per day in her twenties, placed Sophie Dahl and Pamela Anderson on alternate covers of the magazine's June 2000 issue with the question, "Is this the ideal body shape? Realistically curvy Sophie Dahl vs. impossibly perfect Pamela Anderson." When circulation figures came in, they showed that Dahl's cover sold more issues. Jones eventually left *Marie Claire*, after making several belligerent remarks about the magazine industry's—and her own—role in causing eating disorders. After she resigned, Jones chided fellow Brit editors in an article published in London's *Mail on Sunday*, claiming that she had been the target of criticism after she had spoken out against the industry. She claimed that the then editor of UK *New Woman* had accused her of discriminating against thin women, and that the editor of UK *Elle* had accused her of "betraying the editors' code."

Not all editors deny responsibility. "I absolutely, 100 percent believe that the media in general is responsible for the disheartening and depressing reality of negative body image," says Elizabeth Kiester, fashion director of *YM*. "In fashion, we have embraced skinny-skinny-skinny and pretend that we don't. I'm thirty-six years old, and every time I see Gisele, I spiral, so I can only imagine what it does to someone in her peer group." If "real" girls are used in a fashion story, it says so, with a self-congratulatory tone. When Kiester worked as fashion market director at *Jane,* a swimsuit layout once featured a "regular" girl, meaning size 8 as opposed to a 2 or 4. "We didn't draw attention to the fact that she was 'regular'—meaning the headline wasn't 'Swimwear for real bodies' or anything stupid like that—and we got tons of mail from readers saying how much they loved the story," she says. "It was like some sort of cathartic relief or something." Kiester says she's actually had models' photos retouched to appear more "normal"—adding inches to their waists and legs—because it's so difficult to find models at the agencies who are bigger than a size 4.

After much ado, former *Harper's Bazaar* editor-in-chief Kate Betts admitted in a March 2002 *New York Times* feature that she had pulled Renée Zellweger off her magazine's cover over a year ago because the actress, who had just gained weight for *Bridget Jones's Diary,* was too fat at the time. "We wanted to put an actress on the cover because of her performance and her talent, and yet ultimately the decision had only to do with the way she looked," she wrote. "It seemed wrong—or maybe regrettable—to judge somebody by such trivially narrow criteria." Just four months after Betts's article, Zellweger, now many pounds lighter, finally popped up on *Bazaar*'s cover. New editor Glenda Bailey printed a few of the Betts-rejected photos inside the magazine, saying that she didn't think Zellweger was too fat at all. Of course, she had the *thin* Renée on the cover, and that's what matters to newsstand buyers.

In April 2002, *Vogue,* which for years had seemed like it would never show a woman over a size 6 (besides its famous Oprah cover), finally caved in and showed fleshier bodies on its pages, with a feature including voluptuous television chef Nigella Lawson and plus-size model Kate Dillon towering over a diminutive bodybuilder, as well as women of nearly every body type from superskinny Joan Didion to statuesque six-foot-three-inch socialite Alexandra Schlesinger. Editor Anna Wintour, who once told a reporter she probably wouldn't hire an overweight editor, commented on the feature for the *New York Post:* "By depicting the range of female shape, we think that readers and the fashion industry will be struck by how wonderful women can look, whatever their shape is." Perhaps *Vogue* thought it would finally appease all those disgruntled readers who had written in for years about the magazine's exclusive use of skinny models. But it couldn't win. The photo of the size-12 Dillon, in particular, was criticized—readers complained that it made the model stand out too much as the lone, freakish "big girl."

Even if magazines showed heavier body types on a regular basis, would consumers really respond positively? We appreciate the idea of magazines that use larger models. We're glad that they exist. We like the idea of magazines that show more "realistic" sizes. The only problem is that we don't buy them, and then they go out of business. Take *Mode,* for instance, the first fashion and beauty magazine targeting women size 12 and up. The magazine performed respectably, acquiring a circulation of 600,000, only to shut down in September 2001. Ultimately, the publisher blamed the economy for the magazine's demise, not low circulation figures. That may have been true, but interest from readers and advertisers clearly wasn't strong enough to keep the publication afloat. Statistics show that 40 percent of women in the U.S. are size 12 and up. If more of them had subscribed to *Mode,* the magazine would have become a phenomenon, practically immune from failure. But they didn't. And another victory was notched for the skinny model.

ADVERTISING

In 1994, two years after Kate Moss created a media firestorm by posing topless alongside Mark Wahlberg in provocative underwear ads for Calvin Klein, the proto-waif appeared in a print ad for the designer wearing nothing but a white bikini and a vacant expression, sprawled out with one knee gawkily flayed out as if creating a pointy letter *P* with her legs (a curiously popular pose in the waif era), arms raised above her head as if she were pulling on her ponytail. It wasn't hard to see why so many parents feared the influence that the five-foot-seven-inch, 100-pound model would have on their children. Moss's tiny abdomen registered zero fat, her navel looking as though some downward force was attempting to suck it straight into her body. Did the ad make consumers want to buy the white bikini? Perhaps. Did it make us look? Certainly.

In the world of fashion, discontent sells. "People are manipulated in many ways for the sake of profit," says Jean Kilbourne, author of several books on the negative effects of advertising, including *Can't Buy My Love*. "Those who are dissatisfied with their looks, their bodies, their status symbols, make great consumers." If we were completely satisfied with every aspect of our lives, we would never aspire to buy anything else, and the fashion industry would go belly-up. The Fashion Victim looks at clothes that are impossibly beautiful, worn by models who are impossibly thin. She wishes she could own the outfit and look like the model. But if she buys the clothes, she's still faced with the disappointment that she doesn't look as good in them as the model, and the dissatisfaction continues.

In comparison to the magazines themselves, the fashion advertisers' motives are even more conspicuously rooted in money since their explicit purpose is to sell product. "Advertisers promote the myth that purchasing new clothes—just like being a certain size—will lead to happiness, success, power, glamour, romance," says Holly Hoff, director of programs for the National Eating Disorders Association. "So in some ways people are tricked into thinking that being a certain size or wearing a special jacket will make them happier than they are now and this increases sales."

One way fashion advertising contributes to the thin ideal is simply by surrounding us with images, just as magazines do. Even illustrated ads featuring fashionable women virtually always portray them as impossibly thin. A 2001 print ad for Freixenet bubbly featured a chic cartoon lady seated cross-legged at a café in Rome with a stylish bob, big black sunglasses, a tri-band string of pearls, little black dress, glass of champagne, and shoes so pointed they could poke a hole through a wooden board with one swift kick. The most striking thing about the woman wasn't the crocodile bag at her feet, but rather her wiry limbs—her legs and arms were the same sticklike width. Had she been a real woman, her frail ankles would surely have buckled under the weight of the large pearls around her neck if she were to stand. Similarly, the 2001 Steve Madden print and TV ad campaign featured models, computer-distorted to look like they had oversized heads, massive eyes, minuscule waists, and long legs—true Lollipop Girls, whose tiny bodies couldn't possibly support their gigantic noggins. The images looked disturbingly similar to pictures shown on many shocking pro-anorexia websites in which girls doctor images of models and actresses to make them look even thinner. Was it irresponsible advertising? No. Any girl who would look at such a body shape as realistic must surely be delusional. But ads like these were just threads in a larger quilt, weaving together the image that thinness equals coolness.

MODELS

Working in the media, you develop an intimate knowledge of two truths: 1) models aren't physically perfect; 2) they're pretty close. True, models are airbrushed, they're spackled with body makeup to cover bruises, stretch marks, and discolorations, every last flyaway hair is smoothed down, every eyebrow hair is plucked. Their flawless appearance is enhanced by great lighting, great clothes, great locations, a great photographer. A stylist and makeup artist are waiting in the wings to adjust a strap, remove a piece of lint, apply another layer of blush, regloss lips. And once the film is in, to get that one gorgeous photo, you'll have sheets and sheets of others that weren't so gorgeous. Still, everything that's done to make models look lovely isn't magic— they're beautiful girls to begin with.

And the imperfections that models do have aren't visible to the average viewer. "On TV you're not going to see everything, even high-definition TV, the resolution just isn't there," says Randy Brooks, a runway photographer who shoots for various international clients including *Paper* magazine and *Harper's Bazaar Japan*. "Basically, if there's smoke or dust or if the air isn't clean in a big venue like a tent, atmospheric debris can take away some fine detail. There is cellulite, occasional zits and bad complexions, but you're not going to see a bad complexion on a full-length shot taken from a hundred feet away, unless it's a close-up or head shot. And in that case, motion and movement can take away from seeing all the details and imperfections. No one's perfect."

Still, compared to the average person, the model is generally more camera-ready. The Fashion Victim's error is viewing the model figure as attainable. Many people fail to understand the importance of genetics. "If you plant a pear seed, you grow a pear; if you plant a banana you get a banana," says Holly Hoff, of the National Eating Disorders Association. "We wouldn't expect one to be able to change to look like the other." Models, like basketball players and jockeys, are often born with certain physical traits, in this case, being tall and thin. "Many models eat like pigs," says Jeffrey Kolsrud, co-owner and director of Q Models in New York and L.A. "I think what people forget is that many of these girls are very young, thirteen to eighteen, and they don't need to worry about dieting. As they get older, their metabolism changes and yes, then they do have to change their eating habits. If we see that girls are gaining weight, they are asked to diet. We often hook them up with a nutritionist and trainers to help them."

In its four-year history, says Kolsrud, Q Models has had four models who suffered from eating disorders. He and his associates organized an intervention for one girl, convinced her to get help, and arranged to have her mother pick her up so she could be hospitalized. At the time that we had spoken, Kolsrud had just finished dealing with another case. "She came to us with the problem," he said. "Her parents sent her to New York knowing that she's anorexic, so I had the responsibility of finding this little girl help, which she has now." Four eating disorders in four years is a modest figure, at least according to statistics laid out in the book *Glued to the Tube* by Cheryl Pawlewski, Ph.D., which contends that up to 60 percent of models suffer from eating disorders. It's possible that Q Models is the luckiest agency around. Or it could be that they aren't completely aware of all of their models' eating habits. Part of the problem lies in the fact that the definition of an eating disorder is far too open to interpretation. The average person (and the medical community) may consider a diet of a thousand calories a day to be starvation, while a model may think it's perfectly healthy. After all, compared to girls she knows who throw up and abuse laxatives, eating *nearly* enough calories doesn't seem so bad. And let's imagine that the model works out for ninety minutes a day and burns off even more calories. Again, ninety minutes is a lot of exercise, but it's certainly not enough to raise any red flags. Therefore, in her own mind, she isn't doing anything unhealthy and would have no reason to bring the issue up with her agent. She doesn't think she's suffering from an eating disorder, her agency thinks she's naturally thin, everyone's happy, end of story.

Is there pressure for models to stay thin? Naturally . . . just as there's pressure for football players to stay strong, scientists to stay mentally sharp, and artists to stay edgy. In the merciless world of modeling, a girl's weight is often dictated by her agency or a client. If she starts to gain a few pounds from partying or eating or simply growing, she'll feel internal and external pressure to shed them immediately. "Unfortunately, there have been instances where a girl gets let go because she doesn't want to lose the weight," says Kolsrud. "Many times when a girl is put under contract with a company they can stipulate in her contract that she cannot fluctuate more than a few pounds from her current weight." The result is not pretty. In her 1998 book *The World's Best Kept Diet Secrets*, author Diane Irons reveals some of the bizarre tactics models employ to stay slim, such as chewing up and spitting out food and sucking on fruit pits to feed their fantasy of eating.

With today's fashion models, we speak in degrees of thinness. In 2001, the modeling industry saw a war between skinny and skinnier: the sexy Brazilians versus the boyish Belgians. Models who stray the slightest bit from the very flat shape are referred to as curvy. *Vogue* credited Gisele Bündchen with "the return of the sexy model," heralding her as the antithesis of the androgynous waif. But the Brazilian model is far from fleshy. After former UK *Marie Claire* editor Liz Jones hugged Bündchen, who packs a mere 115 pounds on her five-foot-eleven-inch frame, she famously stated, "She felt like a bag of bones." Fellow Brazilian skinny-minnie Caroline Ribeiro has also been called curvy, as has Carmen Kass. Supermodel Heidi Klum has said she's too hippy to fit into sample sizes at catwalk shows. Uhh-hmm.

As a society, we make any model who doesn't fit the average image into a poster child for her body size. Fleshy Sophie Dahl's name is rarely mentioned in articles without an identifier in front of it (like fleshy). By the time the dueling-body-shape covers of *Marie Claire*, pitting Dahl against Pamela Anderson, appeared on newsstands, Dahl was no longer a size 15—she had dropped to a 12. Although her cover won, she sued the magazine for £500,000—results of the lawsuit remained hush-hush. Among her complaints: the magazine had doctored the image, erasing her bra straps so it looked as if she had posed nude, *and* they had reneged on an agreement not to mention her size and not to use her in features dealing with body shape.

While there has been greater media attention given to plus-size models in the past decade, the runway shows that feature larger women are typically hosted by mass-market retailers like Lane Bryant, not by major fashion designers; larger sizes are commonly considered down-market, very rarely designer, and certainly never couture. Diversity on the runway has been more celebrated in recent years, with designers clamoring for "unusual-looking" models, like those with freckled faces, women over forty, even those with disabilities (like double amputee Aimee Mullins, who walked the runway for Alexander McQueen with her prosthetic legs). Larger models are still grouped into this "unusual" category. In August 2000, organizers of Premier Womenswear, the UK's largest show of mainstream and commercial collections, decided to celebrate the fuller figure, after a major survey by British retailer Marks & Spencer revealed that the average British woman is a size 14 (a U.S. size 12) and not a 10 (U.S. 8). They chose three size-14 (U.S. 12) women, selected through a *Birmingham Post* competition, to strut the catwalk amid the conventional models. "When we're speaking of race, culture, or heritage, we call it diversity and celebrate it," says Carol Johnson, author of *Self-Esteem Comes in All Sizes* and founder of the organization Largely Positive, which promotes health and self-esteem among larger people. "When it comes to women's shape, diversity turns into 'flaws.' This makes no sense."

DESIGNERS

Most Fashion Victims realize that models themselves are merely pawns in a larger game. After all, it's designers who control the board. Who can blame us, say designers, we're simply showing our clothes on the bodies they look best on. As Isaac Mizrahi once said about using thin models, "If I were in the furniture business, I'd want my furniture to look its best. If I were in the chicken industry, I'd want the best chickens. It's just good business." Designers use thin models for various reasons. "From a technical aspect, on TV and in film you look one size or two sizes larger than in reality," says BCBG designer Max Azria, who says the best sizes are o and 2. "I look at myself on TV and I hate myself. I look so fat. In my mirror, I'm a little bit healthy, but it's not a catastrophe—but when I see myself on TV or in a movie I'm amazed at how much I am fat. The camera gives you one or two sizes more. If you are not very skinny you will look obese." Photographer Randy Brooks says the camera definitely adds weight. "Due to the laws of physics, when you convert someone from three dimensions to two, you're basically flattening them out," he says. "If you imagine a big roller rolling over your body on the sidewalk, your image would spread out over a greater area. There's your ten pounds." Also, in yet another cruel twist of fate, a 2002 study by researchers at the University of Liverpool found that television makes men look hunkier but women chunkier. When shown images of men and women, test subjects said that both genders looked 5 percent fatter on TV, but quirks in the way we perceive images favored men, giving the illusion of having a stronger jawline. So, to appear thin in pictures, it's necessary to be *very* thin.

Still, who says anyone needs to look thin? Perhaps, as John Tierney suggested in a September 2000 *New York Times* piece, designers don't want any fleshy curves stealing attention from their designs. "Why must models starve themselves?" Tierney wrote. "There is a standard answer in the fashion world: clothes look better on a clotheshanger figure. But maybe designers' egos are involved, too. Maybe they don't want womanly curves distracting from their genius." When Betsey Johnson employed Playboy Playmates for her spring show in 2001, the buxom catwalkers *did* garner more attention than the clothes. Could Tierney be on to something?

Designers influence our perception of size by simply not offering larger sizes. In fall 2002, Karl Lagerfeld said women would have to lose weight to wear his clothes. Designers have an ideal body shape in mind when they create, and it's usually not the bigger woman. Some lines, like DKNY, Ralph Lauren, and Chanel, offer plus sizes but most others don't. And it's not for lack of a market. Some 65 million American women—40 percent of the female population—wear a size 12 or larger. Yet only 26 percent of all women's clothing sales are in the plus-size category. Business at Saks Fifth Avenue's plus-size department in New York has increased more than 20 percent since 1999.

Designers also wield control over the clothes we'll wear, or the lack thereof. We're gradually revealing more skin. Since 1913, the amount of fabric required to clothe an American woman has dropped 64 percent. We bare our thighs when miniskirts are in, we parade our belly buttons in hip-hugger jeans, we show our arms in tank tops. Today, the freedom to wear more revealing clothes is considered to be empowering. Today, when Jennifer Lopez bares 90 percent of her body at the Oscars or when Ally McBeal arrives at court in a micro-miniskirt, we think of them as being strong and independent, not necessarily as hoochie-mamas. "I'm usually shocked about how the clothes are getting smaller and smaller—and I'm no prudish grandma, either," says Rachel, a twenty-seven-year-old editor in Birmingham, Alabama. "I'm usually muttering at the TV, saying things like, 'She's naked' or 'How can they go out there with practically no clothes on?' " And it's not just women's clothes. Menswear has also become increasingly body-conscious. Designers are adding more fitted sweaters and skinny pants to their collections, emphasizing the need for a lean body with well-shaped pecs and arms. As our clothes shrink, so must we. The more skin that's showing and the tighter the clothes get, the more self-conscious we become about our bodies. If we all stomped about in sack-like muumuus every day, we might not feel such a strong compulsion to sculpt our bodies. Some designers' clothes are unforgiving: few people who aren't tall and slim can wear Gucci pants, slinky Hervé Leger dresses hug every inch of flesh (and every roll of fat), skimpy clothes at stores like Bebe and Arden B. aren't flattering to every body shape.

Designers also set body standards by establishing sample sizes, which, in turn, determines the types of models to be used in the catwalk show. In the 1980s, designers used a standard sample size of about a 6 or an 8. In the past five years, the samples have shrunk to a size 2 or a 4. It's not financially viable for designers to create samples in various sizes, so they'll pick one—a size 2, for instance. So their runway show will feature only models who can fit into a size 2. Hence, a show with only one body type. Then, celebrities who want to borrow clothes from a designer must fit into sample sizes (unless the garments are made especially for them), so we see only the very slender stars in the most fabulous clothes, again reinforcing the notion that thin equals stylish.

SEEING STARS

"Frail-looking and emaciated," "rail-thin," "rake thin," "bony-jutting skinny," "stick-thin figure," "dangerously ill-looking," "a figure thinner than a fashion page," "swizzle-stick figure," "nastily bony"—these are all terms that have been used to describe *Ally McBeal* star Calista Flockhart. Ever since the launch of her show in 1997, the actress has endured incessant nosiness over her weight, far worse even than the tornado of speculation that has surrounded many of Hollywood's suspected gay actors. In interviews, reporters frequently comment on any morsel they see touch her lips. People scrutinize the fluctuation of her weight as if it could predict the weather (could see her clavicle today— must mean rain). The media seem to have a touch too much fun coining new phrases to describe her thinness.

In a way, we feel sorry for celebrities because the pressure we feel to be thin is magnified tenfold for them. After being lambasted by the press for her malnourished appearance, Elizabeth Hurley described the pressure to be thin to British *Elle* in 1999: "If it's any consolation, I threw away two-thirds of my wardrobe and lost fifteen pounds after first seeing paparazzi pictures of myself—the celebrity version of a vicious Polaroid." When Minnie Driver packed on twenty pounds for her first film, 1995's *Circle of Friends* with Chris O'Donnell, she told a reporter at the *Toronto Sun* that the weight gain wracked her self-confidence. "I did weigh myself once," she said. "There were tears. It was hard to relinquish the need to be found attractive." Poor Minnie, sympathized the Fashion Victim, until, that is, Ms. Driver appeared at the 1998 Oscars in her red Halston gown looking every bit the svelte starlet. She had reentered the realm of the detestable, yet nonetheless enviable, thin celebrity.

Celebrities have always influenced society's ideal body shape, from Greta Garbo to Marilyn Monroe, Raquel Welch to Audrey Hepburn. But in recent years, as actors and actresses have begun to play an increasingly prominent role in fashion, vigilant attention to their bodies has also intensified. In contrast to models, who typically start out thin, we often see celebrities' weight fluctuate. We witnessed the softer 1980s Madonna transform herself into her sculpted 1990s Madonna. We watched Janet Jackson whittle away at her body fat with grueling workouts to reveal a set of solid abs, and Brad Pitt transform his chiseled physique into an even more chiseled physique for *Fight Club*. Because we see stars dieting and exercising to get these bodies, we think the ideal is somehow more attainable. After all, these people may have been born like us, but they became fashion idols thanks to willpower and hard work (as well as money, which usually translates into a trainer, dietitian, and yoga coach).

The celebrity body may be less dependent on genetics than the model body, but that doesn't leave it any less vulnerable to attack. "I reserve my real ire for Gwyneth—models, for some reason, don't upset me so much, because they look so alien in person: tall, stretched out, and strange," says Rebecca, a twenty-five-year-old writer in New York City.

As much as they appear to flaunt it, most celebrities would rather not draw attention to their weight loss. "I never wanted to be a spokesperson for weight loss," Jennifer Aniston told *W* magazine in 1999. "A few years back, they said I was too curvy. I guess when I was rounder, I was easier to relate to. The media builds you up and tears you down. What the magazine readers are missing is that the glamour they see on the cover isn't real, and it isn't easy. Those pictures take a lot of work. Being thin is hard work!" The publicist of a major actress who had gained and lost a lot of weight within the span of a year requested that her client not to be shown in a *Mademoiselle* story I was editing about celebrity workouts. The terms "reed-thin" and "whippet-thin" had been used more than once to describe the actress's new physique.

Rather than showing real concern for the stars' health (mental or physical), we often joke about their weight. Former NBC executive Lori Gottlieb remembers the long-running joke around the office about a purported *Friends* tag line: "Hot anorexic chicks." (The slogan "Cute anorexic chicks" was actually used by an NBC affiliate in Iowa on a much-protested promo billboard for the show in the late nineties.) "What disturbed me was that instead of saying, 'Since these women are serving as fashion models for young women in our culture, we should make sure they don't look like Dachau survivors,' we were complicit in promoting the cult of 'anorexia chic,' " says Gottlieb, a former anorexic, who wrote the memoir *Stick Figure* about her own eating disorder. "Just seeing these women's bodies shrink season after season was its own very powerful message. Now the not-so-funny joke is that you can track each season by using Courtney Cox's and Jennifer Aniston's weight as a barometer: 'Must be second season, Jennifer's pelvic bones aren't jutting through her capris yet.' "

Still, as much as we shake our heads in disapproval at skinny celebrities, we've made them our fashion idols. In a poll conducted by Britain's *Woman's Journal*, Audrey Hepburn came in just behind Grace Kelly as the most elegant woman ever. As Simon Doonan, creative director of Barneys New York, said in a 1999 Salon.com interview about the beloved sylphlike Hepburn, "I'm sure she had an eating disorder. Everybody has an eating disorder if they're in the performing arts, you know. . . . If they're not Chris Farley they're bulimic. . . . People say things like that as if it's some terrible indictment. 'Oh, she had an eating disorder.' So what? She had a good life and she did a lot of incredible things and she was smart enough to bail on the career and focus on the philanthropic stuff. She has a pretty flawless image." In 2000, Brits voted Victoria "Posh Spice" Beckham the Ultimate Fashion Icon, beating fellow waif Kate Moss for the title. A year later, Beckham admitted that rumors about her suffering from anorexia may have been true, stopping short of actually using the A-word. "I used to chop up bowls of spinach and carrots and steam them. Or I'd just eat peas. A whole family pack of Birds Eye at one sitting," she said in *Posh Spice: My Story*. "But it never occurred to me that I had an eating disorder, because people with eating disorders were thin, and I was still the same size I had always been." At the same time that people were complaining that Jennifer Aniston had lost too much weight, hers became the celebrity face that sold more magazines than any other at the time. Onlookers cringed at the sight of Calista Flockhart's meatless collarbone jutting out over her dress on the red carpet, but instead of a creating a backlash against thinness, it made the socially ideal weight shift downward. So today, Flockhart's body is no longer *such* an oddity in Hollywood.

Celebrities are routinely rewarded by the fashion world for their weight loss. At the 2001 VH1/Vogue Fashion Awards, the Red Carpet Award went to Renée Zellweger, who proved her gutsiness when she showed she was willing to pack an extra twenty pounds onto her waifish frame, said the magazine. Would the *Bridget Jones* actress have won if she hadn't lost the weight and then some? Doubtful. Our perception of body shape is seriously warped when it comes to celebrities. Jennifer Lopez, who won the 1999 VH1/Vogue Fashion Award for Most Fashionable Female Artist, has curiously been grouped with "larger" women, although at five feet, six inches, she weighs in at an unchunky 120 pounds.

VANITY SIZING

One afternoon while shopping for work clothes in SoHo, I stopped in at Urban Outfitters to find some casual flat-front pants. I brought three pairs into the dressing room: chocolate cords with piping down the sides, gray pinstriped trousers, and a pair of dark stretchy jeans. I grabbed my usual size 4—and 6s as backup. Not one fit past my knees. Slightly flustered, I handed the fitting-room attendant my unacceptable picks and went back out to try my luck at the next two sizes. The 8s fit, but more snugly than I had hoped. Could all the sushi I'd eaten the night before have gone straight to my thighs? I passed on the 8s and left empty-handed rather than face the 10s in my closet each time I opened the door. The next week, I tried my luck at the Gap. My thighs swam in 6s. The 4s practically fell off my hips. Oh, my delighted ego!

If someone were to ask me my size, my answer would be: it depends. I have a few size-2 dresses that fit me perfectly, size-4 shorts that could use a good shrink in the wash, size-6 French Connection pants that restrict blood flow when I sit, and a pair of size-10 Mavi jeans that I like to wear baggy. We're intensely affected by those digits printed inside the backs of our clothes. Since so many of us avoid the scale whenever possible, we've begun to use our clothing size as the gauge of whether we're too fat. Using the "does it fit?" method is dangerous, not only because our weight tends to fluctuate throughout each month but also because clothing sizes lack any type of standardization. So a pair of jeans in your size that barely button up could ruin your entire day, when they're actually not "your size" at all.

Since clothing size has the potential to seriously sway our moods, it's become a constant source of frustration for many shoppers. In a 2001 survey conducted for the Woolite Fashion Forum, half of the women queried claimed that their biggest difficulty when shopping was finding clothes that fit properly or flattered their figures. The problem isn't with our bodies, but rather with designers and retailers and their deceptive practice of vanity sizing, adjusting clothes sizes downward to stroke our fragile egos. Fitting into a smaller size may make consumers feel good in the fitting room, but it has created a state of wild disorder in the apparel industry—since everyone is a different size in a different label, no one knows what size they truly are.

It's our own neuroses that have fueled vanity sizing. "Few people know that a garment which measures 36 in the hip will not go on a person with 36-inch hips unless the fabric stretches," says Kim Bennett of Vanity Fair, Inc., which is the largest maker of clothes in the U.S. and owns brands like Lee Jeans, The North Face, Gitano, Chic, and

Jantzen. "But those same people would be horrified to read 38- or 40-inch on a tag that gave accurate measurements. So say we use the 36-inch hip measurement of the person we intended the garment for, the woman who wants to believe her hips are 36. Do we, in an attempt to keep her happy, make sure we have enough ease to fit a 37-inch hip? How about the 38-inch hip? Thus, vanity sizing was invented."

The problem dates back to the early twentieth century. For men, most sizing information is derived from old military studies for equipment and uniform design. Men's sizes today, which are done according to body measurements, are fairly straightforward in comparison to the "2, 4, 6, 8" system of arbitrary numbers employed for women's clothes. Why the gender inconsistency? "With the advent of ready-to-wear, women's clothes were designated by an arbitrary numbering system, perhaps in an effort to not make public their actual body measurements," says Sandi Keiser, chairperson of the fashion department of Mount Mary College in Milwaukee, Wisconsin. "Throughout the last half of the twentieth century women have done much of the apparel shopping for men. As a result, shopping based on actual body measurements helped them to make informed purchases. Even when men shop for themselves, they rarely take the time to try things on. An accurate sizing system is mandatory to provide a satisfactory shopping experience that invites repeat purchases."

The first size survey for women was conducted in 1940 by the U.S. Department of Agriculture. The Department of Commerce updated the standard several times in the seventies to accommodate the broader spectrum of sizes but discontinued the practice in 1983. "Since then, the American Society for Testing and Materials (ASTM) has taken on the responsibility for making sizing standards available to industry and for their revision," says Keiser. "But adherence to these standards is voluntary." The result? Sizing chaos. With no formal set of standards to abide by, designers were free to employ vanity sizing. "After World War II, the current size 6 didn't exist," says Kay King, head of the fashion department of Houston Community College. "Most women who wear a 6 now wore 10s and 12s then. It's been a psychological thing to make women think they are smaller than they are."

As some clothiers shift their sizes downward, others are forced to follow suit or risk being known as the brand that no one can fit into. "As a company trying to sell garments, you really do not want a consumer to try on what they believe to be their size and find it too small," says Bennett. The confusing results can take an immediate toll on the Fashion Victim's self-esteem. "My daughter is seventeen years old," says Bennett. "A couple of years ago she came home from school all upset about her body. After many tears she finally told me she was so fat because all her friends wore size-6 jeans and she wore size 8. Well, at the time, she was buying jeans from some store no longer in business, and all her friends were buying from the Gap. I took her to the Gap and in less than an hour she went from the fattest girl in her crowd to the skinniest, all because she wore a size 4 in Gap jeans."

Many companies have resisted standardization in sizing, instead using vanity sizing as a marketing tool. Consumers know what size they are in a certain brand, and if they buy only that brand, they know there's less stress in the dressing room. Some designers express frustration over the practice, while others accept it. "A DKNY size 6 is a BCBG size 10—everybody knows that," says BCBG designer Max Azria. "I understand. I think Donna [Karan] is very smart. It's a matter of each designer; they look at fashion a little bit through themselves. If you compare Prada to Gucci: Prada works for petite and Gucci more for tall, also Armani works for tall. If I am tall, it will be only Gucci or Armani; petite, only Prada or someone else. Donna Karan is a tall woman; she sees things tall and she understands the psychology of the woman based on the fact that a size 6 will make her very happy. That's very smart . . . it's about understanding the consumer."

The sizing issue has even become a government affair. In June 2000, Argentina's senate approved a bill forcing the clothing industry to make clothes that fit women of all sizes, amid complaints that stores stocked apparel only for thin women. The law would require manufacturers to use exact numeric measurements rather than the arbitrary small, medium, and large sizes that vary considerably from one store to the other. "The fashionable brand names that target adolescents do not want 'chubby' girls using their clothing, because they believe that would hurt their brand name, which is identified with languid, anorexic models," said the bill's sponsor, parliamentary deputy María del Carmen Banzas.

In some cases, designers aren't necessarily *trying* to be deceptive, says Bennett. The design process typically involves what's known as a "fit model," a real-life mannequin who represents the ideal body to the designer. "Visualize a square," says Bennett. "Our garment fits that square perfectly, and we grade it up and down so we fit all sizes of 'squares.' However, everyone is not square. Here comes a rectangle, which is narrow in width but long in height. The rectangle holds the same volume as the square but must buy a bigger size to get the height it needs, and then the width of the garment is too big. The industry fits their 'square' and makes different sizes for all the different squares out there. The rest of us must do the best we can to fit into what is out there. This is why if you have ever come across a brand of clothing that fits you, chances are everything made by that company will fit you. You are their 'square.' "

Establishing standard sizes is also difficult because while measurements are objective, fit is subjective. A teenager may want her jeans to fit tighter than a middle-aged woman of the same size. One man may like to wear his button-down shirts slightly looser than another. If you try something on in a missy or juniors line, don't expect it to fit the same as a woman's garment in the same size. Designers must also take the average age of their consumers into account. As we get older, we typically become wider around the middle, even if we haven't gained weight. Therefore, adult sizes tend to give a bit more at the waist.

All of this sizing confusion has toyed with our emotions. We're elated when we fit into a small size, but depressed when we have to wear a larger one. Fortunately, relief is on the way. In 1997, the U.S. Air Force, along with more than twenty corporate sponsors including several apparel makers like the Gap and Levi Strauss, launched what would become the Civilian American and European Surface Anthropometric Resource project (CAESAR). Over the course of several years, researchers collected 3-D physical measurements of nearly eleven thousand people in the U.S. and Europe. It's hoped that this data will take the guesswork out of creating sizes for everything from airplane seats to jeans.

MANNEQUINS

While catwalk models can't technically be "impossibly" thin, mannequins very often are. In 1950, the average hip measurements of mannequins and women were equal: thirty-four inches. By 1990, the two had deviated by six inches, the average woman's hips measuring thirty-seven inches, compared to the mannequin's mere thirty-one. If a woman were to have the same proportions as the modern mannequin, she would be too thin to menstruate, according to many eating-disorders organizations. Certainly we don't walk by the slender mannequins at Neiman Marcus and force ourselves to heave our Twinkies. But store dummies both reflect our perceptions of the perfect body (they're created according to the body shape that's in vogue) and affect them (we want to be what we see). As many designers insist, clothes hang better on very thin figures. Mannequins stand as a constant reminder of this, and of fashion's inherent cruelty.

"One of the most common complaints I hear is that mannequins are so 'model-like' in size that they aren't realistic," says Bob Beaudin, founder of Redbeau Mannequin Service Corporation in Atlanta, Georgia. "This seems to be the norm in both male and female mannequins in that they have perfect dimensions, unlike real people. The females tend to be small-busted, males tend to have flat bellies and muscular torsos." Plus-sized mannequins tend to be taller with broader shoulders, larger bosoms, and thicker legs. "But they're still well sculpted and couldn't be called 'fat,' " says Beaudin. "I would suppose that the thinking behind the design of mannequins is not to reflect reality, but rather to reflect desire. Customers looking at clothes on a perfectly proportioned mannequin will have the impression that they might look that way in that dress or suit. Many psychological factors at work, I'm sure."

Until 1936, Saks Fifth Avenue thought mannequins with heads were distasteful, that is, until famed mannequin maker Lester Gaba designed a figure known as Cynthia, a papier-mâché figure so lifelike that he sometimes took it to the opera. Mannequins changed with the times (stores showcased Twiggylike shapes in the sixties). Over the years, they became more realistic, getting nipples in the seventies and a visible bulge for male mannequins in the eighties. There have been attempts to produce more voluptuous figures. In 1998, illustrator Reuben Toledo created a size 18-20 mannequin called Birdie, a Rubenesque white body with 38-32-44 measurements for Pucci International. Toledo's fashion-designer wife Isobel dressed the line, choosing to clothe Birdie the same as she would a size 4. "We felt it was time to show our customers that people of all sizes go to hip clubs, restaurants, and so on," she said. But for the most part, the shapes that are still in vogue in window displays and on store floors around the world are overwhelmingly tall and thin.

As with most things, the industry has been so set in its ways that changing to heavier mannequins isn't as easy as making a few phone calls. In 1993, high school students in Seattle convinced the department store Bon Marché to include a wider range of body-shape diversity in its mannequins. The store agreed to add a larger-sized torso form in one of its young women's departments. Although the step seemed like progress, it also revealed the barriers that retailers face. The store couldn't simply add a larger full-length mannequin because the figures are manufactured in a standard misses size 8 or junior size 7. Full-length mannequins in the women's department were larger but were proportioned for the wider cut of those clothes and wouldn't fit the narrower misses or junior dimensions. So, the change couldn't be made without manufacturing completely new mannequins.

METHOD TO THE MADNESS

The funny thing about the Fashion Victim is that she cares *why* a thin person is thin. We sneer at models who chain smoke and who we presume subsist on nothing but melba toast and egg whites. But thin people who clearly work out seldom receive the same level of criticism. Magazines frequently promote workout features as plans to "get fit" and "get healthy," since those terms sound far less vain than "get skinny." But in fact, many fitness models who appear in magazines like *Shape* and *Fitness* have less body fat than fashion models do. Female triathletes and marathoners sometimes suffer from amenorrhea, or lack of menstruation, a condition known to afflict anorexics because of their low body fat. But no one would disparage an athlete. Had Courtney Cox been a world-class marathoner instead of an actress, would anyone have cared if we could see her rib cage? Janet Jackson, whose grueling workout schedule would qualify as overexercise by the criteria of most physicians, is looked upon as a role model—everyone wants abs like hers.

Years ago, I met an accountant who competed regularly in amateur bodybuilding competitions, not the shows featuring masculine-looking women with exaggerated muscles and veins popping up all over, but the more natural contests. No one would look at this woman and consider her unhealthy, just fit. Instead of her ribs, you could see a six-pack of abs. And instead of a gangly, meatless arm, you could see a well-rounded bicep. Her skin encased her body like a surgical glove. Her diet for the month leading up to a competition—a packet of plain oatmeal for breakfast, a bland chicken breast for lunch, and four egg whites for dinner—astounded me. Had that meal plan belonged to an aspiring fashion model, friends would have brought her to a psychiatrist.

Except for a few supermodels like Cindy Crawford and Elle McPherson, the public rarely hears about models' exercise regimens, except to hear that they don't have one. Most models insist they don't diet or exercise—aside from a few exceptions like Daniela Pestova and Claudia Schiffer, who claims she can feel her body sagging if she doesn't exercise for even one day. Years ago, in an interview with DKNY models Mark Vanderloo and Esther Cañadas, the pouty-lipped Cañadas mentioned that neither one of the svelte duo worked out on any type of regular basis. "Mark goes jogging sometimes," she said. "But as for doing 150 sit-ups a day? I don't even know how you count that." Models must incessantly maintain that they're naturally skinny to battle criticism. In 1993, Kate Moss insisted, "I try to eat so I won't be so waiflike, but even if I do, I'm not going to become this voluptuous thing. I do have a sweet tooth, but I don't eat loads. I'll eat anything." Even her then boyfriend Johnny Depp got in on the act in a 1995 *Esquire* interview. "She really puts it away," he said of Moss. "Why punish somebody because they have a good metabolism? Because they digest their food better? It doesn't make any sense."

Similarly, Gisele Bündchen insists she skips the gym and only gets exercise running up and down the stairs at her apartment. Proto-waif Twiggy has said, "I got blamed for anorexia and all, but I always ate well—anything, absolute rubbish." In 1993, Amber Valletta told *People*, "A lot of the girls who are thin can't help being thin. I mean, my best friend, Shalom [Harlow], she's thin and she can't help it, and there are plenty of girls like that. I wouldn't diet. I'm going to eat the chocolate cake if I want to." (Does the image of Amber polishing off a plateful of chocolate cake make you hate her more or less?) In November 2000, an interviewer from Latvia's *Delfi* magazine remarked to Carmen Kass, "You are probably aware that your image is quite often associated with the word 'anorexia,'" to which she replied, "They probably don't know that I'm one of the largest models [laughs]. You have to eat to have the strength to live and work. I wouldn't be able to keep up if [I] starved myself. Healthy eating keeps metabolism in balance. Things you deny yourself hit back later."

Sometimes, models seem confused about the definition of "diet." Linda Evangelista notably stated, "I don't diet. I just don't eat as much as I'd like to." Naomi Campbell redefined the term in a British inter-view in May 2001: "I never diet. I am naturally slim, but I have to watch what I eat and I can't eat too much of it." This after telling *People* in 1991 that her favorite foods are Kentucky Fried Chicken, McDonald's, Raisinets, Mars bars, Snickers, and deep-chocolate-fudge Häagen-Dazs.

In recent years, it seems to have become the mission of many magazines to prove that models, actresses, and fashionistas actually chow down. In a *New York* magazine feature on Anna Wintour, she was seen famously chomping on a juicy, rare burger, sans bun (but red meat—the scandal!). Skinny celebrities have been known to order the most buttery, fat-laden dishes when they dine with reporters. In 1995, at the height of the criticism of Jodie Kidd's weight, news "mysteri-ously" leaked out to Britain's *Guardian* that "Kidd likes nothing better for supper than a Big Mac or a bacon sandwich."

We desperately want to think that every model has an eating dis-order or that she supplements her diet of cigarettes and vodka tonics with laxatives. That would make us feel better. But the truth is that most of them are just naturally skinny . . . and young. When you're young, you're naturally thinner. Your body hasn't developed yet, and your metabolism tends to be very quick. On average, a teenage girl can eat three hundred to six hundred calories more per day than an adult woman of the same height and weight and not gain a pound. Catch up with these models a few years later, when they've left the business, and they look slightly more like the rest of us. Others who are in great shape work hard at being that way. So we wrinkle our noses at their goddesslike images, and love and hate them at the same time.

It's actually better to think that all models are eating healthily and are just naturally skinny, says Holly Hoff, of the National Eating Disorders Association. What's more dangerous, Hoff continues, is to think that all models diet, since it only perpetuates the misperception that *anyone* can diet and become that slim. "Most of us accept our eye color or even our shoe size as influenced by genetics, but when it comes to our weight and shape, people use very extreme eating and exercise rituals to try and fight their genetics and change their natural sizes," she says.

"I HATE HER . . . I WISH I COULD LOOK LIKE HER"

In the end, we can't seem to figure out what we want. We scoff at superskinny models yet diet in an effort to look like them. Weight loss is considered an achievement in our society. We gush to friends, "Have you lost weight?" not out of concern for their health, but as a well-earned compliment. We applaud "before and after" stories of formerly fat folks who have finally controlled their weight, like Ricki Lake, Oprah Winfrey, Richard Simmons, and Jared Fogle, the man who lost 245 pounds eating veggie sandwiches from Subway. We also praise plus-sizers who wear their pounds proudly, like Camryn Manheim and *The View*'s Star Jones.

The sight of emaciated waif models in the early 1990s and shrinking actresses in the late 1990s spawned mock concern in the media, from *USA Today*'s "Walking a Thin Line on Ally's Weight" to *Us*'s "Starved for Success" and *People*'s "Going to Extremes" in 1999. The Fashion Victim tsk-tsked at the "Lollipop Girls," whose heads looked as though they were teetering for dear life on their now-tiny bodies. Yet, the same actresses who had been criticized for dropping drastic amounts of weight continued to be emulated in magazines, and on the red carpet.

We're hypocrites when it comes to other people's weight. Audiences applauded Tom Hanks when he shed over forty pounds for the film *Cast Away*. When Jennifer Aniston lost weight through exercise and a high-protein diet, Fashion Victims had it both ways, criticizing the actress for looking *too* thin but secretly wanting to look like her. We let out a smug "ah-*ha!*" when her personal trainer, Kathy Kaehler, publicly condemned Aniston's supposedly unhealthy low-carb diet. Still, as much as Fashion Victims enjoyed sharing disapproval of her diet, that certainly didn't stop them from stocking up on chicken breasts and protein shakes and abstaining from bread.

What's most disturbing about the fashion—body image link isn't simply that they're connected, but rather that fashion seems to benefit from it so much. It's not only the $33 billion weight-loss industry that benefits from our obsession with our bodies; the profits also filter right back into the fashion industry. Business booms as a result of our insecurity. The Fashion Victim shops when she loses weight, then glumly buys bigger sizes when she's resigned herself to the fact that she can no longer pull her jeans up past her knees. Luckily for the industry, the roller coaster rises and falls quite frequently. We're a society of yo-yo dieters. Approximately 44 million people actively diet each year, yet 90 to 95 percent fail to keep off the weight and actually gain back more weight than they lost. We lose weight, then bounce back to a higher weight, lose weight again, and so on. With every drop and gain, we buy new clothes.

So our downtrodden Fashion Victim attempts to self-medicate her bad mood by shopping—the true retail therapy. She hates how her pants reveal a little belly bulge, the way her denim skirt exposes a touch of cellulite on the sides of her thighs, the way her sleeveless tees display her lack of muscle tone, so she's constantly on the lookout for more flattering, slimming styles. Designers and retailers have attempted to take advantage of the perceived power of clothes to "fix" our flaws. They create bras that lift, girdles that cinch, pants that elongate, jeans that flatter. In 2000, Hanes introduced a pair of panty hose with bun holsters to lift and separate the butt cheeks, dubbed the "Wonderbutt" by one newspaper. When fashion makes you self-conscious about your body, it's also right there to pick up the pieces. In November 2001, Lee Cooper re-released its Pack-it jeans. First made in the 1970s, the jeans were the male equivalent of the padded bra, worn by men in search of a bulging crotch. Those who had previously been too embarrassed to wear skintight pants could now do so with man-made bravado.

Fashion creates the problem *and* the solution.

7

Who Makes Your Clothes?

$5,300   *Price of an Hermès Birkin Bag*

$5,300   *Total three-year earnings of a Salvadoran worker sewing garments for companies like Liz Claiborne and Perry Ellis*

Money doesn't grow on trees. And clothes don't grow on hangers.

For a product that we own so much of, we know relatively little about what it takes to get our clothes from the factory to our closets. Part of the reason? Most people simply don't care. Just as the average person is content to pick up her mail every day without pondering the intricate workings of the U.S. Postal Service, she is also content to pick up new clothes without mulling over the process of garment making.

The garment trade has a long, shady history filled with violence, corruption, and exploitation, from the use of sweatshop labor to the mob's longtime involvement in the industry. But scandal doesn't necessarily hurt business. Controversies over how our clothes are made may come and go, and shoppers' devotion to certain labels and styles may wane for a short time, but fashion always has the power to pull them back in. In 1997, reports surfaced that menswear giant Hugo Boss had manufactured Nazi uniforms during World War II and most likely used slave labor from concentration camps. Analysts immediately presumed that the news would hurt business. Of course, the original misdeed was long over, but some fashion-savvy men were faced with a dilemma: they love the Hugo Boss look, but could their affection for a fine gabardine coat erase this new negative image from their minds? Apparently, it could. The company experienced record highs for both sales and income in 1997 and has grown every year, even expanding into womenswear in 2001.

The practices employed to get our clothes to us aren't always pretty. But, fortunately, the clothes themselves are pretty enough to make us look the other way.

BLOOD, SWEAT, AND TEARS

Each weekday morning for eleven years, millions of people who didn't get enough sugary sweetness in their Froot Loops could get a dose of saccharine from Kathie Lee Gifford. For a good part of the nine to ten o'clock time slot, the *Regis and Kathie Lee* cohost would sprinkle her conversation with tidbits about her perfect home life, her perfect children, and her perfect (or so she thought at the time) marriage. Her face was everywhere: the morning show, TV commercials for Carnival Cruises, plugs for children's charities, a handful of music albums, parades, her own clothing line at Wal-Mart. Life seemed rosy for the former beauty queen, and with true schadenfreude, the public couldn't wait to slam her.

As the late 1990s approached, Gifford backlash was in full swing. In a June 1996 issue of *Allure* magazine, Tara B., a flight attendant and former Kathie Lee fan club member, said of her former idol: "I hate her. She's one of those pushy women who tell you how to live your life. They think they can sing, they think they can act, they never shut up about their husband or their kids or their Lord Jesus Christ." *South Park* creators Matt Stone and Trey Parker mocked the talk-show superstar in an episode, parading the animated Kathie Lee into town in a bulletproof "Popemobile," then making her the detestable target of an assassination plot. Late-night talk-show hosts picked on her for her syrupy vocal albums. In the spring of 1996, Charles Kernaghan, executive director of the National Labor Committee (NLC), a New York–based organization that fights unfair labor practices, produced the nugget that would tarnish the morning-show queen's reputation for good. Kernaghan testified before Congress that garments sold by Wal-Mart bearing the Kathie Lee brand name, under a licensing agreement that earns the store $300 million in sales a year (and earns Gifford $9 million) were produced by underage girls in a Honduran sweatshop called Global Fashion. Gifford, who'd been known for her involvement in children's charities, fired back, sobbing to her television audience, "You can say I'm ugly, you can say I'm not talented, but when you say I don't care about children . . . How dare you!"

The Gifford scandal was like candy for comics. David Letterman compiled a Kathie Lee–themed Top Ten list—"Top Ten New Items from the Kathie Lee Gifford Product Line"—that included such things as a new workout video called "Sweatin' in the Sweatshop," a *Honduras on Thirty Cents a Day* guidebook, and Sweatshop Barbie. Then there was *The "I Hate Kathie Lee Gifford" Book* by Gary Blake and Robert Bly. A sample page from the book's fictional day planner included the notations "Give Frank enema" and "Make out weekly payroll to sweatshop workers." Even venerated newspapers got in on the Kathie Lee bashing. In July 2000, the *Chicago Tribune* ran an article entitled "A Farewell to Kathie Lee, Sweatshop Queen." And a syndicated cartoon depicted her as a dominatrix yelling, "Sew faster!" to a crew consisting of cohost Regis Philbin, husband Frank, and son Cody.

In May 1996, everyone's favorite punching bag had announced on ABC's *PrimeTime Live* that she would be opening all twenty-four assembly plants where her clothing is manufactured to independent monitoring. It seemed to be a step in the right direction, that is, until later that month, when the *New York Daily News* uncovered a sweatshop just blocks from her Manhattan TV studios, where 50,000 Kathie Lee blouses had just been completed. Upon hearing the news, Gifford declared herself "physically sick," so sick, in fact, that she couldn't make it down to the garment shop herself and had to send Frank in her place to hand out envelopes stuffed with $300 in cash to each of the workers as reparations.

What was interesting about this particular scandal was that Gifford herself took the brunt of the criticism—not Wal-Mart. In fact, the superstore managed to keep its hands relatively spotless, while its perky figurehead caught the flak full force. The focus of public attention was both surprising and unsurprising: surprising because activists usually love picking on gigantic corporations (Wal-Mart, of course, being the most gigantic); unsurprising because of who the eventual target was (the supremely unlikable Kathie Lee). Even today, years after her very public humiliation, Gifford's name is still instantly associated with sweatshops.

Thanks to the attention drawn to the role of the celebrity endorser, others—like Jaclyn Smith, for her Kmart clothing line, and Michael Jordan, for his Nike endorsements—caught heat from activists. But in a game of word association, few people would utter the word *sweatshop* in conjunction with either of those celebrities' names. In 1996, Jordan earned $20 million endorsing Nike sneakers and apparel—a sum more than the total annual payroll for the thousands of Indonesians who helped make the shoes, according to the organization Made in the U.S.A. When *Time* magazine raised the question of worker exploitation with Jordan, His Airness replied, "I'm not really aware of that. My job with Nike is to endorse the product. Their job is to be up on that." (Imagine the public uproar if Gifford had responded like that!)

It wasn't the first time sweatshops had captured public attention. Factories of the nineteenth century were notorious for their dangerous, exploitative conditions. It was all too common to hear stories of rats running rampant on factory floors, machine operators losing fingers and arms, and workers receiving mere pennies for their labor. A handful of famous sweatshop stories hang like dark clouds in our history. In 1911, the infamous Triangle Shirtwaist Factory fire in New York City killed 146 of the factory's 500 garment workers. In 1995, seventy-two Thai workers were discovered in El Monte, California, having been held in virtual slavery for seventeen years to sew garments sold at some of America's biggest retailers, including Nordstrom, Sears, and Target (the retailers predictably insisted they were unaware of such conditions). But the dishonoring of Kathie Lee Gifford brought the sweatshop issue an unparalleled level of mass attention. If nothing else, her public humiliation brought much-needed awareness to problems that had slipped under the Fashion Victim's radar for decades.

BLAMING FASHION

Nearly all of the world's biggest retailers and manufacturers have been accused of unfair labor practices at some point. In 1998, journalists exposed child labor in a Benetton subcontractor in Turkey. Nike was accused of using child labor in Cambodia, Adidas, of using prison labor in China and sweatshop workers in El Salvador. Students alleged that Kate Spade was using "sweatshop union-busting tactics" when they picketed outside her SoHo store in 1999. Liz Claiborne was charged with physical attacks against union members. The NLC claims that workers in the Dominican Republic are paid 3¢ for every $12 Victoria's Secret garment they sew. Timberland, a company that frequently boasts of its record of socially responsible business practices, was accused of paying sixteen-year-old girls in China only 22¢ per hour and making them work up to ninety-eight hours a week. And in 2001, Disney nosed out Wal-Mart in the race for the "Sweatshop Retailer of the Year" award, cosponsored by the international group Oxfam and the Toronto-based Maquila Solidarity Network.

For the most part, sweatshops are not simply the result of greedy factory owners trying to get rich off of slave labor. The nature of fashion itself—the apparel industry's drive to sell trends and consumers' unquenchable desire to buy them—has helped fuel the sweatshop problem. "Consumers are manipulated by the fashion media, advertising, and companies that promote planned obsolescence," says Edna Bonacich, Ph.D., professor of sociology and ethnic studies at the University of California, Riverside, and coauthor of *Behind the Label*, a recent book about L.A.'s sweatshops. "The demand for constant change was created by an industry that needs to keep selling goods, even if everyone has enough and more than enough." The Fashion Victim's penchant for Speed Chic, with its revolving lineup of quickly

outmoded trends, has made sweatshops not only widespread but practically necessary. The craziness of constantly changing fashions produces the need for flexibility on the part of garment manufacturers,
explains Bonacich. That flexibility manifests itself as a web of small
contracting shops around the globe that rely on cheap labor.
Manufacturers need swift workers at the lowest prices, and when they
can't get them in one place, they simply move to the next. In order to
jockey for position, factory owners must one-up their competitors by
dropping the cost of their labor, essentially lowering workers' pay
rates to next to nothing. "The race to the bottom is the result of unbridled capitalism chasing after profits," says Katie Quan, director of the
John F. Henning Center for International Labor Relations at the
University of California, Berkeley. "It's a search for cheaper and
cheaper labor, in the hope of reducing production costs and increasing
corporate profit. It's the nature of the beast, and if left unregulated,
the system will scour the world to find the cheapest labor."

The competition is fierce. The race toward the bottom is set in
motion the minute a trend takes flight. Let's say Designer Q shows fla-
menco skirts in her spring line. Not only does Q get the ball rolling to
produce the skirts, but countless other retailers and manufacturers
jump on the bandwagon to copy the trend. They know the trend won't
last long, so it's imperative that they beat their competitors and get
their versions out first. Both Q and her competitors hunt for contractors who promise the quickest turnaround times at the lowest prices.
Q realizes that her usual plant in California won't be able to handle the
order at the price she's looking for, so she simply moves production of
the skirts to Peru, where a factory can make them for $7 per piece. Q's
closest competitor finds a shop in the Dominican Republic that can
make them for only $4.50 per piece. And a discount store gets them in
Cambodia for $3 apiece. After materials, overhead, and other costs are
deducted and the contractor takes his share, how much does the
worker herself earn? Mere pennies.

Compounding the confusion, many retailers around the world
don't even know whom they're really doing business with.
Traditionally, manufacturers would present clothing samples to buyers
from retail stores, then the buyers would decide on the quantity they

wanted to buy and negotiate a price for their store. But in recent decades, says Joe Rodriguez, executive director of the Garment Contractors Association of Southern California (GCASC), there's been a rising trend among retailers to cut out the manufacturers and go directly to the factories—for example, a department store will manufacture its own private-label clothing, such as JC Penney's Arizona Jeans and Macy's Charter Club, to stock alongside its Levi's and Donna Karan. According to the Oakland, California, group Sweatshop Watch, approximately 32 percent of women's apparel sold in the U.S. is manufactured under private labels. And some of it is done well, but many times retailers aren't interested in getting knee deep in all the minutiae of manufacturing, so they end up going to people called jobbers, who may give the impression that they're factory owners when they're not. Jobbers, says Rodriguez, are typically former manufacturers who closed their own factories because there were too many regulations, lawsuits, and labor problems to deal with. They still had the contacts and knowledge of the business, so they became middlemen, eliminating the risk of actually owning a factory. As a result, "retailers think they're doing business directly with the factories but they're not," he says. "They establish these relationships with these people who closed down their factories years ago. [Jobbers] have their own network of subcontractors now, so they take the orders from the major retailers. They don't have a factory, but they know how to take the orders; they have the contacts with the retail world. They take half a slice of that profit but they don't pass that along to the contractors, so it never gets to the rightful place where it should be."

Although we may not be fully aware of the extent of the problem, most of us are aware that at least some of our clothes are made under exploitative conditions. "Consumers certainly bear some of the responsibility," says Richard Appelbaum, Ph.D., professor of sociology and global and international studies at the University of California at Santa Barbara, and coauthor of *Behind the Label.* "Buying on the cheap certainly exacerbates the problem." There comes a point when we have to open our eyes: If you buy a shirt for $9.99, how much do you think the worker who made that shirt could possibly have earned? That's not to say that only inexpensive clothes are made in sweatshops—some higher-priced designer lines come from the exact same factories. But sweatshops flourish more than ever when consumers view clothes as disposable and retail prices are continually driven down. In the past three decades, despite inflation and rising wages in most other sectors, garment workers' wages have dropped to rock bottom. Long before she became a labor advocate, Katie Quan worked as a garment seamstress from 1975 to 1982 in New York's Chinatown. "In those days, I could make $18 an hour on piece rate, sewing women's slacks for a brand called Counterpoint that retailed at Macy's for $45," she says. "By 1995, I was the head of the union in San Francisco, and Counterpoint pants were sewn by my union members for an average of $9 an hour. By that time, they retailed at JC Penney's for just $14.50."

A major reason the garment sweatshop didn't become a dinosaur of the twentieth century lies in the product itself: fabric's pliability makes it difficult to automate the manufacturing process. While the rigid electronic components of, say, a television set can be put together by a machine, the flexible denim for a pair of stretch jeans would be tougher for a machine to maneuver. Certain parts of the apparel-making process can be done by machine, but most of the assembly still requires human hands. So, while manufacturers of other types of goods have been able to shave expenses by mechanizing production, garment makers are left with no other alternative than to cut human labor costs.

And the exact amount of those labor costs isn't left entirely up to manufacturers—a good deal of the decision rests with retailers, who establish their desired profit margin and how much they want to pay for certain garments up front, then set out to find a contractor who can deliver it at that price. Still, in a 1999 poll by the Marymount University Center for Ethical Concerns, most consumers—65 percent—hold manufacturers solely accountable for sweatshops, while only 11 percent held retailers responsible. "[Big-name retailers] set prices on a 'take-it-or-leave-it basis,' and the effect works its way down the supply chain to the workers, who get paid pennies," says Bonacich. Suppose you're a retailer and you want to buy striped turtlenecks for $12 each at wholesale, which you'll turn around and sell for $24 in your store. Of the $12 wholesale cost, the manufacturer spends about $5.40 on fabric, then uses $3 for profit and overhead. The remaining $3.60 goes to the contractor, who pays the worker who made the shirt about $1.44—approximately 6 percent of the total cost. Because of the low price that you, the retailer, set before production even started, the payment that dribbles down to everyone else all the way down the chain leaves only a meager wage for those at the bottom. And a $1.44 rate is considered quite generous in some factories. In shops in California and New York, piece rates for assembling specific parts of a garment can go as low as a few pennies for a seam, six cents for a collar, and seven cents for a sleeve. So, if you crank out a sleeve per minute, you earn a meager $4.20 per hour—far below the $5.75 minimum wage. In foreign countries, the wages dip much lower. In 1996, the NLC found that Haitian workers earned 6¢ for assembling an entire Disney 101 Dalmations children's garment that sold for $19.99 at Wal-Mart—three-tenths of 1 percent of the sales price.

The race for the bottom appears only to be getting worse. Deborah Christiansen, Ph.D., professor of apparel and merchandising at Indiana University, sees no end in sight for manufacturing's move offshore. "The newest development I just heard about this week is the production auction," she says. "Manufacturers are being invited to 'bid' for the business of a company, only in this case the lowest bidder wins. It's the e-Bay of the fashion world—amazing."

WHAT IT'S LIKE

Around the world, conditions at garment factories run the gamut. Some are excellent. Some are acceptable. Some are bad. Some are atrocious. Over the years, the apparel-manufacturing industry has earned a deservedly bad reputation from a history of worker abuses. In the early 1900s, it wasn't uncommon for workers to lose arms, legs, and fingers in machinery. In Ed Cray's book *Levi's*, Hortense Thompson, a fifty-year veteran of the Levi Strauss factory in San Francisco, described the danger of operating a metal button machine in the early 1900s: "One time a lady's hair got caught in the machine.

Her scalp was taken off. She didn't die, but she was in the hospital a long time. People sometimes sewed their fingers. When people were hurt on the job, the company didn't pay medical expenses."

In the many years Richard Appelbaum has spent interviewing sweatshop workers, he says he's actually seen worse conditions in U.S. factories than in Asian ones. "L.A.'s downtown garment district is filled with seventy-five-year-old office buildings that have been carved up into a warren of tiny factories employing fewer than twenty-five workers each," he says. "They're dingy, dirty, overcrowded, with exposed wiring, blocked exits, and inadequate toilet facilities." When he went to conduct his first-ever interview with workers, he entered the elevator of a downtown building, which took him to the sixth floor in total darkness, since the light was out. There, he encountered a half-dozen factories for different companies, "all worthy of Dickens." "There was one toilet serving all the factories on two adjacent floors— no doubt adequate when the building housed a handful of office workers ages ago, but now overflowing with human excrement, since the toilet was malfunctioning," he says. "I'm not saying that all factories in L.A. are this bad, but many are quite bad."

Sweatshop conditions can't always be identified by appearance alone. "I think the misconception about sweatshops today is that a sweatshop is something that's dark and dirty and cramped—an almost nineteenth-century view of what the factories were like in New York," says Dara O'Rourke, Ph.D., an assistant professor of environmental policy at the Massachusetts Institute of Technology and a leading expert on sweatshops and global garment labor. "Actually, there are still many sweatshops like that in the U.S.—really poor conditions, overcrowded factories. But I think there are equally bad or worse conditions in what you might think of as twenty-first-century sweatshop. New factories, built in the last few years in Asia, Vietnam, and China, are quite modern, new, clean, and well lit. They've got all the things that make them *look* fine." But that's only an illusion: the facilities may appear acceptable; it isn't until you delve deeper into labor practices dealing with wages, safety, and working conditions that you realize all is not well. Offenses documented around the world that may not be so easily observable by outsiders include daily friskings, verbal and physical abuse, sexual harassment, and pregnancy checks. Some female workers have even been asked to have abortions. According to a report from the late 1970s entitled "Women Workers in Asia," management at certain factories would often provide pep pills and amphetamine injections to keep the women awake and working, causing some of them to become addicts. Wage violations in the U.S. slip through the cracks when unscrupulous factory owners employ the practice of "buying checks"—workers must pay their bosses cash in order to receive their paychecks. Thus, the figure on the pay stub creates the illusion that workers are earning the federal minimum wage.

Manufacturers are often able to evade the scrutinizing eye of observers by hiring home workers, a practice that's illegal in some U.S. states. Jobbers give women bundles of cut fabric to sew at home; thus workers must take care of the costs of doing business on their own—rent, electricity, commercial sewing machine (which can cost anywhere from $500 to $3,000). It may seem like an ideal setup for some, especially working mothers who then can stay home with their children. But home workers earn less than those in the shop, and the practice makes it notoriously difficult to collect wages: in one case, a Haitian immigrant brought one thousand finished pieces to her boss, who replied, "I gave you two thousand pieces!" He refused to pay her until she worked off the missing pieces. Home working also translates into high production quotas, long hours, and no time off, and it makes tax evasion easier, since some workers are paid off the books. Although it's illegal in California, a 1996 sweep of contract shops in the southern part of the state exposed home-work sites where Guess? clothing was sewn. Eighty percent of the women's clothing produced in Chile is made in home-work shops, as is 30 percent in Mexico and 55 percent in Argentina.

Labor problems often go unreported because many workers have no one to turn to for help. In California, a majority of workers have no representation. Very few, if any, garment shops in southern California are unionized, says Joe Rodriguez of GCASC. He blames it on the contractors' lack of power. "This is the only industry that I know of where the contractor doesn't set the price," he says. "If you need a plumbing contractor in your house, they tell *you*, you don't tell *them* what they're going to be paid. It's just the opposite in this industry. When there's even a hint of union or unionized attempt, the manufacturer or retailer just doesn't give him any work, so there is absolutely never going to be any unionization out here—the union realizes that there's no point trying to unionize that shop because there'll be no work in that shop." In other countries, many workers don't even realize that they have rights. On average, in over two hundred factories inspected by independent monitoring firm Verité, fewer than 10 percent of workers knew their rights on issues of minimum wage, overtime pay, benefits, paid leave, and the right to organize as a union.

HOW SWEATSHOPS TOOK OVER

In the garment business, there is often a fine line between being shrewd and being shady. Companies want to keep costs as low as possible by paying workers less, except pesky things called laws often keep them from dropping too low. What to do? Find ways to dodge the rules.

Today, producing apparel on a large scale is not as simple as finding workers, paying them, and churning out clothes. Manufacturers have to deal with free-trade agreements, quotas, pressure from unions, and, of course, allegiance to the bottom line. In many cases, these necessities have driven them away from the watchful eye of their governments and into countries where sweated conditions run rampant.

MASS PRODUCTION'S MASS EXODUS

In 1973, Petra Mata, a twenty-six-year-old with more dreams than pesos, crossed the Mexican border to start a new life in Texas with her husband. Friends had told her that a woman like her, with only a sixth-grade education and a few phrases of broken English under her belt, would have no problem earning a good living in the U.S., a nearly impossible feat in her homeland. After three years of floundering at low-paid jobs in restaurants and at a tortilla factory, Mata finally landed a position with potential—as a sewing-machine operator at the South Zarzamora Street garment factory in San Antonio, Texas.

Although she had no previous sewing experience, after two weeks of training, she became adept at operating the machinery and continued to sew men's sports jackets for several years. Then, in 1981, Levi Strauss took over the plant to produce Dockers pants and jackets. Mata had few complaints—over her fourteen-year period at the factory, she had moved up through the ranks from seamstress to trainer to supervisor, eventually bringing in a respectable $9.73 an hour. By all accounts, the South Zarzamora Street factory was no sweatshop: workers received health insurance, some sewing machine operators earned up to $12 per hour, and workdays, although occasionally long, weren't brutal—Mata worked about ten hours a day, five or six days a week.

In 1989, Mata and fellow supervisors began to notice foreign visitors—Chinese and Indian businesspeople—walking around, snapping photos and shooting video. "What's going on?" she asked management on several occasions. "Oh, nothing, nothing . . . nothing to worry about," they'd reply. In fact, by all outward appearances, the factory was more than fine. That year, the 1,150 workers in the plant were cranking out an average of sixteen thousand trousers and five hundred jackets a day for the Dockers line, making it Levi's largest plant in the U.S. In July, management awarded each worker a $200 bonus for helping to produce such high profits and honored them with the title of "miracle worker."

Six months later, management called a meeting with the supervisors at the ritzy conference room of a nearby hotel. Mata and her coworkers sat patiently at round tables, wondering why they were there. The doors swung open, and a procession of caseworkers hired by Levi's marched in and handed each person a packet. The plant was closing. "It was like somebody died," Mata recalls.

Production of Dockers pants was moving to Costa Rica, where workers were paid about $1 to $3.80 per hour, some earning less in one day than what Zarzamora workers made in one hour. Some of Mata's fellow employees, mostly night-shift workers, were sent packing that day. Others, like Mata, stayed on for several months to finish up projects, all the while harboring an intense resentment against the work they were doing and the products they were making.

What was even worse than the daunting task of finding a new job was the unsatisfactory severance package offered to employees. Levi's offered each laid-off worker one week's salary for each year served, three months of health-care benefits, and no early-retirement option. To Mata and her co-workers, it was a slap in the face. "When you have a low education and you don't know the language—we know how to work but we cannot beat the system," she says. In order to make ends meet and to put food on the table for their four children, Mata's husband, who had been diagnosed with diabetes at around that time, had to take two jobs—one as a cook and another at a grocery store.

"Ay, dios mio, what are we going to do? Where are we going to go?" Confusion and frustration resonated among all the laid-off Zarzamora workers. Six months after the announcement of the plant closure, most were still jobless. On February 12, 1990, a group of them got together and established Fuerza Unida, "United Force." Each week, the grassroots organization met at Our Lady of the Angels Church in San Antonio, where the laid-off workers could offer a supportive ear to one another and create a plan of action against their former employer. In its first year, membership swelled to seven hundred. With the pro bono services of a prominent labor-rights attorney, the group, headed by Mata and co-coordinator Viola Casares, filed an $11.6 billion class-action lawsuit in April 1990 against Levi's and called for a national boycott of all the company's products.

One of the major charges in the lawsuit was that many workers had suffered occupational injuries, including carpal tunnel syndrome, herniated discs, deafness, and vision problems, as a result of their work for Levi's, and now that they were unemployed, they were left without health-care coverage. Mata even contends that some workers have developed liver and ovarian cancer, which she says may have been caused by inhaling large amounts of lint in the factory and from exposure to chemicals, although no one has ever been able to prove these allegations. The judge rejected the lawsuit, and the workers lost once again on appeal. "They had big, big professional lawyers," says Mata. "They were paying a lot of money. There came a time when we felt, 'This isn't going to work. We don't have a lot of money to fight against this big giant.' "

Still, Fuerza Unida didn't give up—its leaders continued to meet, unsuccessfully, with Levi's executives to try and hammer out a more just severance package. On November 3, 1997, Levi's announced it would close another eleven of its U.S. plants. This time, realizing the extent of its messy PR faux pas in San Antonio seven years earlier, the company offered this new batch of pink-slipped workers three weeks' severance for each year of employment; eight months' notice, medical coverage up to eighteen months, and up to $6,000 for training, education, or relocation costs. For years, the company denied that their flight offshore would be a continuing trend. Then in February 1999, the company announced it would shut down an additional eleven plants, leaving another 5,900 workers jobless. John Ermatinger, president of Levi Strauss's American division, finally conceded, "Shifting a significant portion of our manufacturing for the U.S. and Canadian markets to contractors throughout the world will give the company greater flexibility to allocate resources and capital to its brands. These steps are crucial if we are to remain competitive." In the early 1980s, Levi Strauss owned and operated some fifty plants in the U.S.; by 2002, it was down to only two.

Today, Mata shakes her head whenever she sees a pair of Levi's or Dockers in a store. "We, the workers, help those people to get big houses and live in rich communities and drive the very fancy cars—how many people were there with injuries who made all the money?" she says. "When I was working for them, I'd see Levi's and feel very proud like, 'I make this.' Now, sometimes I feel like I wanna talk to the manager of a store and say, 'How the hell you have these pants here—so much high prices.' My son, he always buys Dockers, and he even pay $46. Oh my God, the workers in Mexico, Honduras, and Costa Rica earn so little. They probably pay so many workers with that $46."

The Levi's story certainly isn't an isolated incident. The lure of dirt-cheap labor and facilities in developing countries in Asia and Latin America has proven too tempting for many manufacturers to resist. At the heart of the problem are free-trade pacts like NAFTA, which phased out tariffs and quotas between the U.S., Mexico, and Canada. A 1999 article in *The Nation* reported that apparel job loss in the U.S. in the four years following NAFTA was more than quadruple the rate of the preceding four years. And as further global trade agreements kick in over the next few years, and tariffs and quotas are eliminated, even more manufacturing jobs are expected to flee to low-wage countries.

Governments in developing countries make no secret of what they can offer big-name corporations, often advertising their abundance of cheap labor. In 1990, El Salvador's government posted this ad promoting its low-cost work force: "Quality, Industriousness and Reliability Is What El Salvador Offers You! Rosa Martinez produces apparel for U.S. markets on her sewing machine in El Salvador. *You* can hire her for 57 cents an hour." They reran the same ad the next year, but this time, Rosa's advertised wage had dropped to a mere 33 cents an hour. The U.S. apparel industry employed about 1.2 million employees in 1950 and reached a peak of 1.4 million in 1973. Today, it employs only about 700,000. And it looks like things will get worse before they get better. Experts predict that apparel and textile employment in the U.S. will decline 23 percent through 2008, whereas employment throughout the economy as a whole will increase 15 percent, reports InfoMat, an information provider for the apparel industry. "In twenty years, the industry had globalized at a phenomenal rate, leaving hundreds of thousands of workers out of jobs," says Katie Quan. And most of the victims of globalization have been women like Petra Mata. "The workers were predominantly immigrant women from China and Latin America who were middle-aged—too young to retire and too old to start new careers," says Quan.

Some critics even question how much the apparel industry's union, UNITE, does to stop the flight offshore. In 1998, Joel Cohen, a labor attorney for McDermott, Will & Emery, testified to a committee of the House of Representatives about the union's practice of collecting liquidated damages. The union engages in agreements with certain manufacturers: keep production in domestic, unionized shops or pay a fee. If a manufacturer violates that agreement and moves production overseas, it must pay the union liquidated damages—a fee that sometimes climbs into the tens of millions of dollars. Here's the shady part: "UNITE, rarely, if ever, forces jobbers to abide by the contractual commitment to give garment production to American unionized shops," said Cohen. "Instead, what it does is allow the jobber to do whatever it wants and it then collects liquidated damages for the contractual violation." As a result, he says, American garment workers lose their jobs to cheaper imports while the union collects money for itself. In the last ten years, the union has collected approximately $100 million in liquidated damages, according to published reports. Does this mean the practice is abused? Not absolutely. Does it mean that the potential for abuses casts suspicion on the system? You bet.

The convoluted network of factories created by the dispersion of manufacturers around the globe has created a situation that has made it difficult to track violations. "A brand like Levi's has a huge global supply chain with thousands of suppliers that makes it virtually impossible for *them* to even know that their clothes are produced under good conditions," says Dara O'Rourke of MIT. Nike uses more than 700 factories in 50 countries and doesn't own any of them. Gap uses over 1,200 factories in 42 countries. Liz Claiborne operates in 40 countries around the world, and no one producer handles more than 4 percent of its production, says Lora Jo Foo, attorney and president of the coalition Sweatshop Watch in Oakland, California.

HUNTING FOR SWEATSHOP WITCHES

As much good as the Kathie Lee Gifford scandal and others like it have done in the past few decades to bring attention to the sweatshop issue, they have also led to a virtual witch hunt, in which a few aggressive antisweatshop activists have played on manufacturers' and retailers' fears of suffering a Gifford-like fate, in turn, helping further fuel the industry's departure from the U.S. In 1998, L.A.–based sportswear manufacturer Karen Kane was targeted due to guilt by association. The company, which did about $70 million in wholesale volume each year, manufactured 75 percent of its garments domestically and the rest in China and Mexico. President Lonnie Kane, whose wife Karen designs the line, testified to the House of Representatives in May 1998 that he had received a call in July 1995 from David Young, an organizer at UNITE, informing him that union reps would be picketing at Goodtime/Song of California, one of Karen Kane's contracting shops, but

Young had refused to explain why. Young reportedly gave Kane an ultimatum: Pull out of that factory or become the focus of protests yourself. Kane told the union organizer that he would think about the situation and get back to him. The next day, Kane received a call from one of his retail stores in Beverly Hills. "Picketers had come into our store, handed out leaflets that referred to Lonnie and Karen Kane as sweatshop operators," Kane recalled. "They blocked our doors and pushed themselves upon our customers, verbally inferring that myself and my wife and Karen Kane, Inc., were operators of sweatshops that take the food out of their and their children's mouths, inferring that they were out of work because of Karen Kane and that they would disrupt Karen Kane's business until we stop working with Song of California."

While no one denies that there are labor rights problems, some insiders say they've been blown out of proportion. "I think many of these workers' advocacy groups are well intentioned," says Joe Rodriguez of GCASC. "But everybody has an agenda. Sometimes to further their agenda they gloss over certain things, state certain things that contain half-truths, exaggerate in some cases." The confusion seems to start with the term "sweatshop" itself. According to the Department of Labor, any business engaged in an operation in violation of minimum wage, overtime, or child labor laws is a sweatshop. But that definition leaves room for gray areas. Rodriguez recalls a press conference at which the DOL released the results of its latest apparel-industry survey. The headline: 67 percent of apparel shops surveyed were found to be in violation of minimum wage, overtime, or health and safety laws, and employees in the same survey had been underpaid by tens of thousands of dollars. This may have been technically correct, says Rodriguez, but numbers can sometimes paint a confusing picture. "You can make statistics say anything you want," he says. "It depends on where you put the emphasis. All of those headlines are 100 percent accurate, but they're so misleading." When Rodriguez dug deeper into the survey, he found some twisting of the truth. It turned out that the sample size of the survey was only about 1 percent of all the garment shops in the state. And that large sum of money that hadn't been paid? Again, it turned out that those thousands accounted for only a minuscule percentage of the total payroll.

"If you were investigating a payroll of, say, $5 million, and only $60,000 of that was badly paid . . . it would be just as accurate to point out that 99.5 percent was paid *correctly* rather than zero in on the dollar amount," says Rodriguez.

Abiding by the DOL's definition—that any shop in violation of wage, overtime, or health and safety laws could be tagged a sweatshop—meant that even the smallest infraction could be damning. One GCASC member was fined because five of its six employees didn't sign their time cards one week (mind you, they only *had* six workers in the entire operation).

"Is this shop considered in violation of overtime rules?" Rodriguez asked the DOL. "Yes," he was told. "So, therefore this is a sweatshop employer?" asked Rodriguez. "Yes . . . it is," came the reply.

Rodriguez raised another example with DOL representatives: if a factory had a 35-inch aisle, instead of the mandatory 36-inch aisle, its owners would be fined, and it would technically be considered a sweatshop. "That's not the type of competition that's killing us—it's the ones that are the blatant abusers," says Rodriguez. "Those are the ones we need to talk about, not the little nickel-and-dime things that they point out in some of these surveys." He believes agencies like the DOL can be swayed by selfish motives: "They take these statistics, lump them all together to make and glorify their headlines and to also add to their job security—because that's how you let the world know that we need to have more of these inspectors and inspections taking place." So, while conditions at the world's factories may be bad, it's possible that they're not as grim as research suggests. Yet these statistics are continually used as fodder for antisweatshop campaigns, and some well-intentioned businesses get caught in the crossfire.

The sweatshop finger-pointing has gotten so bad in recent years that it's stigmatized the entire apparel-manufacturing industry. "Just about everybody that is offshore is considered a sweatshop," says W. Lane Tarleton, general manager of Land Apparel, a company that has manufactured clothing in Honduras since 1997. "When I come to the U.S., people always say, 'Oh, you work in one of those sweatshops, don't you?' " That's not to say that there aren't an overwhelming number of exploited workers earning mere pennies to assemble the clothes and shoes we wear every day. But, as many in the garment industry would attest, targeting those companies with the biggest names, but perhaps who commit the lesser evils, may not do the most good.

Under the constant threat of bad publicity, droves of U.S.-based manufacturers have figured it would be easier to hit the road and set up shop in foreign countries, far from the scrutiny of government and activist groups. In the mid-1990s, American antisweatshop activists turned up the heat on numerous big-name corporations, including Guess?. In 1996, five of the company's contractors were cited by California inspectors for illegal home-sewing operations. Then a class-action suit accused the Los Angeles–based manufacturer and sixteen subcontractors of paying workers less than minimum wage, leading to heated protests by activist groups. In January 1997, the company announced that it was relocating 40 percent of its production to Chile, Peru, and Mexico, where the company's stitchers would earn $20 to $40 a week, compared with about $5 an hour for their Californian counterparts. The move left only 35 percent of the jeans maker's production in L.A.; just three years earlier, it had manufactured 97 percent of its clothing in the U.S.

AND THEN THE GARMENTS LEFT GOTHAM . . .

Nowhere was the exit of apparel manufacturing from the U.S. felt as much as in New York City. In the late nineteenth century, as consumers began to clamor for ready-to-wear and large numbers of immigrants from Eastern and Southern Europe began to flood Ellis Island, New York's garment industry thrived. Mass production in the city began with coats and suits, and within several decades, dresses, shirtwaists, and undergarments were also being turned out in factories. As a major port and the fashion center of the U.S., it only made sense that New York would remain one of the world's most vital hubs of garment manufacturing.

Today, the New York City Garment District, a progressively splintering region on the west side of midtown Manhattan, encompasses approximately 34 million square feet extending from Fifth to Ninth Avenues and from 35th to 41st Streets. Delivery workers wheel racks of clothes and pushcarts with bolts of fabric on and off commercial trucks, in and out of lobbies. Wholesalers, contractors, buyers, and other local workers emerge from their buildings to the sidewalks below to smoke, talk (loudly) about business, grab a kebob from the vendor at the corner, spy on their competitors. While shoppers at Sephora, a few blocks up in Times Square, sniff the scent of fashionable perfume like Michael Kors or Marc Jacobs, pedestrians in the Garment District breathe in a less pleasant olfactory cocktail of truck exhaust, grilling onions, and that "new fabric smell," caused by the chemicals used to treat some textiles. At the multitude of wholesale showrooms on ground level, it's far less common to see first-rate designer garments than it is to see Sears-type cookie-cutter evening gowns and bright skirt suits hanging in the windows.

In the early twentieth century, factories began moving to Chinatown—the city's *other* garment nucleus—because rents tended to be cheaper downtown, since the area, still mostly occupied by immigrants, had yet to be taken over by big business, luxury apartments, or major retailers. Some two hundred garment factories cropped up there over a time span of several decades. As unattractive as the sights can be today uptown in the Garment District, they're ten times worse in the famous area near Mott and Canal Streets. Above the grimy sights on the sidewalk—napkins and newspaper bits floating in fluorescent green puddles, vendors selling counterfeit Gucci sunglasses and Prada handbags next to storefronts piled high with stinky fish stacked on ice—are dank factories lined with workers toiling silently at sewing machines. Even though New York's apparel-manufacturing industry had never enjoyed a sparkling reputation for its treatment of workers, the shifting of many factories into Chinatown made it easier for labor violations to slip through the cracks. Since many of the Chinese workers were illegal aliens, they often owed their smugglers large debts and would pay them off over time from their wages. Many workers didn't speak English and had no knowledge of U.S. labor laws, meaning they were largely a desperate work force with no one to turn to for help.

The New York apparel industry flourished up until the 1960s

when overseas competition began to eat away at the city's dominance. In 1987, the city planning commission passed a zoning ordinance intended to keep the garment industry in the Garment Center, creating the Special Garment Center District. The rules required building owners to set aside 50 percent of all space on side streets in the garment center for manufacturing uses. Then, in the mid-1990s, the dot-com boom brought a flood of well-funded businesses to the area in need of office space. Landlords began ignoring the district's zoning ordinance, since well-funded techies were willing to pay twice the rent of the garment business. When there wasn't space, building owners made space. Crooked landlords knew that designers can't afford the bad publicity caused by sweatshop allegations and used this knowledge to their advantage. For example, activists picketed outside a building at 43rd Street and Fifth Avenue in September 2000. The building's owner, Chase Manhattan Bank, had charged upscale womenswear-designer Elie Tahari of running a sweatshop on the third floor and threatened him with eviction for violating safety regulations and building codes. But by all appearances, Tahari's operation was far from a sweatshop. The designer claimed that he was being evicted so his landlord could charge rents more than 60 percent higher than what he was paying. "In many cases, it is a matter of greed," says Jonathan Bowles, research director at the Center for an Urban Future, a New York City–based think tank that conducted a three-month study of the Big Apple's fashion industry. "Not surprisingly, landlords want as much as they can get for their properties, and they know that apparel manufacturers can't stay in business if they pay much more than $10 or $15 per square foot in rent."

As the U.S. economy took a turn for the worse in the late 1990s, retail sales waned, leading to even more business closures. By 2000, employment in the New York garment sector had fallen to 78,200, down from 104,415 in 1991, according to the Labor Department. In contrast, the number of apparel and textile manufacturing jobs in Los Angeles has risen 22 percent since 1993. Not that the Garment District and Chinatown are ghost towns, complete with tumbleweeds and slack-jawed yokels, but it's not hard to see the effects of the apparel industry's departure. According to Danniel Maio, a partner at Identity

Map, a New York mapmaking firm that has surveyed the New York Garment District since 1994, rents at some buildings increased up to fourfold, reaching impossibly high levels for many fashion tenants, whose products and labor costs had been discounted 20 to 60 percent. Even before the World Trade Center attack on September 11, 2001, which further devastated the industry, Maio says that empty garment factories were a common sight. "Quite often, I see factories with ten to fifty machines being worked on by one to three people with the lights dimmed [to save electricity costs], which I didn't observe during the first five years of the survey." For the first time in its history, fashion-industry employment now represents less than half the overall jobs in the New York Garment District's core. When manufacturers departed the U.S., "Made in . . ." labels from countries like Taiwan, Honduras, Mexico, and China became far more commonplace. And even products that still claim to be American made aren't always what they seem . . .

MADE IN THE U.S.A., OR *IS* IT?

If you were dropped by parachute onto the idyllic island of Saipan, the largest island in the Commonwealth of the Northern Mariana Islands (CNMI) 125 miles north of Guam, you might think you'd landed in a Japanese paradise. Tourists, mostly flying in from Japan, flock to the island's karaoke bars, sushi restaurants, and Japanese-owned beach-front luxury hotels. Vacationers can laze on the beach, wade in the warm waters, play a round of golf, snorkel—all the activities you might expect to participate in on a perfect island getaway.

Saipan, bordered on the east by the Pacific Ocean and on the west by the Philippine Sea, has a rich, although bloody, history. Most tourist attractions here are places where fierce battles took place during World War II, including a few massive "Banzai Cliffs" where Japanese soldiers and families leapt to their deaths to avoid capture and the caves where soldiers hid out until as late as 1952, not knowing that the war had ended. There are fifteen official dive sites where visitors can get an up-close look at sunken battleships. What's not featured on any tourist map, however, are any of the thirty-four garment factories that have popped up on the island since the late 1970s.

After the war, the Japanese were forced out (only, ironically, to return years later as tourists), and a covenant made CNMI a U.S. territory, like Puerto Rico, in 1978. Living in the commonwealth isn't exactly like being an American citizen. Inhabitants don't pay U.S. taxes and they can't vote. The agreement gave the U.S. the authority to conduct foreign affairs and defense for the fourteen thousand citizens, while reserving the right to build military bases there. And, in a move that some today have branded a major mistake, the U.S. government allowed the commonwealth to set its own immigration, minimum wage, and customs policies.

The local government's lenient laws opened the door for a massive influx of garment factories and laborers. Since the island was a commonwealth of the U.S., manufacturers could avoid paying duties on materials coming in and garments going out, sidestepping expenditures totaling $200 million a year, meaning they could produce a shirt that would normally cost $10 for just $5. Without adequate regulations, Saipan didn't just allow sweatshops to exist, it practically invited them. In the past five years, garment contractors on the island have been cited for more than a thousand OSHA violations. Officials established a system of short-term work permits, allowing workers from places like China and Korea to enter the commonwealth for a year. Today, foreign guest workers make up more than 90 percent of the garment industry workforce there, constituting more than half of the Marianas' total population of seventy thousand. Many workers have been forced to work twelve-hour days, seven days a week, without overtime compensation. Some have been forced to sign "shadow contracts," which waive some of their rights, such as freedom to practice their religion, ask for a raise, or even date. Chinese workers would customarily pay employment brokers in their homeland up to $10,000 in recruitment fees in exchange for helping them obtain work in Saipan, then they would be obligated to pay off the debt over time. It wasn't until they started working that they'd realize this wasn't the plum setup they had bargained for. The workers would earn far less than their recruiters promised and have no one to complain to. If they were fired, they would still be responsible for repaying their employers. It was, in effect, indentured servitude. The CNMI set its minimum wage at $3.05 per hour, about half of the federally mandated wage in the States—and a deceptive figure since garment workers are nearly always paid by the piece rather than by the hour. And thanks to the CNMI's sloppy customs system, imported textiles and other materials were not routinely checked upon arrival, letting fabrics from countries that had been subject to quotas and tariffs slip through the cracks.

Had these injustices occurred in any other country—say, Burma or Nicaragua—they might not have seemed so shocking to the average American. After all, abuses like this do go on every day around the world. But what was different was that products that came from Saipan could be legally slapped with a "Made in the U.S.A." label, a loophole of sorts that several major brands such as Calvin Klein and Fila took advantage of. Saipan may have been a U.S. commonwealth, but the island was far from American shores and its economy mostly run by Chinese businessmen, so the treatment of workers frequently followed Chinese rather than American customs (contrary to what people might expect when they see a "Made in the U.S.A." label). What was worse, it appeared as though U.S. officials were blissfully unaware of any problems on the island. In 1998, Republican congressman Tom DeLay of Houston was invited to Saipan as a guest of the government. About one hundred other high-ranking U.S. congressmen and other officials have attended similar trips. On DeLay's trip, he did take time to tour several factories and barracks, which were no doubt gussied up before his arrival, but the rest of his getaway was spent snorkeling, playing golf, and attending a fancy dinner thrown in his honor. "Even though I have only been here for twenty-four hours," he told a crowd of his fellow attendees, "I have witnessed the economic success of the Marianas."

In 1999, three separate lawsuits were filed on behalf of more than fifty thousand workers against twenty-six U.S. clothing companies and their contractors in Saipan, seeking more than $1 billion in damages. Eighteen of the retailers, including Calvin Klein, Donna Karan, J. Crew, Liz Claiborne, and Tommy Hilfiger, settled almost immediately for $8.5 million, also agreeing to have independent monitors regularly inspect factories. The remaining eight companies, which held out and chose to fight, included Gap (the company that does the most business on the island—$200 million, according to Global Exchange), Target, Levi Strauss, and The Limited.

Consumers who read about the Saipan scandal rightfully felt deceived. A Roper poll of American consumers found that the "Made in the U.S.A." label was considered a positive attribute by 95 percent of the people. Sixty percent of respondents in another poll indicated that the country of origin is at least somewhat important to them when making purchasing decisions. Thanks to our stereotypes of various countries, certain country labels carry cachet; others, stigma. For many consumers, the country where a garment is made is an indicator of quality. "I'm a snob about where my clothes are made," says Angela, forty-eight, a sales consultant in Gaithersburg, Maryland. "To me, certain countries represent a certain quality. For instance, I prefer fabrics and workmanship from Italy, gold jewelry from Italy rather than Turkey, wool and cashmere from England and Scotland, leather goods from Italy, cotton goods made in the U.S. To me, countries like Taiwan indicate mass-produced goods." For others, seeing the name of a certain country is a signal that a garment was made under good (or bad) working conditions. "I prefer to buy clothes that were made in the brand's country of origin, especially if it's Europe or the U.S., only because I know that there are established and respected labor laws in these countries," says Roxanne, a twenty-nine-year-old writer in London. And clearly, consumers have no uncertainties about what constitutes an American-made product—in a 1996 survey, only 14 percent of consumers strongly agreed that a product that had 50 percent American parts and labor should be considered "Made in the U.S.A." The Saipan case opened many consumers' eyes to the fact that there's only so much we can know about where our clothes came from.

DOES THE FASHION VICTIM CARE?

Today, supporting the existence of sweatshops is on a par with singing the praises of animal testing—many people may secretly be grateful for the benefits that come from these activities (sweatshops help consumers keep more of their hard-earned money; animal testing means fewer trial-and-error experiments on humans), but few have the audacity to support them publicly. So consumers are put in this odd position: They're torn between the perceptible, everyday advantages they derive from sweatshops (cheap clothes) and the notion that they're *supposed* to oppose sweatshops.

A RELATIVE MESS

There are plenty of dreadful jobs I can't imagine holding, like garbage collector for one. But if there were no garbage collectors, we would be inundated with trash, and I dare say the world would come to a stinky halt. Of course, if we wanted to, we could create less trash and make garbage collectors' lives easier. Likewise, the sweatshop worker has become an unnecessary necessity—we don't really need all the clothes we own, but we've convinced ourselves that we do.

Fashion Victims hate to think that workers are being exploited, but we love our inexpensive clothes. We feel some level of pity toward workers who earn pennies for each shirt they make, but usually not enough to do anything about it. We shake our heads at news of big-name retailers caught up in sweatshop scandals, but don't stop shopping at their stores. According to surveys, we're a society of caring consumers. In a survey conducted by Marymount University's Center for Ethical Concerns in 1999, three-quarters of those polled said they would avoid buying from a retailer that they knew sold garments made in sweatshops, and 86 percent said they would pay an extra dollar on a $20 garment if there were a guarantee that the garment was made in a legitimate shop. But, as we know, the average consumer is far more virtuous on paper than in the store. Agreeing to pay an extra dollar is one thing; the inconvenience of finding out where all of our clothes come from is something entirely different. Unfortunately, finding out if a particular manufacturer or retailer uses sweatshop labor isn't as easy as flipping over the price tag. Very few consumers take the time to read online or published reports on businesses that violate labor laws, and, as of right now, there's no established way for consumers to look at a garment and instantly tell that it was made under good working conditions. And although American consumers say they prefer U.S.-made products, that's only when they're *looking*. In reality, though, very few really go out of their way to even check the tags on clothes they buy. A poll conducted by the Crafted With Pride Council found that only 29 percent of consumers surveyed knew the origin of their clothes. Perhaps the Fashion Victim cares where some of her clothes are made (when it suits her purposes for, say, an Italian-made jacket or French-crafted scarf), but for most lower-ticket items, she doesn't even read the label.

The majority of clothes shoppers aren't overly concerned with sweatshop workers—most feel so far removed from the lives of these low-paid laborers that it's nearly impossible to understand what they go through. In 1995, *Dateline NBC* producer Minnie Roh conducted an eight-month investigation into the world of the New York garment factory, working undercover assembling sweatshirts in a Jamaica Avenue, Queens, sweatshop. She toiled amid ten other sewing machine operators in a small, narrow room sewing sleeves onto shirts. On her first day, her boss explained that she would be paid by the piece—seven cents per shirt. Roh calculated that if she were to turn out one shirt every two minutes, that would be $2.10 an hour, or $16.80 for an eight-hour day—$3.05 per hour less than the U.S. minimum wage at the time. But she underestimated how much work it would be. She took no breaks (despite her grumbling belly and aching back) but was able to crank out only fifty-three shirts on her first day. So, for an eight-hour workday, she earned $3.71—barely enough pocket change to afford a hot dog and soda in New York.

Hearing about the experiences of someone like Roh puts a completely different spin on sweatshop labor: Here was someone who didn't seem so foreign, so far removed. Someone with the same expenses, the same standards of living, as many New Yorkers. It's easier to be shocked at a $3.71 New York wage than by a four-cent Burmese one, only because most of us are pretty clueless about living in Burma. Roh's story conjures up the temptation to compare: in my freshman year of college, I made $5.50 an hour working at a bookstore—in one hour, I earned more than she did in an eight-hour day.

In most industries in the Western world, we're spoiled by good working conditions. We complain about our jobs—no room for promotion, mediocre benefits, high stress. We gripe about our brand-new computers when they freeze up. We whine about how much our dental insurance sucks for not covering every cent of a root canal. At one of my old jobs, a co-worker complained that there was no way to make mochaccino in the floor's automated coffee machine. The point is that we even *have* all these things to complain about in the first place. If any of us abandoned our cushy white-collar work environments for just one day to slave away in a garment factory, we would be singing a different, undoubtedly more bluesy, tune.

THE SWEAT SMELL OF SUCCESS

Oddly, in our culture of workaholism, it's become all too easy for us to brush off the plight of sweatshop workers. They toil for over seventy hours, six days a week, often with no paid overtime. Well, so do many white-collar workers in the U.S. who slave in front of computers instead of sewing machines, our unsympathetic side tells us. (I sometimes clocked seventy-hour-plus workweeks on this book in my one-bedroom apartment with no overtime pay—oh, the perils of being a sweatshop writer.) Sweatshop workers are often not allowed to take vacation time. Again, walk into an investment bank on Wall Street, and you'll find industrious people who haven't taken time off in years.

It's ingrained in the psyche of most Americans that hard work can lead to success and *really* hard work can lead to even greater success. Stories abound of stockbrokers, entrepreneurs, and other professionals pulling themselves up from their meager beginnings to make a name and a fortune for themselves. Americans are the worst of the workaholics. My European friends go on holiday at least four times more frequently than anyone I know in the States. According to the World Tourism Organization, U.S. workers have fewer vacation days than those in any other country—just 13 per year, compared to Italy's 42, Brazil's 34, and Japan's 25. A report by the International Labor Organization (ILO) showed that the average American worked 1,978 hours in 2000, up from 1,942 hours in 1990. The ILO determined that the average Brazilian and British employee worked some 250 hours, or more than five weeks, less than Americans per year. Germans worked roughly 500 hours, or twelve-and-a-half weeks, less than their American counterparts. Even the industrious Japanese have more days off of work than the Americans. Since so many of us work so diligently, it becomes more difficult to pity others who also work hard. Pain is a sign of hard work, and in a society where being productive is a virtue, pain is power. As a result, a callous part of us feels unsympathetic toward the industrious sweatshop worker.

The injustices start to become a little clearer when we put them into terms we can all understand. At subminimum wage earnings, workers have to get creative about housing, often piling a whole group into one tiny apartment. A real meal becomes a luxury. Not only is good food out of reach financially, but sewing machine operators, like Roh, often work straight through lunch, barely looking up from their work-stations even once. The $25 that most people wouldn't think twice about shelling out for a shirt would take many garment-factory workers months to save up for. A Cosmopolitan at chi-chi nightspot Lotus in Manhattan's meatpacking district costs about $11—that's three days of sweatshop labor down the hatch!

Sweatshops are an utterly unsexy topic in the sexy world of fashion. At first glance, Fashion Victims don't care how our clothes are made, as long as they're relatively cheap (and as we've discussed before, "cheap" is a completely subjective term), up to date, abundant, and don't fall apart after one wearing. It's not that we're completely heart-less—it's just that our judgment is clouded over by this veil of industri-ousness, so we actually delude ourselves into thinking that the wretched jobs of sweatshop workers are helping *them*. One of the most common statements consumers make about sweatshops is: "Aren't we helping developing countries by putting factories there?" After all, a seamstress who earns 23 cents in China (the average hourly wage for sweatshop workers there) is earning 23 cents more than she would with no job. And if sewing-machine operators are earning 59 cents an hour in El Salvador, we assume that the cost of living in that country is lower than ours. But the living wage—the amount necessary to meet immediate needs (food, housing, child care), save some money for long-term purchases or emergencies, and provide some discretionary income that can filter back into their local economy—in El Salvador is $1.18 an hour. And while Americans believe that workers in Mexico are paid lower wages because their day-to-day expenses are cheaper, in reality, basic goods such as bread and milk are cheaper over the border in the U.S. In Mexican maquiladoras—factories set up specifically to export products into the U.S.—workers earn the equivalent of $25 to $50 a week in an area where a pair of pants costs $15 to $20.

When it comes right down to it, introducing garment factories into a Third World country may help the workers in one way or another, but we shouldn't delude ourselves into thinking it's an act of charity. "Obviously, when you're unemployed, having a job is better than not having one, but I don't think it's right that U.S. companies use the vulnerability of others to their own benefit," says Edna Bonacich. "They can afford to pay much more than they do, and they should. Of course, this is a collective problem. They all have to agree, or be forced, to accept higher standards."

Many consumers seem to like the idea of a share-the-wealth system. "I think if the designers and top executives were willing to take a pay cut, most fashions wouldn't have to rise in price," says Chrissy, a twenty-eight-year-old homemaker in Hazleton, Pennsylvania. "The mark-up on clothes is extremely high—I notice this when there's a sale and clothes are marked to a fraction of what they originally cost. If the stores were really taking a loss, they would've all gone out of business years ago." Clearly, no one is suggesting that a sewing-machine operator in Hong Kong should earn anywhere near the $2.3 million per year The Limited's Leslie Wexner takes home, but bringing them even a few dollars closer would be a huge help. "One has to also look at the juicy compensation packages the top brass in retailing and manufacturing design provide themselves with and wonder, 'How much is enough?' " says Richard Appelbaum. "Could a little of the wealth be redistributed downwards? To a woman making fifty cents an hour in Honduras, a 50 percent increase to seventy-five cents an hour could make a world of difference. Would it really price a Disney sweatshirt out of the market? Couldn't a Disney exec take a slightly smaller increase in pay next year to cover the cost of a few thousand employees getting a twenty-five-cent hourly raise?"

WHAT'S BEING DONE
SELF-SCRUTINY

If you took everything that clothes makers said at face value, you'd think every company was not only doing its best to ensure good labor practices, but that it had actually succeeded in saving the world. In a random peek at fifteen websites of major apparel and athletic-wear retailers, I saw that every one had a section entitled "Social Responsibility," "Human Rights," or some such, presumably to reduce the number of e-mails the manufacturers receive inquiring about their labor practices. In warm, fuzzy corporatespeak, they say things like "We all share a responsibility for improving the world in which we live" (The Limited); "We're passionate about human rights" (Reebok); "Integrity is at the heart of who we are" (Sara Lee). Through their corporate and public affairs departments, companies engage in damage control when negative news hits, such as the discovery of child labor in a Cambodian factory. But they also attempt to get the jump on criticism, providing their own brand of corporate spin.

In October 2001, Nike released its first-ever Corporate Responsibility Report. The fifty-six-page document shocked many labor experts because of the company's openness about accepting some blame: CEO Phil Knight uncharacteristically admitted, "We made mistakes. . . . We deliberated when we should have acted and vice versa." But fessing up to one's sins is only a baby step in the right direction. Six months after the Nike report was released, Oxfam International, a worldwide partnership of agencies working to end poverty, found that workers making Nike products in Indonesia were earning full-time wages of only about $56 a month. Although the country's legal minimum wage had increased that year, the cost of living had also risen, so workers may have been earning more than they had twelve months earlier but they were also spending more for necessities like food and fuel.

In its report, Nike also attempted to debunk the idea that corporations pocket huge profits at workers' expense. Materials account for up to 70 percent of the cost of the average Nike shoe, it said. Plus, the company has to pay for shipping, duties, and insurance, as well as everyday business costs like taxes, design, research, administration, and so on. So the fact that a worker is paid a dollar to make a $100 shoe doesn't necessarily mean that the company's executives are rolling around naked on the other $99. At the same time, big companies aren't exactly losing money for the sake of workers. According to a February 2001 article in *Clariant* magazine, gross margins (how much more a customer pays for a product than it costs the company to make it) for fashion brands are typically in excess of 60 percent. That's quite impressive compared to the gross margins on computers (typically 20 to 25 percent), cell phones (30 to 40 percent), and fast food (20 to 30 percent).

Over at Sara Lee, which manufactures Hanes and other activewear lines in a network of factories in five countries, each of the company's suppliers must sign a contract agreement certifying that they've met the requirements of the company's Global Business Practices, and staffers perform periodic random audits of each facility. "Should questionable behaviors come to light, our production contract agreement would be voided and our production would be moved to another facility," says Duane Hammer, vice president of planning and inventory control at the company. It may be a good policy on paper, but as labor activists have argued, when manufacturers continually pick up and leave, it never really fixes the problem. Relocating may punish the factory's owners, but it also penalizes the workers by leaving them unemployed, until, that is, the next manufacturer—who may pay them even less—comes along.

INDEPENDENT MONITORING

Many companies have attempted to appease labor rights activists by hiring independent monitors to keep tabs on the factories they work with. They can then broadcast the fact that they passed these third-party audits with flying colors. Unfortunately, studies show that these findings aren't immune to manipulation. "There are potentials for conflicts of interest for firms who make money off auditing to deliver audits that keep their clients happy," says MIT's Dara O'Rourke, who has visited several dozen garment factories around the world. "You want to keep clients happy; you want to make sure they continue to hire you. I don't know if that leads to intentional misstatement of fact, or just going a little softer on issues, or occasionally overlooking things or making sure the checklist leaves out the finer details."

In September 2000, O'Rourke published a report funded by the Independent University Initiative questioning the effectiveness of PricewaterhouseCoopers (PwC), the world's largest private monitor of labor and environmental practices. In 1999, PwC performed over six thousand audits of garment factories for companies such as Nike, Disney, Wal-Mart, the Gap, Jones Apparel, and others. O'Rourke tagged along on a number of inspections in China and Korea and caught a whole host of problems that the PwC auditors missed, like overtime violations, lack of protective equipment, falsified payroll records, and hazardous chemical use. O'Rourke found workers spraying clothes with cleaners made from benzene, a known carcinogen, without wearing safety gear. "So they're getting direct exposure to something that will give them cancer at high enough doses," he says. "Those kinds of problems are ones that auditors like PwC often miss because they're not trained to look at these things." Also, O'Rourke found that workers were frequently coached by managers about what to say or threatened that they'd lose their jobs if they told the truth. "Workers aren't stupid," he says. "They know a management consultant is a consultant to the *management*, not to them. They know they're not safe telling them things, so they sometimes censor themselves."

One of the major flaws in the system is that social-auditing firms entered into the situation before they had the trained personnel and general know-how to do the job right. Many of the companies already had financial offices around the world, so they figured, "Hey, look, we've got this office in Shanghai with a bunch of people who speak Chinese, and we can get them there tomorrow to your Disney factory or your Nike factory," says O'Rourke. But auditing a garment factory isn't as simple as sending a financial accountant into a plant with a clipboard and a checklist, which many companies did. "People go to school for years to learn how to do health and safety audits, so you can't expect an accountant, even a really smart accountant, to figure it out in a few minutes," he says.

Even though it's known that independent monitoring has weaknesses, that doesn't stop companies from trumpeting their passing marks. But as O'Rourke explains, "Flawed monitoring can do more harm than good—it can divert attention from the real issues in a factory."

IN SEARCH OF A TELL-TALE SIGN

So let's say that one day the Fashion Victim becomes a truly caring consumer, willing to expend extra energy to dig up the humble history of each and every new garment she buys. As it stands right now, that's not an easy task. In 1998, UCLA freshman Arlen Benjamin set out to trace the origin of a Fruit of the Loom shirt she bought in her campus store. After getting nowhere with phone calls to the company's corporate headquarters, she took a trip to San Pedro Sula, Honduras, with her mother, Medea, a human rights activist. The pair located five factories in the area making Fruit of the Loom products but were turned away from each one. They ended up talking to local union leaders, who finally shared some of the horrors of the Honduran sweatshops with them. Even after their globe-trotting, the Benjamins still got to see only a small portion of the picture . . . imagine how little the average consumer knows.

When respondents in a 1999 Marymount University survey (*The Consumer and Sweatshops*) were asked, "What would most help you avoid buying clothes made in sweatshops?" 56 percent said a fair-labor label would be the most helpful, while 33 percent preferred a list of companies and stores that have been identified as using or tolerating sweatshop labor. But it's often not as easy as singling out certain companies, since labor conditions can vary even within one company, from factory to factory. Many labor rights activists, like Katie Quan of the John F. Henning Center for International Labor Relations, suggest buying only clothes with a union label, under the assumption that unionized workers were probably paid a decent wage. But that requires an effort—something most Fashion Victims aren't willing to exert. Most consumers don't have instant access to union-made clothes at every store they frequent. And the union label may not offer much reassurance, after all. A study showed that three-quarters of UNITE's New York factories are sweatshops by the union's own standards, violating wage, hour, and safety regulations.

So can we ever know if our clothes were sewn under good working conditions? I posed the question one day to Dara O'Rourke. After half-heartedly giving me the obligatory answer that some brands *are* better than others, he paused and conceded, "If you sewed it yourself, you might know."

DOES PRICE INDICATE QUALITY?

Have you ever had the sneaking suspicion that you're getting ripped off, paying more for designer goods simply because they have the name of some arbiter of fashion plastered on them? Many Fashion Victims operate under the illusion that their name-brand merchandise is crafted in designer-owned factories by specially trained, well-paid laborers. Not so, as we've learned from hearing many sweatshop stories. "I think there's not much correlation between the price of a product you would buy at the mall and the likelihood it was made in a good factory," says MIT's Dara O'Rourke.

Many of the priciest luxury fashions do require expert tailoring and would therefore need to be made by more skilled hands. And high-end clothes tend to be more expensive because there are fewer of them in existence. "When you manufacture millions of T-shirts, your costs are lower," says Margie Voelker-Ferrier, coordinator of fashion design at the University of Cincinnati. "When you make a few hundred, the cost per piece goes up tremendously." Higher prices are also indicative of an attitude: a garment simply feels like it's worth more when it costs more. To distance themselves from the knockoff artists who've been stealing their designs and reinterpreting them in cheaper forms for years, the world's elite prêt-à-porter designers have created a new luxury niche some have called demi-couture—ready-to-wear clothes that use more elaborate embroidery and finer fabrics, and that have prohibitively high price tags, a practice meant to appeal to wealthy shoppers' desire for exclusivity (and keep out the gauche poor folks).

A price is also the culmination of a whole chain of events that occurs before an item of clothing makes its way into your closet. Companies incur many expenses to get those clothes into your hands, and you pay for them at the register. When you fork over your credit card to purchase a Ralph Lauren sweater, you're not just paying for an angora scoopneck . . . you're also buying a piece of the entire image that the company has built. Ralph Lauren's Polo line will spend $187 million on advertising and marketing this year. The apparel, footwear, and accessories sector spends about $1.4 billion in advertising each year. Staging and publicizing a single fashion show can cost several million dollars. At the store, prices are inflated yet again to cover the retailer's costs for overhead, advertising, salespeople, and so on. The retail chain Men's Wearhouse spends $50 million a year on TV and radio advertising. When you buy a suit at that store, you're paying a portion of that $50 million bill.

At the same time, when we see bridge lines and other middle-of-the-road designer garb being made in the same garment shops alongside cheaper brands, it raises the question: Does a higher retail price always mean it's better? Voelker-Ferrier says the issue isn't quite so cut and dry. "It isn't about being made 'better,' to a certain degree," she says. "Is a BMW better than a Ford? Yes, there is a difference, to some extent. When you take a micrometer, you find that every connection measures the same; every detail is looked after. In designer clothes, it's the same. The patterns are curvier, fit better, etcetera. Maybe the designer worked with the fit model to get the perfect fit. All those costs must be factored in." O'Rourke isn't so sure. "For those super-high-fashion women's clothes that are produced in France, Italy, and Japan that get up in the thousands of dollars, that may be true, but certainly not in any kind of retail stores that normal people shop at," he says. "The Armani Exchange T-shirt that costs them about a dollar to produce, they sell for $120. It's not at all about the cost or quality of that T-shirt—it's the exact same quality as the one down the street for $8—it's about the brand."

. . .

Sweatshops aren't the only dark cloud in the history of garment making. Just as consumers are oblivious to injustice on the path their clothes take from sweatshop to store, they're also blissfully unaware of the killings and corruption that have taken place for nearly a century in what used to be the hub of garment making: New York City.

THE MOB TAKES MANHATTAN

In 2001, the gangster played muse to many a designer. In January, the mob ruled at Yohji Yamamoto's menswear show in Paris—models flaunted the designer's fall wares for wiseguy wannabes, like charcoal suits in thick wool, eight-button tweed coats, and caps straight out of *The Godfather, Part II*. In February, New York designer Mark Montano enticed audience members to his "Gangster Girl" show with clever invitations written in newsprint font to resemble the FBI's Ten Most Wanted list. The collection included such mob-influenced creations as the "Hands Up" coat, "Back Stabber" dress, "Gangsta" pantsuit in fuchsia plaid wool, and the crowd favorite—the "Bullet Hole" dress, a breezy frock that had actually been shot through at the gun range. Then a month later, Italian designer Gai Mattiolo sent models down the catwalk at his Milan show in mafioso chalk-striped suits, sumptuous fur coats, and black trousers.

The irony of the dapper don–themed garb in 2001—and in nearly every prior year—was that the Mob's influence has run deep throughout the apparel industry's history. And the corruption hasn't been restricted to the distant past. On April 5, 2001, a month after Mattiolo's swanky Italian show, a jury in federal district court found Anthony Spero, purported consigliere of the Bonanno crime family, guilty of ordering four gangland hits in Brooklyn and running an eight-year loan-sharking conspiracy during the early 1990s. It's estimated that New York rag traders were being squeezed as much as $4 per hanger by the Bonanno family to transport a truckload of garments, often no farther than a few city blocks. Today, with independent operators free to operate without fear of Mob retaliation, the going rate is under 25¢, just 17¢ at New York's All Star Trucking.

Mob rule over the garment trade has been a crime epic that has spanned the industry's entire existence. Beginning during Prohibition and extending into the 1990s, La Cosa Nostra—purportedly made up of five crime families in New York City (Bonanno, Colombo, Genovese, Gambino, and Lucchese)—schemed, swindled, and terrorized business owners and individuals out of billions of dollars. Hundreds of millions of those dollars came from the garment industry alone, an expense that has ultimately been paid by you, the average consumer. How could such atrocities occur? It was frighteningly easy.

UNION CORRUPTION

In the 1920s, garment making was the gangsta rap of manufacturing: a profitable industry with a dark side rooted in violence. Just as a few infamous hip-hop moguls muscled their way into power in the music industry in the early 1990s, shady Mob figures utilized intimidation, sabotage, and violence to control businesses in New York's Garment District. But as wealthy as a few rappers became, with their diamond-studded Rolexes, their Bentleys, and $500 bottles of Cristal, the garment racket of the 1920s was far more lucrative—and dangerous—work.

The first true Garment Center Mob boss was Louis "Lepke" Buchalter, whom FBI director J. Edgar Hoover would tag the "most dangerous criminal in the U.S." in 1939. In the 1920s, Lepke and his partner Jacob "Gurrah" Shapiro became known as the Gold Dust Twins thanks to their Midas touch. Unions and other trade groups would hire Lepke and Gurrah to do their dirty work. This corruption was integral to Lepke's rise to power and vice versa. As labor investigator Michael Moroney, former consultant to the federal Organized Crime Strike Force, says, mobsters in the 1930s didn't simply infiltrate unions; they established them. "The five crime families of New York are the foundation of American trade unions," says Moroney. "Without the support of the Mafia, and government officials who have winked at them, most unions simply would not exist."

For years, according to Burt Turkus, former Brooklyn assistant DA and coauthor of the mob book *Murder Inc.*, Lepke and his partner, using threats of labor strikes, violence, or sabotage, shook down manufacturers and trucking bosses for anywhere from $5,000 to $50,000 apiece—still a lot of money today, but a fortune back in those days. Noncompliant shop owners had to fear beatings, bombings, arson, kidnappings, and other perils at the hands of the Twins. In 1933, J. Joseph, an importer of rabbit fur who had been doing business with a non-Mob shop, had acid thrown in his face as he sat on a bench outside his home. Going to the police wasn't an option—if the cops weren't in Lepke's pocket, they generally didn't care about the lowly rag traders, who were mostly lower-class immigrants.

It's been officially estimated that Lepke extorted anywhere from $5 million to $10 million dollars from the garment trade every year during the 1930s. In today's money, that would have totaled over half a billion dollars. During the 1920s, according to *Murder Inc.*, more than 60 percent of the clothing worn in the U.S. came from the New York region. Therefore, it's likely that three out of every five garments bought in that time period had come from a company being shaken down by Lepke.

The FBI began inquiring into the racketeering tactics of the Gold Dust Twins in 1932. It was estimated that Lepke himself ordered the murder of at least seventy men in his career, and many other orders were issued by men under his control. Shortly after he surrendered on August 24, 1939, Lepke was sentenced to prison on antitrust and narcotics charges. He was later tried and convicted on a state charge of murder. On March 2, 1944, his belly filled with roast chicken, shoestring potatoes, and salad, Louis Lepke Buchalter died in the electric chair at Sing Sing prison.

Still, the boss's death didn't bring about the end of union corruption. According to Bob Fitch, author of *The Assassination of New York*, it has continued right up to the present day. In 1997, the Department of Labor's Office of Labor Racketeering charged the garment union with running a Garment Center labor-peace racket in tandem with the Gambino and Lucchese crime families.

LOAN SHARKING

Lepke left another legacy from the 1920s. Twice a year, garment makers were at the mercy of buyers. Representatives from stores around the country would come to check out the Garment Center's wares to stock their stores for the season. There was no limit to the courting of buyers with sex, drugs, liquor, bribes, anything that might sway them, according to Ernest Volkman's 1998 book *Gangbusters*. Because of Prohibition, alcohol was the bribe of choice. Lepke's friend Lucky Luciano hooked him up with fellow criminal Thomas Lucchese, who soon began providing the Gold Dust Twins with cases upon cases of the finest imported whiskey for use as enticements. Lepke and Lucchese became close friends and were soon brainstorming to come up with new misdeeds. They happened upon an idea, unique to the garment trade, that would change the face of crime in New York City for decades to come: loan sharking.

Clothes makers needed large amounts of short-term capital to pay for labor and materials in order to have their goods ready for the biannual visits from buyers. This was risky. If a style failed, the manufacturer might not be able to pay back a loan. So banks generally steered clear of the industry, but shop owners had nowhere else to turn. Then Lucchese came up with a proposal: he'd loan them $50,000 for twenty weeks at a weekly interest rate of $2,500. The mobster would double his money; the shop owner would get his clothes made, collect money from buyers, and pay back the loan. If payments couldn't be met, Lucchese would offer another option: he'd wipe away the debt and assume ownership of part of the company instead. The deal may have seemed unfair to some entrepreneurs but certainly topped the alternative—paying in pain. Reports indicate that he owned at least seven shops outright. Lucchese had brilliantly used criminal tactics to create the illusion that he was a legitimate businessman. In the late fifties, when Robert F. Kennedy subpoenaed Lucchese before the Senate Labor Rackets Committee, the mobster declared, "I am a dress manufacturer," then took the Fifth Amendment to Kennedy's next eighty-seven questions.

Lucchese died of a brain tumor in 1967. After a lifetime of crime, his only criminal conviction was for an auto theft he'd committed in the early 1920s.

TRUCKING

Like Lepke's legacy of corruption, Lucchese also left something for posterity: trucking. During his reign, Lucchese had gained control of the Garment Center's trucking outfits by striking deals with corrupt Teamsters Union locals. "He could charge whatever he wanted for trucking services," writes Volkman in *Gangbusters*. "Because a squad of goons made sure no competing trucking outfit entered the Garment Center, there was no alternative." When Lucchese died, he transferred his power in the Garment Center to his son-in-law Thomas Gambino, who just happened to be the eldest son of his friend, legendary mob boss Carlo Gambino.

Using violence and intimidation, the Gambinos extended their control of trucking from the Garment District manufacturers to the sewing shops in Chinatown and maintained their stranglehold for thirty years. The family seized ownership of the district's most important trucking company, Consolidated Carriers Corporation, and acquired interests in other businesses. Its seven directly controlled firms grossed an estimated $40 million a year, and about $12 million in net profit. By the mid-1980s, the mob operated an astounding 90 percent of the trucks that serviced the garment district, according to a 2001 article in *City Journal*.

On a daily basis, the mob's presence was hard to ignore. But it was particularly difficult on those unlucky days when business owners had to face their oppressors. In the early 1990s, a production manager for New York designer Nicole Miller testified that once, when he tried to use a small non-Mob trucker, trench-coated goons showed up and stood around menacingly, hands in pockets, until the frightened independent operator fled. Shop owners and workers seethed over the authorities' lack of control over the situation. In a 1977 series of investigative reports entitled "The Mafia: Seventh Avenue's Silent Partner," *Women's Wear Daily* reported that "Cosa Nostra, our thing, could call New York's multibillion-dollar clothing industry their thing, because just about every piece of clothing made there is touched by the hands or the money or the influence of organized crime." It wasn't like deals were being made in dark alleyways and seedy strip clubs à la *The Sopranos*. According to *WWD*, local garment manufacturers and union officials were so brazen as to sit down with gangsters in the discreet darkness of fashionable restaurants or busy bars and cocktail lounges and amiably discuss the day's business trials and tribulations.

District kingpin Thomas Gambino, honored as the garment industry's Man of the Year at a 1981 dinner at the Plaza Hotel, benefited personally in a big way. By 1992, investigators estimated his personal wealth at $75 million. Meanwhile, however, the garment industry suffered. As vicious stories of violence and sabotage became more frequent, businesses increasingly fled. The mob had crushed a once-burgeoning trade. The mob tax levied on the rag traders was passed on to the consumer in the form of higher prices. Authorities estimated the price tag for Mob control was 7 percent on each Gambino-trucked item. Consumers would pay an extra $15 for a $200 shirt, money that would go directly into the Gambinos' pockets, tax free.

Finally, in 1989, after bugging the Gambino family offices, Manhattan DA Robert Morgenthau caught Thomas and his brother Joseph Gambino talking about their mob-owned trucking firms on tape. They were arrested in late 1990. Morgenthau reached an innovative deal with them: in exchange for not going to jail, they agreed to get out of the business and pay $12 million to fund a special monitor to oversee the industry for five years and sell off mobbed-up companies. The arrangement transformed the industry. It took almost two years for shop owners in the area to believe that the Mob was really gone and that they could sign up with new truckers without fearing reprisal. Soon, some seventy-five independent truckers flooded into the district. The cost of shipping plummeted.

UNTOUCHABLE

Even with all the convictions, the deals, and the bad publicity, both Mob and non-Mob corruption didn't vanish completely from the Garment Center. Some crime families have disappeared entirely, and others have shrunk 50 to 90 percent from their size thirty years ago, says James O. Finckenauer, Ph.D., director of the International Center at the National Institute of Justice. Still, as of 2001, the estimated "made" membership of La Cosa Nostra is eleven hundred nationwide, with roughly 80 percent of the members operating in the New York metropolitan area (made men, or "soldiers," make up the main crews). In addition to the made members, there are approximately ten thousand associate members who work for the families, says Finckenauer.

The mob's involvement in the garment industry was weakened when the Gambinos were brought down, but some activities continued. In 1993, two Paterson, New Jersey, brothers, Joseph and Raymond LaBarck, who headed a 1,200-member local of the Amalgamated Clothing and Textile Workers union, were convicted of operating a seven-year racketeering scheme based on threats and violence and accepting more than $400,000 in bribes from employers to ensure labor peace. Three years later, Joseph Iannaci, a Colombo family representative on the payroll of the Greater Blouse and Skirt union was charged with shaking down the group for nearly half a million dollars from 1989 to 1995. In 1998, the FBI indicted twelve Garment Center mobsters, including the Lucchese family's acting boss, Joseph Defede, for racketeering and extortion. That December, Defede pleaded guilty to extorting hundreds of thousands of dollars from Garment Center businessmen.

For nearly a century, the losses incurred by businesspeople in the garment industry at the hands of the Mob were passed along to the public in the form of inflated prices. Even today, consumers continue to feel the aftershock. We pay, not only in higher prices, but also in the sad reality that the American garment-manufacturing industry could have been one of the strongest in the world but has instead consistently deteriorated over the decades. In a 1997 report, New York City mayor Rudolph Giuliani wrote, "The mob tax inflated prices for every-one, lowered the quality of goods and services, and forced too many honest people to live in fear. The perception and reality of this prob-lem provided yet another reason for businesses and investors—and jobs—to stay away from New York City." The corrupt, violent reputa-tion of the garment-making industry scared off many businesspeople and deterred others from even entering the trade. The industry never had a chance to grow.

8

Wear and Tear

Il faut suffrir pour être belle.
>*—French saying meaning "One must suffer to be beautiful"*

Oww!
>*—James Brown, "I Feel Good"*

"It was the middle of September in 1927—the year Charles Lindbergh crossed the Atlantic, the year of the first electronic television transmission—and Isadora Duncan had her sights on a hot little sports car . . . and its owner, Benoit Falchetto, a young stud who had caught her eye one night while she was dining out with friends. The fifty-year-old American dancer, who some today call the pioneer of modern dance, convinced the "Greek god" Falchetto, a man nearly half her age, to take her out for a test ride one night along the Promenade des Anglais in Nice, France.

Isadora was known for her slightly eccentric, but always chic, fashion sense. On stage, her penchant for dancing barefoot in revealing costumes (at least by the standards of the day) frequently shocked her high-society audiences in London and Paris. She was a known fashion plate, "alternating loose classical robes with designer gowns— Poiret, Soeurs Caillot, Lucile," says Peter Kurth, author of *Isadora: A Sensational Life*. Paul Poiret, the era's enfant terrible, made her a special outfit when she went to Bolshevik Russia in 1921. Playwright George Bernard Shaw, who met her in 1918, later recalled that she was "clothed in draperies" and that her "face looked as if it had been made of sugar and someone had licked it . . . rather like a piece of battered confectionery."

On the night of Isadora's ride with Falchetto, a breezy September 14, the dancer dressed in her customarily chic manner, wrapping a six-foot-long red silk scarf twice around her neck and letting it drape across her left shoulder. Her friend Mary Desti pleaded with her, "Isadora, please put on my black cape, it's quite cold."

"No, no, my dear, nothing but my red-painted shawl," she replied.

Falchetto, also suspecting that his driving companion's shawl wouldn't keep her sufficiently warm on such a brisk night, and in a convertible no less, offered her his leather jacket. But Isadora simply threw her long scarf around her throat, shook her head no, and waved back to her friends, crying, "*Adieu, mes amis! Je vais à la gloire!*" ("Goodbye, my friends! I go to glory!") Falchetto stepped on the gas. As the car rolled forward, Isadora's flowing scarf flew back and its eighteen-inch tassels caught in the spokes of the rear wheel, winding around it like a spool of thread. The force broke her neck and severed her jugular vein. She was killed instantly.

Decades later, the death of Isadora Duncan is still the subject of much curiosity among hobbyist investigators, who devote entire websites to the discussion of the case's details, right down to arguing over precise specifications of the car. (Six-cylinder or four-cylinder? Did it have mudguards? Was it a Bugatti or an Amilcar?) The demise of the great dancer and consummate Fashion Victim was a freak accident for sure, but it brings up an interesting point about our fixation on dress: Had Isadora not put style first, would she have lived to see another day?

FASHION HURTS

Random accidents, like the one Isadora fell victim to, are bound to happen. After all, we live in a world in which thousands of emergency-room visits each year are blamed on sponges and loofahs (mull *that* one over for a minute). In 2001, the long feather on an *Italian Vogue* fashion editor's hat caught fire on a candle at a dinner party, incinerating the entire chapeau in front of her fellow guests. In 1991, a forty-year-old Boston woman was fatally injured when her clothes got caught in an escalator. According to Britain's Home Accident Surveillance System, trousers account for nearly six thousand falls each year, and slipper-related accidents send about twenty-seven thousand people to the emergency room annually in that country. Certainly, in a world where anything can happen—lightning or an errant tree branch could strike at any moment, and don't forget those treacherous loofahs—clothing accidents are relatively unpredictable. But there are other risks that Fashion Victims take on . . . often knowingly. We're otherwise intelligent people, yet when it comes to fashion, all sensibility flies out the window.

For centuries, people of various cultures have endured pain and tolerated risk for the sake of fashion, from the bound feet of Chinese women to the neck-stretching rings of Burma's Padaung tribe to the massive horse-hair petticoats of Queen Victoria's time to the toe-pinching stilettos of today. Westerners act flabbergasted at the sight of a native tribesman with a six-inch shard of ivory poked through his nose, but are the customs we use to signify our membership in a given group any less weird?

Discomfort is all relative, and what we are willing to put up with changes from one period to another. In the mid-1990s, it was still uncommon for American women to wear thong underwear. In 1998, the year an editor at *Glamour* wrote a short article about her first thong, the revealing panties were still widely considered something that only strippers and European women wore—certainly not something comfortable enough to be appropriate for everyday wear. But consumers came around, and by today millions of women have learned to tolerate perma-wedgie as a trade-off for getting rid of panty lines.

Likewise, during times when baggy pants are in fashion, we laugh at the days of uncomfortably tight jeans. But check back in a few years when those restrictive styles are back in vogue, and the same people will be singing a different tune—no doubt in a soprano voice. Tattoos used to be something that only sailors and bikers got, but once body art came into vogue, models, actresses, and fashionistas were rushing under the needle to get little butterflies, flowers, and tribal lines etched into their skin. And modern-day women scoff at the idea of mashing their bodies into corsets, yet they'll endure blisters, corns, bunions, and sore arches to look good in strappy high-heeled sling-backs.

After a while, we grow accustomed to the pain, and even forget that it's there. My boyfriend and I went for a walk in Central Park one Sunday morning with two friends of ours, Alex and Myra. The first thing I noticed were Myra's three-inch-high straw platforms. Every half hour or so, one of us would ask her, "Are you sure your feet are okay?" and, being a true fashion trooper, she'd reply, "Oh, yeah, I walk in these things all the time." After two full hours of walking, *my* feet were aching a bit, and I was wearing sneakers. Maybe Myra had the toughest soles in town; perhaps she had conditioned herself to endure discomfort in her feet in the same way that kung fu masters train themselves to tolerate pain in their hands. Maybe her feet were naturally impervious to pain. More likely, they did hurt and she just didn't say anything. But who hasn't done something similar? When I go out with friends during the winter months, I typically wear sleeveless dresses, halters, and tanks—essentially the same things I would wear if it were eighty-five degrees out (I do cave in and wear closed-toe shoes, however). Meanwhile, other people are bundled up in wool turtlenecks and sweater coats. And whenever anyone asks "Aren't you going to be cold?" like Myra, I shake off their concern. In Hollywood, underdressing in chilly weather is par for the course. Just check out the red carpet at the Golden Globes in January or at any movie premiere scheduled in winter—the actresses still schmooze the media line, teeth chattering because they insisted on wearing sleeveless, backless numbers with slits that require Brazilian waxes. Dressing sexy at the risk of catching a cold seems worth it at times like these. But trade-offs like this aren't restricted to special events. The Fashion Victim goes through a similar process of weighing pros and cons whenever she gets dressed.

In the nineteenth century, physical pain equaled visual pleasure. The circumference of a skirt, the elevation of a wig, the tightness of a corset, the height of a heel—the more extreme they were, the more they signaled to others that their wearer was part of the fashionable upper class. Then, in the latter part of the century, growing numbers of women became more physically active in everyday life and began playing sports as well, a difficult undertaking thanks to the fashions of the time. The reformers of the Rational Dress Movement fought for more sensible styles that wouldn't increase a woman's danger of falling while skating or of taking an embarrassing tumble from her bicycle. In 1868, Rational Dress supporter Ellen Gould White wrote, "A bad circulation leaves the blood to become impure, and induces congestion of the brain and lungs, and causes diseases of the head, the heart, the liver, and the lungs. The fashionable style of woman's dress is one of the greatest causes of all these terrible diseases."

Fashion has historically been blamed for an array of health problems. One of the most vilified articles of clothing is the corset. In the film *Moulin Rouge*, each of Nicole Kidman's intricate, wasp-waisted outfits took thirty minutes—and help from assistants on the set—to lace up. Before filming Kidman broke a rib during dance practice, then broke it again getting fitted for a particularly tight corset. "I stood there and I remember just, sort of, the blood draining from my face [and] thinking, gosh this doesn't feel right," she recounted. During one interview, the poor corseted actress grabbed her side and squeaked out a constricted giggle to the reporter, saying, "I can't laugh!" And this was just for a movie. How could anyone have tolerated the pain of such bone-crushing garments on a daily basis?

The first corsets date back to the first half of the sixteenth century, when aristocratic women began wearing what they called "whalebone bodies," because many of the early varieties were literally made of bone. At first, they were limited to upper-class women and girls, but they eventually trickled down to women of the middle and lower classes, who wore less ornate versions. In the late nineteenth century, the popularity of the corset caused a massive medical backlash. *The*

Lancet published more than one article a year from the late 1860s to the early 1890s on the dangers of tight lacing. At the time, corsets were blamed for everything from tuberculosis to hysteria to breast cancer, although it's now believed that the most likely physical side effects were fainting, atrophy of back and abdominal muscles, and deformed ribs. "Corsets were blamed for a good deal of ailments that doctors at the time didn't know the cause of and it was easy to use the corset as a scapegoat," says Isabella, a custom corset maker in California. "Yes, they do manipulate the bone structure when worn from early adolescence on, but not when corset wearing starts later in life, which is basically how they are worn now. And they don't alter the body much at all when only worn on occasion." The corset comes back into fashion every once in a while, and a small population of fans, like Isabella, continues to wear them all the time. She admits that there is one drawback: she has to watch what she eats, and not just to maintain her weight. "Anything that makes you bloated in the least will quickly make the corset uncomfortable," says Isabella. "Small portions are a must."

Admittedly, fashion has also been the target of unfair attacks down through the years, drawing criticism not only from doctors and scientists but also from religious and reformist groups attempting to promote modesty by portraying purportedly impious trends as unhealthy. Some Rational Dress campaigners attacked the corset on medical grounds, not because they had actual scientific proof but because they thought the push-up/pull-in garment was a profane item of clothing that would surely lead women down the road to promiscuity. Similarly, in Swaziland, a country where at least a quarter of its one million people are infected with HIV, government officials blamed the miniskirt for causing the country's AIDS epidemic. The country had prohibited all miniskirts for morality reasons in 1969, until authorities realized the law was unenforceable among the general public. And then the government managed to ban short skirts again in schools in 2000.

THE CRAZY THINGS WE DO

Why do we subject our bodies to such torture? "Vanity, vanity, vanity," says Beverley Jackson, author of *Splendid Slippers*, a book about

Chinese foot-binding that described the tiny slippers women would wear over their deformed feet. Some theorists attribute our tolerance for fashion-inflicted pain to our innate desire to charm the opposite sex, much like the peacock showing off his brightly colored feathers to woo potential mates. But our willingness to squeeze, contort, tighten, push up, lift, and separate, and to tolerate general discomfort for the sake of fashion goes beyond mating. After all, we're creatures with rampant egos who have plenty of *other* people to impress with our dress. We tend to dress more comfortably when lounging alone (we know we don't need to impress our cats and goldfish) and put up with uncomfortable clothing more often when we dress to impress—stiff collars for a black-tie event, four-inch stilettos for a birthday party, control-top panty hose for an important conference. And the boost in self-esteem we get from knowing we look good when we're around others is enough to keep us going. "As we say in the biz, 'Beauty is pain'—half joke, half truth," says Penni, twenty-nine, a television production coordinator in L.A. "When I look good, I carry an air of confidence around me. There's nothing like receiving compliments on how you look. It just confirms that all the hard work we go through to look good is worth it."

As much as we want to stand out from a crowd, we also tolerate pain to fit in. It's human nature to follow the herd. Even the most painful and seemingly grotesque practices can become fashionable if they're adopted by the right people early on. That's just what happened with Chinese women hundreds of years ago. Legend has it that the most desirable concubine in a particular prince's court would dance seductively on her toes, with ribbons binding her feet. The practice caught on among the other concubines, then eventually breached the palace walls and spread throughout the country. Soon, mothers all over China were breaking their daughters' feet, fracturing the arch as if to make the toes touch the sole of the foot, and confining them to life as beautiful cripples. The practice, which essentially began as a bizarre fashion trend, continued until the early twentieth century.

Girls in China whose feet were bound often didn't have a say in the matter. We, on the other hand, have control over what we do to ourselves, but the drive to be fashionable is so strong that it can make us abandon our own common sense. Our desire to overstuff our closets with trendy clothing has created a situation in which we're compromising not only our comfort but also our health and safety, from crippling high heels to the toxic chemicals that are used to make and clean our overabundance of clothes. Our hunger for fashion also affects our health in less direct ways—through the environment. Nearly one-quarter of all pesticides used in the U.S. are applied to cotton, according to the Sierra Club. More of these chemicals are sprayed on cotton than on any other crop. Petroleum-based synthetic fibers like nylon and polyester create air pollution and take generations to degrade in landfills. The United States–Asia Environmental Partnership (US-AEP) reports that the textile industry uses 133 billion gallons of water each year, discards 237 million pounds of knit fabric (of which about 65 percent is recycled), and discharges 30 percent of its reactive dyes into wastewater. The apparel industry in New York City alone generates about 384,000 tons of waste per year, according to the department of sanitation.

There are surprisingly many ways in which our clothes can physically harm us. Here are a few of the biggies.

SHOES

Rebecca, a twenty-one-year-old dance teacher in Yreka, California, wore a pair of new white sandals, open at the toe and in the back, while she was traveling in Japan—a sightseeing visit that required a lot of walking. "By the time I got home, I had blisters and my feet were bleeding from the sandals," she recalls. She could have stopped at any number of stores along the way to pick up a pair of comfy slippers or walking shoes, but decided to stick it out. "I had spent about $50 for those shoes because they were really cute and I thought they'd go perfectly with my white shorts," says Rebecca. "Instead, I got blisters and a bloody mess."

The Fashion Victim is willing to put up with all sorts of pain for the sake of fashion. In a 2001 survey of 1,724 women by the American

Academy of Orthopaedic Surgeons (AAOS), 74 percent of respondents reported that they wore high heels; 80 percent said their feet hurt. The survey also found that, for either fashion or career reasons, 59 percent admitted to wearing uncomfortable, even painful, shoes for at least an hour each day. The AAOS estimates that foot problems cost the U.S. about $3.5 billion a year, and that 75 percent of these problems are caused by ill-fitting shoes.

Shoes are dangerous, and we're not just talking about those $500 titanium-heeled sandals with razor-sharp $3^{1}/_{2}$-inch "killer" heels that Manolo Blahnik removed from his collection in 2001 for fear of causing security problems at airports. Horror stories aren't hard to come by. "I've seen loads of toenails that have gone black from too-tight shoes and had to be removed because they were flapping off, usually from a shopping spree in inappropriate footwear," says Leah Claydon, D.P.M., a podiatrist in Melbourn, Great Britain. "I've seen thousands of corns that can only be caused by too-tight high-heeled shoes, and in one extreme case, a corn on a little toe had become infected, which led to a bone infection and amputation of the toe, and it nearly cost the woman her life."

For people who wear high heels more than a few times a week, the pain frequently goes beyond short-term problems like blisters and sore arches, says Claydon. They'll typically notice that it becomes very hard to walk barefoot without getting pain in their calves. "This is because the steep angle raising the heel slackens the Achilles tendon," she says. "Over time, the tendon shortens, making it very difficult to put the heel to the floor when barefoot—the only way you can achieve it is by pronating the foot [rolling it inward]. This in turn internally rotates the knee and hip, which in turn tips the pelvis forward, throwing the person's body weight in front of the body and increasing the lumbar curvature of the spine—imagine what damage that does!"

It's not just skinny spikes that cause trouble. In 2001, a team of Harvard researchers found that a wider heel may be better for feet, but it tends to be harder on the knees. Both wide and skinny heels increase the force placed on the knee joint, explains head researcher Casey D. Kerrigan, M.D., associate professor of physical medicine and rehabilitation at Harvard Medical School. "The reason that wide heels cause slightly higher torques [more twisting] is probably that greater body force is transmitted through the heel with the wider heel." Also, women tend to think that wider heels are less harmful, so they typically wear them for longer periods of time. Ultimately, this can cause osteoarthritis of the knee. If you wear heels throughout your twenties, you might not feel the effects for many years. "Wearing high heels probably has a cumulative effect over many years, and women typically get knee osteoarthritis in their sixties," says Kerrigan.

Shoes can even be an occupational hazard. Remember when supermodel Naomi Campbell famously tripped wearing Vivienne Westwood's eight-inch turquoise "mock-croc" platforms in the designer's 1993 Paris fashion show? The poor diva was so frazzled when she had to wear sky-high platforms at a later show that she hid, trembling, behind a pile of clothes. During the March 2002 Gucci show in Milan, British model Michelle DeSwarte fell to the catwalk when her ankles gave way atop a pair of four-inch heels. She picked herself up but fell again and continued on bare feet. Later that evening, at the Versus show, she was informed by the show's stylist that if she couldn't manage the high heels, she would be pulled from the show. This time, she managed to stay upright. In 1997, Emma "Baby Spice" Bunton tumbled from four-inch-high platforms and sprained her ankle and wrist while filming a TV show in Turkey.

In February 2000, a group of Nevada waitresses organized a campaign called Kiss My Feet to fight against the policy many casinos have in place dictating that waitresses have to wear at least a 2½-inch heel. For twenty-one years, Wanda Henry was a Las Vegas cocktail waitress and wore high heels much of that time. "Waitresses sometimes go home with blood in their shoes," Henry told the *Las Vegas Sun*. After hearing so many complaints from waitresses, Senator Maggie Carlton of Las Vegas introduced a bill that would prohibit an employer from disciplining or discriminating against a worker with a "medical condition" that keeps her from complying with the business's dress code. In March 2001, the notoriously fashionable Singapore Airlines announced that its female flight attendants would have to change from sandals to designer shoes (sling-backs with a chrome buckle and ankle straps designed by Pierre Balmain) during takeoffs and landings as a

safety precaution, after one of the airline's planes crashed in Taipei
and flight attendants who survived the crash said their standard-issue
open-toed sandals flew off their feet, leaving them to walk barefoot
through debris. Then in January 2002, a former flight attendant sued
Singapore Airlines (they have an awful lot of shoe problems, don't
they?) for $100,000, claiming the dainty sandals she was forced to
wear squeezed her toes together. The damage to her feet, she said,
required two operations to fix.

The platform shoe craze that swept through Japan from the late
1990s to the early 2000s brought with it numerous embarrassing accidents and even a handful of deaths. In August 1998, after hearing
about a student who tumbled down a flight of stairs while wearing platform shoes, Professor Teruko Ishii of Aoba Gakuen Junior College in
Tokyo, who studies clothing-related issues, was prompted to survey
the entire student population of over 540. Twenty-three percent of all
students said they had fallen over while wearing platforms. Of these,
almost half had been injured as a result of their fall, and three of them
had even broken bones. In 1999, a twenty-five-year-old nursery
school teacher fell while wearing her five-inch stacks; she cracked her
head on the sidewalk and died. Also that year, a twenty-year-old
female driver hit a thirteen-year-old girl on a bicycle because her
platform shoes prevented her from braking properly. In March 2000,
a nineteen-year-old girl was killed when she crashed her car into a
utility pole, an accident police blamed on her inability to hit the brakes
quickly enough because she was wearing six-inch-high platform
shoes. Later that year, a thirty-year-old woman crashed into an eight-
year-old boy at a pedestrian crossing, killing him, because her platform shoes prevented her from driving properly. The wave of injuries
and deaths caused local authorities in Osaka to prohibit motorists
from getting behind the wheel when wearing platform shoes—driving
while under the influence of fashion.

Although any mishaps that occurred would surely be considered
the wearer's fault, since common sense should clue a sensible person
in to the fact that the shoes are risky, Japanese platform-shoe manufacturers began to worry that the rising number of injuries could lead
to lawsuits, so they began attaching warning labels to the shoes. One

company's label read: "Because the heels of the shoes are high, please be careful when you run or go up and down the stairs. Be especially careful when you drink because you can be wobbly. We, the producers, will be very happy if you keep these points in mind when you enjoy the trendy fashion."

Still, a little pain and peril aren't enough to reform the glutton for podiatric punishment. Beth, a twenty-seven-year-old fashion editor in New York City, owns three pairs of skinny-heeled Jimmy Choo boots. "They're so amazing-looking, but they're three inches high and not at all comfortable," she says. One time, she made the faux pas of wearing them to a friend's wedding, where she was a bridesmaid. "That was the biggest mistake because, as part of the wedding party, you're expected to trek to distant lands to take pictures," she says. "By the time dinner started, the boots were off and I was barefoot." The fact that her feet had swelled and ached for days afterward didn't stop her from wearing the boots again, or from remaining a devoted Choo lover. "The shape of the Jimmy Choo heel is just perfection," she says. "It's so sleek and sexy at the same time. It makes everyone's foot look truly amazing." And that's the key: beauty prevails over comfort for the Fashion Victim.

Even doctors themselves admit to wearing high heels every now and then. "It's about feeling sexy," says Dr. Claydon, who wears them when she goes out after work. "Everyone feels slinkier in high heels: it alters the gait to enhance that Marilyn Monroe walk, high heels make your legs look longer, contract the calf muscle, giving definition, and make your ankles look slimmer and your feet look daintier." If a medical doctor—who has received more negative reinforcement than the average woman, thanks to the horrors she's seen in her practice—can't resist the lure of cute, uncomfortable shoes, how do the rest of us stand a chance?

TIGHT CLOTHING

For a friend's summer wedding one year, I bought a strapless, baby-blue Tocca dress in a size 2, probably a size too small for me, but it looked chicly snug in all the right places—when I stood up, that is.

Sitting down was another matter altogether. After about an hour at the reception, my ribs started feeling compressed, as if someone had been gradually tightening a vise around my midsection. I couldn't dance or sit. I could barely eat (even the smallest morsel of prime rib would stretch the limits of the dress). I received numerous compliments on the dress that day, including one from a woman who approached me near the oyster table to tell me that her husband couldn't take his eyes off me (was this a good or bad thing to be hearing?). But by the end of the night, when I unpeeled myself from the constricting frock, my entire torso aching, I wondered if it was worth it—okay, I wondered for about two seconds and came to the conclusion that, yes, it was. It was more important to me to look good than it was to feel comfortable. I squeezed into the dress for another wedding a few months later.

Why are we willing to put up with this? Unlike high heels, which are inherently flattering since they lengthen the look of the leg, the appeal of tight clothes depends on the rise and fall of trends. Just think about those supertight acid-washed jeans of the eighties: it wasn't an intrinsically flattering style, but people wore them because they were in at the time. It goes to show how Fashion Victims can fall for the most uncomfortable trends, like skintight jeans or constricting corsets. And months and years after the trend dies, we will puzzle over how we could trade free breathing and comfort for style.

But besides the constricted breathing and achy muscles and joints we expect to get from sucking in our tummies, other side effects can arise from wearing tight clothes, including digestive troubles. In 1999, Dr. Octavio Bessa, a physician in Stamford, Connecticut, noticed a curious coincidence among a group of his male patients who constantly complained of stomach problems, including heartburn and distension. Though they seemed to be in good health, all wore trousers at least two inches too small for their waists. When they switched to baggier pants, the pain disappeared. In the UK, William Dickey of Altnagelvin Hospital in Londonderry coined the term "designer dyspepsia" to describe problems caused by our modern-day fondness for restrictive "hold-in underwear," which he says has led to "a massive increase in cases of dyspepsia—the build-up of gas bubbles produced

as part of the normal digestive process which the body cannot release."
Imagine yourself nibbling on shrimp cocktail at a dinner party only to
spend the rest of the night with a talkative belly because your pants are
too tight. Not pleasant.

In addition to those bothersome digestive maladies, tight clothing
can also block blood flow, which can cause a number of vascular problems. Tight-waisted clothes create what Manhattan vascular specialist
Ken Biegeleisen, M.D., refers to as the "tourniquet effect." "If a stocking pressed harder at the top than at the bottom, it would be sort of like
tying a tourniquet around the thigh, which would cut off circulation,"
he says. Wearing pants with a tight waist could do the same thing, not
letting blood properly flow upward from the legs. "Veins carry 'old'
blood—blood that has already delivered its oxygen and is trying to go
back to the lungs for more," he explains. "Good valve function is essential if the 'old' blood is to move up the legs, against gravity, and return
to the lungs." When blood flow is blocked, it can pool in the veins and
cause varicose veins—stretched-out, dilated leg veins with poor valvu-
lar function, which can become swollen and painful, not to mention
unsightly—in people who are genetically predisposed.

Over the years, scientists have also attempted to establish causal
relationships between tight clothes and other, more serious diseases.
In their controversial 1995 book *Dressed to Kill*, medical anthropologists Sydney and Soma Singer blamed bras for causing breast cancer,
claiming that compression constricts the lymphatic system, the
body's natural means of ridding itself of toxins. Then in 1999, C. J.
Dickinson, professor emeritus at Wolfson Institute of Preventive
Medicine, theorized that tight clothing could cause endometriosis, a
painful condition that strikes about 5.5 million American women, and
one of the top three causes of female infertility. The endometrium, the
tissue like that which lines the uterus, develops into small, usually
benign growths outside the uterus, such as in the ovaries or on the fal-
lopian tubes. Since these lesions are actual pieces of uterine lining,
they still behave like it, responding to the woman's monthly cycle and
trying to shed, except they have nowhere to go, so the result is often
internal bleeding and formation of scar tissue. Interestingly, in

countries like India, where women wear loose-fitting clothes, there are far fewer reported cases of the condition. After inspecting more than twelve thousand Indian medical journals, Dickinson uncovered only four cases of endometriosis in the last thirty years, compared to more than five thousand reports or articles on the disease in the same time frame in journals from developed countries, about half of them from the U.S.

The connection between tight clothing and serious disease has yet to make the transition from hypothesis to fact—leading breast-cancer experts discredit the validity of the claim that bras cause breast cancer, and the link between endometriosis and restrictive clothing is far from being proven. But it still wouldn't hurt to loosen up a little. Generally, what's comfortable is healthiest. Just as wearing flat, cushiony shoes would be best for our feet, wearing less restrictive garments would be better for our bodies. And while free-flowing clothes will come into fashion at certain times, the pendulum will inevitably swing the other way soon afterward. And Fashion Victims will grin and bear it.

FLAMMABLE CLOTHES

In the late-night hours of November 4, 1995, twenty-five-year-old Laura Hollister, a first-year business student at Northwestern University's Kellogg School of Business, was returning home from a party. The following hours are a blur. She awoke the next morning at 9:30, looked in the mirror, and called her parents. "Fire, burner, pasta. Fire, burner, pasta," she repeated. Her parents phoned a nearby friend who called paramedics. Hollister was helicoptered to a hospital and remained under medical supervision for the next six months, receiving treatment for the third-degree burns she received on over 55 percent of her body.

Meanwhile, investigators pieced together the events of that night. It appeared that Hollister had reached for something in the cabinet above the stove; her shirttail brushed against the electric burner and ignited. Evidence around the apartment showed that she had tried to stamp out the flames on the counter, then in the bathtub, and eventually ended up passing out on the bed, where bits of burned clothing were found.

To Hollister's parents, the accident wasn't a fluke. They filed a product-liability lawsuit against Dayton Hudson, the parent company of Hudson's, where Laura's mother had purchased the plaid button-down six years earlier. But the shirt met federal flammability standards, and the Hollisters were unable to prove that an alternative fabric would have prevented the accident. At the time of the district court's ruling in May 1998, Hollister's medical expenses had ballooned to just short of a million dollars. She received nothing from Hudson's.

The U.S. Flammable Fabrics Act (FFA) was passed in 1953 after a number of accidents involving brushed-rayon "torch" sweaters and children's cowboy chaps that would blaze in seconds. Throughout its half-century of existence, the FFA did succeed in pulling many dangerous products from the market. In May 1997, Levi Strauss recalled 57,000 fleece shirts that violated the FFA. Later that year, Guess? recalled 2,300 women's fleece jackets because they violated federal standards, burning faster than newspaper. In October 2000, Max Azria was fined $75,000 for selling chenille sweaters that failed the same test. In August 2001, The Limited agreed to pay $500,000 to settle government charges that it knowingly imported and sold flammable children's pajamas and bathrobes. The most commonly recalled garments are those made from materials like chenille, fleece, and terry cloth. "Fuzzy fabrics have greater surface area for flame to spread," explains Carol Easley, lab manager of textile testing services at the University of Nebraska. Think of it this way: Fire in a dense forest spreads faster because flames leap from branches and from one tree to the next. Easley notes that the same concept applies to fuzzy materials. She also points out that fabrics have different burning characteristics, which result in different injuries. "Synthetic fibers burn with greater smoke and flame toxicity than natural fibers," says Easley. "These fibers also tend to burn 'hotter,' just like a melting plastic, resulting in more severe burn damage to skin."

As helpful as the FFA has been, by the 1960s members of Congress began expressing concern that people would be given a false sense of security by the act, that they would wrongly assume that anything manufactured under those government guidelines was "safe." "Be careful—a lot of clothing out there, when exposed accidentally to even a small flame, can become tornadoes of flame," Michael Weinberger, an attorney and author of *New York Products Liability* told the *New York Press*. "Many garments burn extremely rapidly and give off huge amounts of heat. It's shocking to consumers just how flammable their clothes may be."

In order to comply with the FFA, fabrics must pass the 45-degree-angle test—the same test that was employed back in 1953. A two-by-six-inch swatch of oven-dried fabric is placed inside a holder in a metal cabinet at a 45-degree angle. It's then lit with a gas flame for one second, and the time for the fabric to burn down its entire length is recorded. The fabric fails if the flame spreads faster than four seconds for plain-surface fabrics and seven seconds for raised-fiber fabrics: The experiment is repeated five times, and any fabric that fails at least twice is unsuitable for sale in the U.S. A passing grade, however, doesn't necessarily mean a fabric is truly safe. "About 99 percent of all fabrics involved in serious burn cases pass the general apparel test," says Joe Urbas, Ph.D., president of Pacific Fire Laboratory in Kelso, Washington.

"The truth is that most clothing manufacturers are extremely lax in fire safety," Weinberger told the *New York Press*. "The companies that go out of the way in keeping clothing safe are one in a hundred. Where they spend their money is on lobbying and keeping antiquated regulations in place. Imagine if regulations for tires or wiring had never changed since 1953! Yet with clothing we accept it. If you saw some of these women and children in burn centers you'd be outraged." Today, between three and four thousand people are treated in emergency rooms each year for burns suffered after their clothing caught fire—about 200,000 victims whose lives might have been different if the FFA had been stricter since the first laws passed in 1953.

Another problem with the outdated FFA is that it doesn't take into account all the modern-day things we do to our clothes. In 2001, *Consumer Reports* found that using liquid fabric softener on cotton clothing makes it more flammable because it fluffs up the fibers. The magazine's researchers also conducted studies on how various drying methods affect flammability. When they used the government protocol—hand washing and line drying—all garments met the federal standard. But, as we know, that government standard was passed in the 1950s, when most homemakers washed and dried their clothes without the aid of the wonderful technologies we have today. When the researchers repeated the test using the more modern method—machine washing and machine drying—several garments failed the flammability tests, and most burned faster than the line-dried swatches. Again, it was the fault of the fluff factor. Electric dryers fluff up individual fibers, producing a more fertile ground for fire to spread.

There's no reason to believe that your clothes will spontaneously combust at any moment. But too many of us are under the false impression that our clothes are more flame resistant than they actually are because they've been tested by the federal government. Of course, no clothing company sets out to hurt people. That would just be bad business. But some do try to squeak by with the lowest level of compliance to save money. So it's important that consumers themselves be aware of the risks.

CHEMICALS

We're all living in a chemical soup.
—*Lance A. Wallace, environmental scientist*

Most of us take for granted the many high-tech innovations in the apparel industry—all those chemicals that are used to dye, strengthen, remove stains and wrinkles, waterproof, make flame retardant, add sheen, and supply our clothes with the myriad other characteristics they now possess. Most Fashion Victims are happy to overlook these substances, just as we ignore the additives in the packaged foods we eat—it's the "what we don't know can't hurt us" mentality.

Some chemicals, though, pose alarming health risks. Benzene, which is used to remove stains and fingerprints from fabrics before packaging and to produce some synthetic fibers, has been identified as a known carcinogen by the Department of Health and Human Services. To make clothes permanent press and wrinkle free, manufacturers apply a finish made from formaldehyde, that same stinky liquid used to embalm cadavers and dead animals for dissection. "Formaldehyde is listed as a suspected carcinogen, which means that there is only weak evidence for it contributing to cancer," says Tom Kelly, senior research scientist at Battelle, a technological development company in Columbus, Ohio. "The more immediate health effect of formaldehyde is that it may be an irritant, and some sensitive people can suffer allergic-type reactions from skin contact or inhalation."

Consumers are usually exposed to only minor amounts of these chemicals by the time a garment reaches them. Most day-to-day risk can be reduced by washing new clothes, which is especially recommended for clothes worn by babies or people with allergies. "About a 60 percent reduction in emissions was achieved by washing permanent-press shirts once," says Kelly. "Sensitive people may want to wash clothes more than once before wearing them—it can't hurt." Factory workers, who aren't provided with adequate protection on the job, bear the brunt of the risk. Garment workers exposed to high levels of these chemicals may be at increased risk of cancer, dangerous allergic reactions, and respiratory troubles.

What's most disturbing about this widespread use of chemicals is that our hunger for fashion creates the demand for them. If we didn't buy so many cheap garments to keep up with the latest trends, there would be much less need for these potentially dangerous compounds. In the grand scheme of things, it's not only workers who are at risk but also the environment itself and, in turn, the general public. Industrial waste often makes its way into the air, water, and soil. Before the weaving process, a gelatinous film called a size is applied to strengthen fibers. The American textile industry consumes about 200 million pounds of these chemicals each year—and more than 90 percent is disposed of in wastewater. According to the US-AEP, size chemical disposal is one of the largest industrial waste streams in the U.S. Starch, the most common primary size component, accounts for roughly two-thirds of all size chemicals used in the country. Polyvinyl alcohol (PVA), the leading synthetic size, accounts for much of the remainder. Synthetic sizes, which are not as biodegradable as starches, can pass through conventional wastewater-treatment systems and are often linked to aquatic toxicity in receiving waters, according to the US-AEP.

It's possible to get by without so many chemicals in our clothes—just more expensive. Three years ago, Esprit developed an experimental line of clothing called the E Collection, using cotton grown without toxic insecticides and shrink-proofing the clothing with a special mechanical process instead of with formaldehyde. The company test-marketed the clothes at about 30 to 50 percent above its regular prices, which was actually less than the garments really cost to make. The line ultimately bombed.

While the average consumer probably won't lose sleep over the possible short-term effects of these chemicals because of the relatively low risk they present in our daily lives, there is one widely used toxin that we should all pay closer attention to.

PERC: THE DIRTIEST TYPE OF CLEAN

Some days, Brian Olson, owner of 45th Avenue Cleaners in Portland, Oregon, brings his little shih tzu mutt, Benji, with him to work. "He's cute, everyone loves him—he sits on the floor in front and says hi to all the customers," says Olson, who is the president of the Oregon Dry Cleaners Association. Once in a while, though, someone will express concern. "It never fails—'Certified Environmental Drycleaner' on the window, environmental awards hanging on the wall, and not a trace of solvent odor in the air, yet *someone* will ask, 'Aren't you worried about him breathing the fumes?'"

For twenty-two of the twenty-seven years he's been in business, Olson has used the chemical solvent perchloroethylene (perc)—for the first five years, he used Valclene, a type of freon that's now banned because it allegedly depletes the ozone layer. You see, the process of dry cleaning is actually not dry at all. Clothes go into a machine with the solvent and are tossed about. The solvent is drained and vaporized from the fabric, then the garment is dried, pressed, packaged, and handed off to you when you come to pick it up. Despite the stigma associated with the dry-cleaning industry over concern that perc is harmful, Olson insists he isn't worried about Benji's health or his own. "I'm more worried about the cigarettes I smoked for twenty years," he says. "We used to clean delicate stuff in a bucket with our bare hands and hang it to air-dry back before anyone ever thought about health or environmental issues. We would breathe [perc] in all day. Cleaning plants used to reek of it. Who knew any better? No one. It's just the way it was."

The Germans introduced perc in the 1920s, and it caught on with the American dry-cleaning industry in the 1940s. By the 1950s, most U.S. dry cleaners abandoned petroleum solvents, which had a dangerous tendency to explode into flames, in favor of the more stable perc. Today, it remains the most popular dry-cleaning chemical, used by about 85 percent of the thirty thousand dry cleaners in the U.S.

Although many dry cleaners, like Olson, maintain perc's innocence, the chemical has been associated with some scary health problems throughout the years. Studies have linked it with everything from headaches, nausea, dizziness, and irritability to higher miscarriage rates, infertility, increased risk of certain types of cancer, and even death in dry-cleaning workers. The EPA has classified it as a probable human carcinogen. The National Institute for Occupational Safety and Health also lists it as a potential human carcinogen. Several cleaners have gone public with their suspicions that perc made them sick. Joe Whang, owner of Cypress Plaza Cleaners in Orange County, California, believes the chemical contributed to problems with his thyroid gland. The problems started in 1995 when he began losing weight and his eyes began to bulge. In all, he lost thirty pounds. His symptoms mysteriously—or not so mysteriously—disappeared after he switched his shop to a special water-based process.

Still, no one has been able to prove with certainty that perc causes major illnesses. There haven't been any conclusive studies proving that perc does indeed cause cancer, so researchers are left to qualify their claims with wishy-washy statements like "Scientists do not know . . ." Why the uncertainty? It's because of medical ethics, says Lance Wallace, an environmental scientist with the EPA. Unfortunately—or fortunately, depending on how you look at it—scientists can't test potentially cancer-causing chemicals on humans, so it's difficult to determine their effects on us. "By testing animals at high doses, we can determine that some chemicals cause cancer," says Wallace. "But do these same chemicals cause cancer in man at low doses? Usually the answer is that we don't know." It's also tough to isolate specific chemicals in everyday life that may cause disease—a man with cancer who lives above a dry cleaner may have gotten the disease from any number of other toxins he's exposed to on a daily basis.

So, as far as whether or not perc is harmful to the average dry-cleaning customer, the jury is still out. What we do know is that dry-cleaning customers are exposed to the chemical. Clothes, particularly those that haven't been properly cleaned, can actually give off fumes. Tests have shown that dry-cleaned clothing placed in a closed car next to a bag of groceries can contaminate food in less than an hour. And in an EPA test, when researchers put dry-cleaned clothes into a bedroom closet then tested perc levels in the closet, bedroom, and adjacent den, they found levels as much as 190 times higher than the New York guideline ($100mg/m^3$). And airing clothes out doesn't help to reduce the levels by much. The EPA researchers aired dry-cleaned garments outside for six hours; the amount of perc in the fabric was reduced by only 20 percent.

It all sounds very scary, but, again, will this level of exposure cause cancer or any other illnesses? The average person probably isn't in immediate peril (meaning you won't pass out from storing your dry cleaning in your bedroom), but the long-term effects are still unknown. "While it's true that there is perc exposure in the home due to out-gassing, the degree of exposure is so small that it's very unlikely to cause any adverse effects," says Mike Kamrin, Ph.D., professor emeritus at the Institute for Environmental Toxicology at Michigan State University. That's not to say perc is totally safe, either. "The first rule of toxicology is that everything is toxic—nothing is harmless," adds Kamrin. "This includes water, oxygen, etcetera. Whether or not toxic effects occur depends on the dose."

Aside from dry cleaners themselves, another group is exposed to high doses of perc: people who live in buildings with dry-cleaning businesses—an estimated one million Americans. Fumes travel upward through air vents, windows, and walls. In one New York study, researchers found perc levels in residences above dry cleaners that were hundreds of times higher than state guidelines. And watch out if you do your grocery shopping near a cleaner. In Germany, it's illegal to open dry-cleaning businesses near food shops. Not so in the U.S. and in other countries, like the UK, where they're commonly located in supermarkets. Investigations of food taken from grocery stores near dry-cleaning facilities revealed perc levels more than three hundred times as high as concentrations in foods from stores not near a dry cleaner, according to a 1992 FDA report. Fatty foods in particular, like butter, seem to soak up the wafting fumes like a sponge.

Living near a dry cleaner poses another hazard: water contamination from spills. "Perc is a 'sinker' solvent," explains Olson. "It weighs more than water. If the ground is contaminated and the solvent reaches the water table or drinking wells, it can be a major mess to deal with." Massachusetts residents exposed to perc-contaminated drinking water in the early 1990s had a risk of leukemia two to eight times higher than normal and a fourfold increase in bladder cancer, according to the Archives of Environmental Health. We'd like to think that most dry cleaners take every safety precaution necessary, but stories do surface about deliberate offenders. In 2001, Michael Rosenberg, owner of Avenue Cleaners in Farmington, Connecticut, was tried for illegally dumping perc near his business for nearly a year, contaminating the wells of two nearby homes. Two barrels of waste, marked with Avenue Cleaners labels (doh!), were found near a reservoir that at one time had been used for public drinking water.

On a larger scale, dry cleaning presents a threat to the environment as a whole. Approximately 70 percent of the perc used by cleaners in the U.S. is released directly into the atmosphere, according to the EPA. And perc's breakdown product trichloroacetic acid (TCA), a chemical originally produced as an herbicide, has been linked to deforestation and ozone depletion in European studies.

By far, the population with the highest risk of perc exposure consists of dry-cleaning workers. Those who work in shops that use older equipment are particularly at risk for inhaling harmful levels of perc. A

September 1993 report in the *Sydney Morning Herald* found that the chemical is still being exhaled from workers' lungs hours after they've left work. Still, many owners and operators take the risks in stride. "Just like most solvents, perc is hazardous; no one argues that," says Olson. "The vapors will make you dizzy and ultimately, in high concentrations, cause severe headaches and unconsciousness, even death. As to whether or not it causes cancer, well, Greenpeace says it does. Other independent agencies say it doesn't. There simply isn't any evidence to support either theory." Still, Olson dismisses any causal relationship between perc and cancer. "I personally knew two perc dry cleaners who died of cancer in their eighties," he says. "My dad also died of cancer in his eighties. He ran movie theaters. I guess I could argue that popcorn causes cancer too! The point is, we don't know, and until we do, we need to operate with caution. That's just common sense."

Clean Freaks

One reason perc has even become such a problem in the first place is that Fashion Victims dry clean far more than they have to. In 1998, Procter and Gamble, maker of at-home dry-cleaning alternative Dryel, reported that only 20 percent of the clothes taken to the cleaners are actually dirty. Tests show that most "dry clean only" items can be safely washed at home. "We have found that often the more expensive designer items state 'dry clean only' because they have not undergone rigorous testing," says Trisha Schofield, an editor at *Good Housekeeping*'s British edition. "Usually, we say that if a garment is not tailored or structured and is made from a washable fabric without an obvious finish, you can risk washing."

Why do we dry clean? Consumers hand their clothes over to a professional for several reasons. Convenience, for one—it's much easier to bring a dress to the dry cleaner than it is to figure out how to launder it ourselves. We send it away; it comes back hung and neatly pressed. Second, our perception of cleaning methods has been warped by a self-serving apparel industry. Clothes makers have convinced us that dry cleaning is best. Many companies engage in a practice known as lowball labeling, putting "dry clean only" labels on washable clothes. This not only makes it less likely for a garment to be damaged but also transfers responsibility to the dry cleaner. When a consumer buys a garment, washes it according to the instructions on the care label, and the garment gets ruined, it costs manufacturers time and money to deal with customer complaints and returns. Under current Federal Trade Commission rules, manufacturers need to list only one safe care method on a label, even if other methods are also safe. "If they 'prove' dry cleaning works, why go through the expense of proving anything else?" says Olson. As a result, a large number of clothes are labeled "dry clean only" when they can be safely washed with regular detergent and water.

Cleaners, even though they may know a better way to clean a garment, are required by law to follow the care labels. If they go against the instructions and wash a garment in water instead, they're then liable for any damages that may occur—not a risk most cleaners want to take. The blame is transferred from the clothing manufacturer to the dry cleaner—the person who didn't follow the label. But some do break the rules. "We are 'cleaners'—we clean clothes," says Olson. "We use the best and most practical method possible for each item, whether washing or dry cleaning."

In addition, some clothes are tagged with the "dry clean only" label when they can safely be washed in water because the label has come to symbolize a certain level of quality. The Fashion Victim's snobbish attitude toward pricey garments has helped fuel a boost in dry cleaning. Manufacturers of high-end clothes are more likely to slap a garment with dry-cleaning instructions. While the label would dissuade many shoppers from buying a $20 top, it would mean something entirely different to a person buying one for $300. With more expensive garments, consumers often don't trust tags that suggest anything except dry cleaning, anyway. (Throw my Gucci sweater in the wash? No way!) Plus, they would rather be safe than sorry and not risk ruining the item. Just imagine buying a $400 designer jacket that said, "Hand Wash or Dry Clean." Wouldn't you be inclined to dry clean it?

Digging Up Dirt

For all the uncertainty that surrounds perc, the federal government has remained relatively silent. In their 1999 book *Toxic Deception*, Donald Fagin and Marianne Lavelle raise questions about why the U.S. government has done so little to regulate perc usage. They cite a 1998 EPA report, six years in the making, that unveiled frightening statistics about dry-cleaning health risks perc poses to consumers and workers. The report also stated that there's virtually no difference in quality between dry cleaning and a new multistep process of wet cleaning called Green Clean, and in fact, Green Clean turns out to be more economical. Curiously, though, the report still offered no proposed action. The problem, the authors said, was that the EPA's stance was to not interfere with the marketplace. "Companies such as Dow (a manufacturer of perc) and Exxon (a manufacturer of hydrocarbon solvents) aggressively sell dry cleaners on the presumed benefits of their products," they wrote. "Is it too much to ask that regulators play a balancing role in warning them of the risks?"

Perc also wields more financial influence in Washington than the environmentally friendly Green Clean. Two months before a 1994 dry-cleaning breakfast held on Capitol Hill, according to Fagin and Lavelle, Republican Jon Christensen of Nebraska received a $1,000 campaign contribution from the PAC operated by Dow. In April 1995, fellow attendee Martin Frost, a Democrat from Texas, received $2,000 from a couple who owned a dry-cleaning establishment in Irving, Texas. Christensen got a total of $4,000 from a couple in Omaha who listed themselves as "Martinizers," a class of franchisees who have been particularly active on the lobbying front.

Although the federal government may be slow to promote change, some states are trying to push greener cleaning alternatives on their own. Michigan, for instance, has prohibited dry cleaners from operating in residential buildings for several decades, and New York is currently considering measures that would do the same. Some states have tried to make life tougher for dry cleaners who still use perc, hoping to drive more business owners to the alternatives out of convenience. Day

Suehiro, owner of Merry Go Round Cleaners in Beverly Hills, California, has used the solvent for a quarter-century. "We've never experienced any negative health effects from it," she says. "But there are many rules and regulations that have increased our expenses and made it more difficult to operate, namely more paperwork, more fees, and regulations."

Still, one of the reasons perc and other chemical solvents continue to be so dominant in the dry-cleaning industry is that they're backed by some of the biggest corporations in the world, including Dow Chemical and Exxon. The healthier alternative, Green Clean, hasn't been promoted to cleaners with the same major marketing gusto because it lacks a powerful backer. Dry cleaners, mostly being small businesses, get their information chiefly from other dry cleaners and from vendors of chemicals and equipment. Since chemicals and expensive equipment aren't needed with Green Clean, vendors aren't pushing it. There's also this low-lying skepticism within the dry-cleaning profession as well as in the general community—we have this sneaking fear that our clothes will come back from the Green Cleaner's less than perfect.

Dry cleaners simply don't have the funds to switch to safer alternatives, even if they wanted to. You may cringe when you pay your dry-cleaning bill, but it's not as if these businesses are pocketing huge profits. "Look at the prices cleaners charge," says Brian Olson. "Compare them to twenty years ago. Compare that to the cost of rent, cars, housing, food, etcetera." In 1980, Olson went to work at a shop in Portland, Oregon, that charged 95¢ for a shirt and $6 for a two-piece suit at the time. "I drove by that shop last week, and the sign in the window said 'Shirts $1.20' and 'two-piece suits $6.95,'" he says. Prices have stayed relatively the same for consumers, but the expenses of dry cleaners have skyrocketed. "In 1980, perc was under $2 a gallon; it's now over $30 with tax," says Olson. "A new perc cleaning machine cost about $6,000 to $10,000 in 1980. They now cost $30,000 and up."

The modest profit level in the industry means that many businesses are slow to upgrade to new, safer machines. A big source of pollution is out-of-date equipment, which Olson says isn't entirely rare.

"Unless the new equipment is mandated by the government, [dry cleaners] can't afford to upgrade," he says. "The consumer will have to accept higher prices or quality will continue to decline," he says. The problem is that dry cleaning is a competitive business. In New York City, for example, it's not unusual to see two competing businesses located a block away from one another. If one shop raises prices to $2 per shirt while his competitor keeps his rate at $1.50, the more expensive shop will lose customers. They can't afford to hoist prices, yet they can't afford not to.

So the entire issue seems to hinge on money: The government needs to funnel more dollars into researching the health and environmental effects of perc; business owners need to put more cash into updating their equipment; consumers need to loosen their purse strings to pay higher prices. Until this happens, we'll have to live with the possibility that something as simple as cleaning our clothes could gradually be the death of us.

USED CLOTHING

Recently, I spent an hour sifting through a thrift store, a massive four-story warehouse in Brooklyn, the type of place where New York's fashionistas know they can score a $5.50 suede jacket or $7 ball gown if they search hard enough—racks upon racks of faded blue jeans, ski jackets, leather skirts, shoes, even underwear. The clothes were so cheap, especially those in the buck-per-pound bin, that it would no doubt cost more to launder them than it would to actually buy them. As I was leaving, I saw a woman remove her sandals and slip on a pair of moccasins she had just bought to wear out of the store. She then took a button-down shirt out of her shopping bag and slipped it on over her tank top. At the risk of sounding totally phobic, let me just say that I had to wonder whose body had touched those items before hers. In addition to the big yuck factor, unwashed used clothing can also pose a health hazard.

Clothes can be contaminated through airborne, physical, or body-fluid contact, says Gang Sun, Ph.D., a textile chemist at the University of California, Davis. "When clothing is contaminated, germs can survive for days and even months, which is the reason that countries were taking those measures to control foot and mouth disease. In 2001, Latvia and Lithuania banned imports of used clothing from Britain. Regular laundering can wash off many micro-organisms, but not thoroughly. Chlorine bleaching is recommended for bio-contaminated clothing. But when you use chlorine bleach, the issue of color is a concern for most apparel products."

In 2000, the Panafrican News Agency reported that millions of people are exposing themselves to serious disease when they wear items that have been worn by someone else and exposed to toxins. According to the news service, clothing can present a multitude of threats, from radioactivity to ringworm and skin infections. Serious illnesses such as leprosy, tuberculosis, and anthrax may also be spread from close contact with infected clothing. Cheap used garments imported from the U.S. are popular in Africa, and about a third of garments that are brought to U.S. textile recycling centers are exported to be sold in other countries. "The majority of clothing is processed—rarely ever cleaned—and inspected," says Bernie Brill, executive vice president of SMART (Secondary Materials and Recyclable Textiles) in Bethesda, Maryland. "Seriously soiled garments are simply discarded. It's economically impossible to launder the clothing." The problem is that toxins and diseases aren't always visible.

Most thrift stores in the U.S. don't launder donated apparel for the same reason recycling plants don't—they can't afford to. "We don't wash the clothing we sell—it would significantly increase the cost of our bargain buys," says Ashley Tapley, communications manager of Thrift Town Stores, a chain of sixteen outlets in Arizona, California, New Mexico, Texas, and Utah. "We don't sell anything that looks unsuitable for sale, but we're unaware of any diseases in the clothes. To date, the Fed has not required any special handling of used clothing. But I personally always wash my thrift-store purchases as a rule of thumb." The Salvation Army and Goodwill also don't wash donations. "We don't have the capability to wash the clothing before it's sold," says spokesperson Janice Joubert. "I will say, though, that most donors donate clothing that they probably have cleaned themselves. As the clothing is sorted, obviously soiled items are discarded and designated unsellable."

Clothing can spread certain diseases just as easily as, say, a subway pole; and few savvy commuters would get off a subway car and eat finger foods without washing their hands. But we might be doing something just as unsanitary when we put on a shirt we bought a few days ago from a thrift store. Becky, a thirty-three-year-old beauty-shop owner and self-professed thrift store junkie in Clearwater, Florida, says she never washes the clothes she buys before wearing them. "What I don't know about doesn't concern me," she says. "Until I hear about cases in my area or more cases in general, I probably won't wash things unless they're in poor-looking shape."

Most used clothes won't cause a problem worse than, say, a rash from perfumes, skin parasites, or other irritants left on a garment from the previous owner. On the off chance that there are any germs or diseases left on clothes, though, transmission is a risk that's ultra-preventable, and therefore you'd be silly not to nip it in the bud right away with a little soap and water.

9

Compassion in Fashion?

If loving you is wrong, I don't want to be right.

—*Homer Banks*

The desire to push the envelope is inherent in the process of creation. But sometimes fashion crosses the line and enters into turbulent territory—a realm where being provocative and cheeky is indistinguishable from being offensive, even cruel. This leaves the Fashion Victim in an ethical tug of war that's surprisingly not so easily solved: Stick to your beliefs? Or stick to fashion?

MORAL FIBERS

Blenheim, Ontario, population 4,800, is a world away from the fashion centers of Milan, Paris, London, and New York. Situated forty-five minutes east of the steel towers and smokestacks of Detroit, along southwestern Ontario's "banana belt," the town is known as "The Heart of the Golden Acres" for its rich, rolling farmland, peppered with apples, strawberries, corn, cucumbers, and tomatoes. A few times

every decade, Blenheim catches the eye of some major media producer, usually one in need of some feel-good filler. One time CNN
featured hometown boy Joe "Gentleman Joe" Lessard, Senior, who had
edged out his son, Joe "Sultan of Spit" Junior, in the 23rd Annual
International Cherry Pit Spitting Contest by propelling a pit nearly
seventy-two feet.

Blenheim residents, as a whole, aren't overly concerned with
fashion. Topics of discussion around town are usually more in the
realm of the area's vexing influx of black crows than of Halle Berry's
Oscar gown. If a Manolo Blahnik sample sale were to roll into town,
you'd find more people in the stands rooting for the local high school's
Bobcats than ogling discounted leather pumps. Most people in
Blenheim dress without the conspicuous intent to impress. Farmers
wear denim because it's durable, not because it's fashionable this season. Women will dress in head-to-toe black, but only for a funeral, not
because it's hip and minimalist. People kick about town wearing
sneakers because they're comfortable, not because Anna Wintour said
they're in.

The fashion world barely registers on Blenheim's radar, and vice
versa. But on Easter Sunday, 1997, the town found itself at the heart of
one of fashion's longest-running controversies.

. . .

At 1 A.M. on that mild March 30, a white van rolled up alongside the
outskirts of Blenheim's Eberts Farm, headlights off, producing only
the muffled sound of tires chewing on rocks. The terrain, as usual, was
virtually unnavigable in the dark. If it weren't for the yowls of a few
restless animals and the unmistakable barnyard smells, you might not
know what type of place you were in. Although the soil would have
proven excellent for growing sweet corn or flaxen wheat, Eberts Farm
wasn't in the business of producing the same luscious foodstuffs as its
neighbors. The farm, owned and operated by father-and-son team Bill
and Tom McLellan, had raised mink on its slice of the Golden Acres
for twenty years.

It was just by luck that the van's occupants—Gary Yourofsky, 26;

his uncle Alan Hoffman, 47; Hilma Ruby, 59; Robyn Weiner, 25; and Patricia "Pat" Dodson, 48—had ended up at Eberts that night. The Michigan residents had awoken that morning as on any other, met up at a local animal sanctuary called Pighoppers, and spent the day there helping with farm chores. At around 7 P.M., they piled into the van and headed east. For two weeks they had been convening to brainstorm, map out, and fine-tune a plot: to break into a fur farm in Ohio and set its animals free. So they rode down to Ohio, filled with nervous anticipation. When they reached the town, excitement turned to panic when they realized it was nearly impossible to locate the farm in the dark. They drove in circles for hours, passing the same infuriating trees, rocks, open fields. Rather than abandoning their plan completely, they decided to regroup, huddling in the van and quickly hammering out Plan B. As luck would have it, just two weeks earlier, Ruby had been arrested at Eberts Farm and charged with breaking and entering, mischief, and theft when she had helped release 250 animals. "I'm sure I could find it again," she said. The group rerouted, cruising up Route 401 toward Blenheim.

As they sat at the periphery of Eberts Farm, the "Michigan Five," as they were later called—dressed in the fur-farm saboteur's uniform of black sweatpants, sneakers, jackets, gloves, and hoods—swore a pact: "If we get caught, no snitching." Then all except for Dodson, the driver, piled out and scaled the farm's five-foot perimeter fence. Inside were six large sheds, housing about twenty-four hundred individually caged minks. Each person had a designated mission. Guided by a sliver of moonlight and small flashlights, Yourofsky and Weiner started at opposite ends of the sheds and opened cages; Hoffman cut holes in the perimeter fence to accommodate fleeing mink; Ruby spray-painted anti-fur graffiti on the sheds and confiscated the valuable breeding cards hanging over each cage that detailed each animal's pedigree.

Forty-five minutes later, the ground, once a stagnant pasture covered with mud, feces, and hay, had become a squirming sea of animals. Mink scurried in every direction: some toward the fences, some back toward the sheds. A particularly distraught one leapt at Yourofsky's

chest when he opened its cage. "It startled me briefly," says Yourofsky.
"But he knew I was the good guy, and he quickly scattered off with the
others." As he approached the fourth shed, nearly home free,
Yourofsky's instinct told him there was danger ahead. "Wait. Stop.
Something's not right," he whispered to Weiner. Seconds later, two
headlights beamed through the darkness. A voice bellowed, "Hey, you
motherfuckers, I can see you."

Earlier, a neighbor had spotted Dodson circling the area and had
grown increasingly suspicious of the van's Michigan license plates.
The vigilant local called law enforcement, and the Ontario Provincial
Police stopped Dodson on the road. Authorities rushed to the farm and
quickly grabbed Ruby and Weiner. Yourofsky and Hoffman managed to
run off to a local convenience store and call a taxi but were nabbed
when police stopped the cab they were in and found the two of them,
covered in dirt and mink feces, in the back seat. When officers
searched the van and the intruders, they found a bottle of hydrofluoric
acid, a walkie-talkie, latex gloves, paint thinner, several bags of clothing, maps to other fur farms, and instructional "eco-terrorist" literature. The Michigan Five spent Easter in jail.

Even though the group's plot had been partly foiled, their plan
still caused irreparable damage to the farm. According to Tom
McLellan, about 1,100 out of 1,542 runaway minks were eventually
recaptured, but at least 300 others died from pneumonia, killed each
other, or were hit by cars when they ventured onto the roadways. "The
worst part is that many of the dead animals were pregnant females—
each female will produce about nine kits," he told the *Detroit News* the
day after the raid. "Many of the recaptured females, which usually give
birth near the end of March, are beginning to abort their young
because of stress."

Media branded the raid a blunder on the part of the activists,
since so many of the animals died as a result, a common complaint
after many fur-farm freeings. (Among other common concerns, newly
freed animals create an imbalance in the local ecosystem. In a 1998
raid of Britain's Crow Hill Farm, sixty-five hundred liberated minks
wreaked havoc around town, killing chickens, hens, birds, and family

pets like guinea pigs, cats, and hamsters. The assault on their animals caused the area's residents to take up shotguns and sticks against the minks.) But Yourofsky, as well as other ardent activists, stands by these types of actions. "The minks were going to die anyway; at least they had a shot at freedom," he says.

The raid was a huge blow to Eberts Farm. Instead of producing its expected 16,000 animals that summer, Tom McLellan estimated the figure to be closer to 3,500. And since the minks' breeding cards had been destroyed, there was no way to prove the remaining stock's line-age, meaning the farmers couldn't get top dollar for their finest breeds. With no proof of pedigree, future stock bred from the remain-ing mink would also be devalued. One hour's sabotage had ravaged a twenty-year-old business.

It was believed that insurance would help pay for most of the McLellans' losses, but getting insured ever again would be difficult. Years later, the family filed a $3.5 million civil suit—$2 million in gen-eral damages, $1 million in specific damages, $500,000 in punitive damages and legal costs—and were eventually awarded $770,000. But the terrorism didn't stop with the break-in. Activists published Tom McLellan's address and phone number on the Internet, encouraging followers to let the fur farmer know "what a wretched mistake he is making by pursuing a lawsuit against accused freedom fighters." The website No Compromise, a support site for the underground eco-terrorist group the Animal Liberation Front (ALF), even followed up the contact information with these taunting words of encouragement, "Tom and his wife really hate to be woken up in the middle of the night." The Michigan Five received fines (some of which were paid by animal-rights support groups) and relatively light criminal sentences, the heftiest being Weiner's two-year jail sentence, which she was allowed to serve out by performing four hundred hours of community service for cooperating with prosecutors. Yourofsky was sentenced to six months at the maximum-security Elgin Middlesex Detention Center in London, Ontario, but released after seventy-seven days. At the time, Bill McLellan sounded unwavering in his determination to rebuild. "Even if it took ten years," he swore, promising not to be intimidated by bullies. Eberts Fur Farm has since closed.

FUR IN FASHION

The raid on Eberts Farm made big news in Blenheim. Outside of the immediate area, though, it was merely cause for people to roll their eyes at the ridiculousness of the situation—it was just another episode in the long-drawn-out controversy over fur. In fact, the incident stirred mixed emotions. On the one hand, people sympathized with the hardworking farmers. No one likes to see down-to-earth country folk getting a raw deal. On the other hand, public opinion at the time had swung so strongly toward the "fur is wrong" camp that it was difficult for many people to truly feel sorry. In the mid- to late 1990s, the raid on Eberts Farm and the dozens like it around the globe weren't all that shocking. Although the McLellans had clearly suffered from a crime, they weren't the most pitiable of victims by virtue of their reviled profession. The bulk of consumers turned away their heads in indifference—fur seemed all but obsolete anyway.

Then, just three years after the Eberts raid, fur didn't seem quite so dead anymore.

. . .

On Monday, February 21, 2000, a little after 5 P.M. Milan time, Prada debuted its fall/winter 2000–2001 collection. The fashion house, a perpetual favorite with the media, celebrities, and other designers, left no doubt from the onset that the new line would yet again be one of the most watched of the season. Models meandered onto the pink runway showcasing a parade of ladylike, 1940s-inspired ensembles. Among the offerings:

A vivid red coat with a fur collar fastened casually around the neck.

A midcalf-length skirt suit with fox collar tied askew.

A belted trench coat accented with a delicate detachable fur collar.

A diaphanous floral dress paired with none other than . . . the ubiquitous fur collar.

In a matter of minutes, there was little question as to what the season's hottest trend would be.

In the months following the shows, many a fashion magazine heralded the fur collar, or "tippet" as it was known to some, as the season's trend to watch. The collar figured prominently in Prada's print ad campaign that year. Paparazzi snapped photos of celebrities like Jennifer Jason Leigh and Amanda Peet in full Prada regalia, fur collar fastened fashionably off center, further solidifying it as the new must-have item. By fall, Prada's fur collar had already been knocked off in nearly every color, style variation, and price range. Stores like Express and Urban Outfitters stocked their own faux-fur versions. Macy's peddled a rabbit collar for $58, and Saks Fifth Avenue carried Adrienne Landau's fox-fur collar for $300. Clothiers across the globe cashed in, thanking Ms. Prada only minimally for propelling sales. "It's true that we could sell our fur tippet very well last year since the trend came with the good reputation of Prada," said Bruce Nakai, managing director of Nabro Corporation, a Hong Kong manufacturer that began selling raccoon, fox, and rabbit tippets in September 2000 for about $60 to $250 each. "But we've sampled other new fur neckwear before Prada's was on the market. The tippet, in fact, was worn by justices of the court and clergy in Europe many years ago, so it's not a new or special design."

Certainly, many designers besides Prada had used fur that season, and in seasons past. Fur had been steadily climbing in popularity in the latter part of the nineties. Beginning in the middle of the decade, retailers reported increases in sales: in 1996, Detroit's Bricker-Tunis Furs saw gains of 25 percent; Morris Kaye & Sons Furs in Dallas and San Antonio increased sales by 15 percent; and sales by Flemington Fur, in Flemington, New Jersey, rose 25 percent. Years earlier, journalists had begun trumpeting the return of fur. In March 1998, Jeffrey Weiner of the *International Herald Tribune* said: "Women seem to be wearing fur with a clear conscience and an irreverent disregard for status. The new image of the fur wearer is smart and young, sexy and flamboyant . . . fur now has an edgy ultra-modern look." In 2000, Eric Wilson of *Women's Wear Daily* declared that "the demand for fur is probably the strongest it's been since . . . the stock market crashed [in 1987]."

Still, in recent years, no other style had inspired the same mass-media attention and acceptance of fur by the average consumer as the

Prada collar. It seemed to provide an excuse for every Fashion Victim
who had been intrigued by but nervous about fur—the Fur Curious.
Those who disdained fur's haughty rep could now get the luxury without the overt snobbery. The Fur Curious could justify the purchase of a
fifteen-inch strip of fur much more easily than they could a five-foot-
long coat. Those who were concerned with the animal rights issue
could feel less guilty, since fewer animals were killed. And less fur
meant less money. Shoppers who couldn't afford to shell out gobs of
cash on a fur coat could show their status in smaller increments.

For the first time since the 1980s, skins appeared to be picking
up steam among the masses. Fur's pint-sized reintroduction helped to
usher in a new era of luxury. In 2001, even greater media attention was
given to designers' fur offerings: a $225 coyote hat from Ralph Lauren,
a $5,000 fox chubby by Oscar de la Renta, and a $95,000 sheared-
mink coat from Fendi. In 1999, British *Vogue* editor Alexandra
Shulman remarked that "covering fashion and excluding fur is rather
like reporting on Europe and not mentioning the euro." The October
2000 cover of American *Vogue* proclaimed, "Fabulous Furs: The Look
of the Moment," reminding readers that "the fur coat, of course, is still
an essential element in any haute closet." A year later, the magazine's
September issue showed a whopping 110 fur items. And the *Vogue*
Holiday Gift Guide packaged with the November issue possessed a single sponsor—Saga Furs of Scandinavia, which occupied all twenty-five
pages of advertising in the fifty-two-page supplement.

Fur trade groups, as is their job, proclaimed fur's comeback.
According to the Fur Information Council of America (FICA), annual
retail sales of fur in the U.S. rose by 21 percent in 2000 (the largest
gain since 1988), from $1.4 billion to $1.69 billion. The difficulty in
making blanket statements about the state of the fur industry has
always been that success is largely dictated by geographic region. Parts
of the southern United States, for example, may experience no growth,
with some companies even going out of business, while sales in the
Midwest may be skyrocketing. But according to FICA, 88 percent of
U.S. retailers reported gains in 2000. The rise of fur didn't appear to
be confined to any one region.

Nevertheless, for each statistic the fur industry released boasting its product's burgeoning popularity, there was a counterpart proclaiming the opposite. "I don't think fur is making the comebacks the industry says it is, but the fact that they're *saying* it is has made some people believe it," says Elaine Close, a veteran animal-rights activist in Portland, Oregon. "That's the problem with just convincing the public: it's fickle. Then, as a result, you see some more designers using fur today who in the past said they wouldn't because they felt it was unpopular." Likewise, People for the Ethical Treatment of Animals (PETA) refuted fur's alleged newfound panache. And for some average consumers, fur still failed to become a hot-ticket item. "Honestly, I don't know anyone who wears fur, nor do I know who might be the next to buy a fur garment," says Jamie, twenty-seven, an accountant in Stamford, Connecticut. "The people I know aren't really into the whole glamour-and-diamonds look anyway. They like lots of simple fabrics and interesting textures as opposed to fur . . . [they don't] even [wear] faux fur."

The Fashion Victim, so impressionable and ready to jump on the next hot trend, was both tempted and tortured by fur's revival. Suddenly, shoppers who never imagined they'd wear fur were faced with the question, *Should I?*

THE RISE AND FALL AND RISE OF FUR

Animal skins have been used as clothing since the earliest times. Kings and queens, emperors, workers, clergy, warriors, politicians, children, royalty and commoners have wrapped themselves in fur throughout history. Badger, fox, seal, and otter furs were used extensively for capes and jackets in medieval Scotland. During the fifteenth century, a tribe of South American Indians, the Chinchas, made robes of chinchilla fur. Manchu ladies in China wore fur-lined robes in the nineteenth century. In recent times, fur's popularity peaked in the 1980s, when full-length mink coats, sable jackets, and plush fox hats identified their wearers as part of the new consumer class. Coming out of the synthetic-fiber era of the 1970s, fur seemed the ultimate in luxury. U.S. fur sales reached a high of $2.3 billion in 1987.

Alas, as with many fads that grow too big (disco, Leonardo DiCaprio, Cabbage Patch Kids), fur's surging popularity triggered the inevitable backlash. In the 1980s, in Britain, groups like Lynx launched massive anti-fur billboard campaigns. One effective ad of the era showed a woman dragging a bloody fur coat behind her with the caption, "It takes up to forty dumb animals to make a fur coat. But only one to wear it." Meanwhile, fur wearers were accosted on sidewalks around the world by activists wielding cans of red spray paint. The actual number of people who were harassed is unknown, but the many attacks that did occur were woven together into a sort of anti-fur folklore. Children of the eighties grew up believing that being attacked with spray paint was the standard consequence of wearing fur. Anti-fur literature circulated, filled with gruesome descriptions of how animals are gassed, drowned, battered, clubbed, and anally electrocuted. Only the most sadistic of us didn't wiggle in our seats at least a little.

As the "Me Decade" came to a close, the tide turned against conspicuous consumption, and fur, by association, began to symbolize everything that was wrong with the eighties. Fur not only became associated with cruelty, it also symbolized the ugly greed and selfishness of the times. Extravagance had suddenly become horribly passé. As we moved into the era of grunge—a period epitomized by flannel shirts and army-issue cargo pants—avoiding fur became easy. People had begun to see fur, despite its obvious warmth, as purely a luxury. With so many other fibers available to us, and considering the surplus of clothing accumulated in our closets, a fur garment was by no means a necessary addition to anyone's wardrobe. By 1990, anti-fur sentiment had become the norm. Fur's free fall bottomed out with sales under the $1 billion mark in 1991.

Even amid waning sales in the 1990s, however, fur never completely disappeared. According to FICA, one in five American women today owns a fur coat. Worldwide, the fur industry produces about 30 million pelts annually from farmed animals alone. In the U.S., there are still about 1,500 retailers, 100 manufacturers, and 350 fur farms (down from 1,221 in 1975). Nevertheless, fur's popularity was on an obvious decline.

Then, to the surprise of many, fur's fizzling embers began to burn bright again in the late nineties. New technologies—like one employed by Fendi, which perforated pelts—made furs lighter and more manageable. The biggest names in fashion experimented with different types of fur. In 2000, in addition to her fur tippet, Miuccia Prada used raccoon. Alberta Ferretti used hamster *(ewww)*, Narciso Rodriguez, fox, Galliano, chinchilla, Marc Jacobs, mink, and Gaultier, sable. Nearly every major design house and many smaller designers worked with skins that year. Fashion Victims quickly took notice, draping luxurious fox wraps over their shoulders and tying plush rabbit scarves around their necks. Fur in the new millennium still symbolized wealth and prestige but was now not wholly restricted to the superwealthy. Now every consumer could get a piece of the action. Fur entered the marketplace at every price: from a $100,000 chinchilla coat down to a $15 rabbit cuff.

Some argued that fur's temporary unpopularity hadn't happened because people thought wearing it was wrong, but rather it had just fallen temporarily out of fashion. "Fur wasn't dead. It just wasn't popular," said Sandy Parker, of *Sandy Parker Reports*, a weekly newsletter that reports news and trends in the international fur trade. It makes sense that fur's comeback would be during the same year that the eighties revival came into full swing again on the catwalk. In her show for Versus, for example, Donatella Versace put Gisele Bündchen in a tight turquoise Lycra dress, all big back-combed hair and bright-red lips reminiscent of the flashy neon decade. Likewise, Maxmara evoked the eighties with its officewear: loose belted cardigans and slouchy moleskin trousers. Amid these retro looks, fur fit right in.

People who had staunchly opposed fur changed their minds for the sake of fashion. Naomi Campbell was slightly ahead of the curve in her change of heart. In January 1994, the supermodel appeared with four other models in Paris wearing only a banner that read *Plutôt à poil qu'en fourrure*—"Rather nude than wear fur." She spoke for PETA on shows such as *Dateline NBC* and *MTV News*, appeared on the cover of the group's catalog, and signed its "Models of Compassion" petition, promising never to model fur. Then on March 7, 1997, at the Fendi fall/winter show in Milan, Campbell created a firestorm of controversy by sashaying onto the runway in an oversized Russian sable. PETA canned her as their spokesperson four days later. "Integrity may not mean much to you, but it does to us," wrote campaign director Dan Matthews to the supermodel. "Your name and image will be removed from all future PETA literature, as it is a disgrace to the many animal-friendly fashion leaders who have both hearts and spines." Campbell continued to offend, sporting a shaggy mohair dress under a matching gray-striped fur coat at Fendi the next year, and a fur jacket over silk trousers at the Gai Mattiolo show a year after that. After catching some pretty heavy flak for her change of heart, Campbell told Britain's *Daily Express* that she likes fur but doesn't wear it often and would never wear the fur of an endangered species. The media relished her brazen duplicity, but Ms. Campbell wasn't alone in her fickleness.

Fur became a prime example of the blinding power of fashion—of how the drive to be stylish can sometimes cause the temporary desertion of one's morals. True, some fur wearers never wavered in their pro-fur stance. But others, who had deep-down moral misgivings about fur, bought it anyway simply because it was in fashion. The drive to follow when the fashion pack moves in a given direction (even if it's a direction you disagree with) is so strong that people are willing to compromise their beliefs. I, embarrassingly, admit that I fell into the trap myself, coming close to buying a Prada fur collar even though I had considered myself mildly anti-fur for years. I didn't buy it but felt ashamed later on that the thought had even crossed my mind. Jeff Stone, Ph.D., assistant professor of social psychology at the University of Arizona, sees fur fashion as an example of conformity in action. "Many conformity effects occur regardless of what values, attitudes, principles, and beliefs a person brings to the situation," he says. "The power of other people to shape our behavior sometimes overrides our own moral convictions."

Fashion Victims who may have had some doubts rationalized their decision to wear fur. Jennifer, a thirty-five-year-old website editor in Hollywood, owns several furs, including a silver fox and a chinchilla, as well as mink collars and cuffs. "I'm an animal lover, but I guess a hypocrite at that, because I do wear leather and fur," she says. "Some collars I have are faux fur, but I prefer real fur. The funniest thing I've found is that I buy a lot of vintage collars that were originally on jackets and coats. That way, I always delude myself into thinking that the animal would've been long dead by natural causes." Some consumers didn't seem to know what to think, like Rebecca, a twenty-year-old dance teacher in Yreka, California. "I think fur is wrong, but I do agree that it's fashion and it looks good," she says. "So at the same time, I like it—it looks really good on certain people."

HOW FAR FOR FASHION?

Throughout history, fashion has had a devastating effect on animals. The great auk, a three-foot-tall, penguinlike, flightless seabird, was hunted by the Victorians for its feathers until it became extinct in 1844 when two fishermen killed the last breeding pair and smashed the last egg. In 1962, Jackie Kennedy wore a leopard-skin coat to meet with the U.S. ambassador to Rome. Soon, Elizabeth Taylor and Queen Elizabeth II were seen wearing the spots, and by the 1970s, the animal was almost wiped out in Africa and the U.S. banned the import of leopard skins altogether.

Over the years, questions have been raised about the ethics of using other animal products, including leather, snakeskin, feathers, alligator, ostrich, pony, even wool (activists argue that it's cruel to keep sheep just to shave them). Entire species may have been wiped out by fashion, but demand for fur and skins continues. The January 2000 issue of *Vogue* featured the omnipresent Gisele Bündchen draped in python for the feature "Skin on Skin." "From python to ostrich, we've succumbed to the seduction of wildly exotic leathers," the magazine read.

Fashion Victims often try to convince themselves that animals aren't harmed. In 1999, more than a hundred socialites and celebrities, including model Christie Brinkley and Manhattan social maven Nan Kempner, were subpoenaed to testify before a grand jury for buying shahtoosh shawls at a charity function in 1994. The delicate wraps, woven from the fur of a Tibetan antelope called the chiru, had been made illegal in the U.S. in 1979 when chiru numbers dropped from several million at the beginning of the last century to less than 100,000. By the 1990s, there were just 65,000. The socialites claimed *they* were victims too. Legend had it that Himalayan tribesmen collected the shed hair of the ibex goat to weave these shawls. "I *believed* the story about people picking the hair off bushes in the rocks," Kempner told *New York* magazine. "It wasn't until much later that it came out that there were mass slaughters of these animals." Unlike cashmere, which is combed from a goat, shahtoosh, from the chiru's undercoat, can only be removed after skinning the animal. Three to five chiru are shot and skinned for each shawl. But fashion has a way of making us believe what we want to believe.

Although leather is used more frequently than fur, it's often considered less offensive, since it's a by-product of cattle, which are raised and slaughtered anyway for food. Fur, on the other hand, is strictly a by-product of fashion. Consumers often don't group fur and leather into the same category. "I don't necessarily think fur is wrong for everyone, [it's] just not right for me," says Susan, a thirty-four-year-old biochemist in Seattle, Washington. "Fur has such a negative stigma these days. To those who judge fur wearers: if you wear leather, it's pretty much the same thing." Some anti-fur folks themselves even waffle on the issue of leather, which has far more applications in clothing and footwear, making it much harder to get by without it. Elaine Close, the activist from Portland, gave up eating meat long before she stopped wearing leather. "The main reason I was wearing leather shoes was, at that point, you couldn't find any nonleather shoes that were nice," she says. "But then I realized that's really stupid—so what if I wear ugly shoes the rest of my life? Is that really so awful? When I realized that that was what I was thinking, I forced myself to stop, and I was lucky enough that a couple years later they started making really nice nonleather shoes. I mean, I don't want to sound too self-righteous because I can definitely see how people are susceptible to that." Even long-time vegetarian Drew Barrymore relaxed her strict anti-leather stance for the sake of fashion in August 2002. "I just don't put restrictions on myself anymore," she said. "I didn't wear certain designers because I didn't want any animals to suffer for beauty and stuff, and so I literally was dressed by Old Navy at one point."

WHY FUR RETURNED

Through the years, new advancements have made fur lighter, more comfortable, and more accessible to the average buyer. Moscow mathematician-turned-fashion-designer Yelena Yarmak uses an advanced technology that can actually make fur look like silk. The threads can then be woven into a jersey, creating a smooth finish. Yarmak also uses new high-tech know-how to experiment with colors, like bright greens and blues, and prints—she's even created mink jackets that look like leopard skin. "The new technology is the fruit of three years of work," says Yarmak. "It lets me make mink look like chinchilla, while keeping it much lighter and more durable." But it wasn't technology alone that scored fur its newfound popularity.

THE GREAT DISCONNECT

The major force behind fur's perseverance through the ages is our detachment from it. Convincing ourselves that we're not accountable allows us to enjoy some guilt-free pleasure. Some people think hunting is despicable, but they'll have a butcher dish up their meat for dinner. Others gasp at the sight of forests being cleared by bulldozers on TV, yet they feel no guilt about building a new home or using a ream of paper to distribute memos at the office. Still others shake their heads when they read about underwater ecosystems being disturbed to carry out offshore drilling, yet cruise around town in their gas-guzzling SUVs. We don't mind benefiting from someone else's dirty work.

We also don't seem to mind killing what's nameless. Thousands of kids gave up eating bacon and refused to smoosh spiders after they read *Charlotte's Web*—they began to associate pork with Wilbur and spiders with adorable Charlotte. If you lived on a farm and named one of the cows (Bessie, Mabel, or one of those other goofy cow names), you might have a hard time sending her to the slaughterhouse. When we don't feel a personal connection to an animal, we don't feel as bad about its death. Most Westerners are horror-struck at the thought of eating a cat or dog—like some of our neighbors to the east have been known to do—yet suffer no qualms about ordering a filet mignon or bucket of chicken. Few people have ever had a mink, fox, or chinchilla for a pet. Few people have even *seen* a mink, fox, or chinchilla up close. So when a man buys a coat with a plush mink collar, he's not launched into flashbacks about his poor pet Mikey the mink from his boyhood. But talk of a domesticated animal being used for fur, and you'll incite some real rage. Pet owners were appalled when news broke that the Burlington Coat Factory had, unwittingly, been selling coats lined with cat and dog fur. Believe it or not, the use of cats and dogs in the American fur industry, as well as abroad, has a long history. A. L. Belden's 1917 book *The Fur Trade of America* states, "Hundreds of thousands . . . of domestic felines, all dear to some one, are annually slaughtered for their fur . . . it is nevertheless a profound mystery how so many become commercial prizes without their devoted owners obtaining an inkling of their destiny."

With many of the animal-based goods we use, there's a disconnect between a product and its origin. A package of ground beef at the supermarket bears no resemblance to a cow. A can of tuna tastes so dissimilar to the fresh fish that it's often a wonder how they're one and the same. The immaculate white leather on a pair of new sneakers conjures no image of cattle in our minds. And how many of us stop to think of gelatin coming from animals when we eat Jell-O? As Carol Jacobs, author of *The Sexual Politics of Meat,* once wrote, "There's a linguistic dance done around butchered flesh. We don't say a lamb's leg, we say leg of lamb. We take away the possessive relationship between a lamb and his or her leg. Animals are not mass terms. Water is a mass term. You can add or take away water, but you can't change what water is. We falsely perpetuate the idea that meat is a mass term, that it never adds up to a living animal."

Some of the fear of wearing fur has dissipated because much of it bears little resemblance to the actual animal it came from. In 1992, fur's popularity had dwindled so much that manufacturers began experimenting with new techniques that would "disguise" fur. Now, a woman could know that she was wearing a fur coat and enjoy feeling the softness against her skin but wouldn't have to fear walking down the street in it. A September 1992 issue of the *New York Times Magazine* included a feature entitled "Furs in Disguise." It described new technology that allowed fur to be woven, textured, and patterned into all sorts of colorful, mod looks. In 2000, *Harper's Bazaar* featured a $95,000 Fendi mink coat, one of only fourteen made—and dyed red, fuchsia, lavender, blue, black, and umber—that looked more like velvet that had been printed with a pattern.

Toward the end of the century, high-tech advances made faux fur look even more like the real thing. Now, we could give someone the benefit of the doubt: maybe she was wearing *faux* fur. When stylist Phillip Bloch works with clients who don't like fur, he'll remove a real fur collar on a coat from, say, Dolce & Gabbana, and replace it with faux fur, then do the old switcheroo when he returns it to the designer. So when you see a celebrity wearing a coat lined with "fox," it's possible that your eyes are deceiving you.

MARKETING

Just a thirty-minute drive north of Copenhagen, in Sandbjerg, Denmark, stands a magnificent farmhouse estate, the type of domicile you'd expect to see in the pages of *Sotheby's Domain* magazine wedged between the Neoclassical Palace in Evian, France, and the Waterfront Country Estate in Salzburg, Austria. In addition to a stunning turn-of-the-century thatched-roof mansion, the twelve-acre property also houses a dazzling pool, as well as a fountain, fish pond, and courtyard, lush trees, and perfectly manicured hedges. Inside the historic house, you'll find a few unexpectedly modern touches—funky light fixtures, bright sofas, an electric-blue rug, and then there's the fur . . . lots of fur. The Danish estate is no ordinary residence—it's the home of the Saga Furs International Design Center (SIDC). Since 1988, Saga has welcomed over twenty thousand professionals from around the world—fashion designers, furriers, trend forecasters, teachers, and design students, among others. Designers at all levels are lured by an all-expenses-paid five-day getaway at the sprawling estate. During their stay, designers relax at the estate, enjoy gourmet food in the mansion's dining room lined with fine art, take field trips to a local fur farm, and learn about the newest fur techniques in one of Saga's on-site workshops. Offering snazzy trips is a common practice in marketing and publicity (I was once invited to an all-expenses-paid weeklong trip to Italy by makers of Parmesan cheese, of all things), but Saga's program has been particularly successful at enticing participants, probably because designers can come away from the experience with a new set of skills (not just a few cases of Parmesan cheese).

Saga was formed in 1954 as a joint marketing organization by the fur breeders' associations in the Nordic countries of Denmark, Finland, Norway, and Sweden. Today, it represents a worldwide market share of 82 percent of farmed fox skins and 66 percent of farmed mink. In 1995, the organization launched its Scandinavia's American Designer Initiative (SADI) to encourage more designers to use fur. One of its activities was to target fashion schools; representatives took trunkloads of furs to final-year design students.

New York designer Mark Montano visited SIDC in October 2000. "Saga Furs is an incredible organization, much like Cotton Inc. or Dupont," he says. "They teach you how to use fur properly and allow you to try your own techniques with the help of technicians. Most design teams from all over the world go to the Saga school. They also teach you how fur is made and how the by-products are used. When Cotton Inc. sponsored my show, they gave me cottons to use. Saga will do the same, though they do not sponsor shows."

Watching the fur industry throw truckloads of money into marketing is understandably frustrating for animal-rights activists. "The fur trade has put considerable effort and money into a PR offensive aimed at persuading designers to use fur in their collections," says Mark Glover, head of British animal-rights group Respect for Animals and one of the founders of the 1980s group Lynx. "These are fickle, sometimes shallow people who can be susceptible to this type of approach. It just underlines the scale of the task we have ahead." *Cosmopolitan* UK fashion director Shelly Vella, who has been involved with the Respect for Animals campaign against fur in Britain for many years, agrees. "What is really frustrating is that the companies who suffered the lack of demand for fur in the UK began to feed money into student design programs, offering money and free usage of fur supplies, hence struggling young wannabe fashion designers had a new resource at their fingertips," she says. "Morals fell by the wayside. Clements Ribeiro were also approached by Saga Furs, who sponsored one of their shows, and hence fur was in fashion once more." Vella disparages the U.S. in particular. "The American market seems to give fur the big stamp of approval, celebrating the different pelts being used and almost mocking the anti-fur supporters by shooting pictures of fur coats in woods with guns, etcetera," she says. "Personally, I was shocked by how the American designers reembraced fur, even those designers and supermodels who previously rejected it. Fashion is fickle after all. Fur is big money, and the companies who produce fur coats were hardly going to lay down and die, so clever pushes financially, including sponsorships, have ensured their reentry into the retail environment."

Consumers are impressionable—they don't need to see a real person on the street wearing a style to recognize it as a trend. For instance, let's say camouflage-print tops come into fashion this fall. Magazines begin to show them, stores begin to stock them. A fifteen-year-old would know that camouflage-print tops were hot this season without ever seeing one on an actual girl. Similarly, as fur's new popularity was continually hyped by Saga and other marketing organizations, the hype became a self-fulfilling prophecy. Fur industry groups made a push for designers to use more fur by offering free pelts, the use of their facilities, and opportunities for advertising relationships. Several designers took them up on the offer and produced fur garments for their upcoming shows. The fashion media, always looking for a trend to tie together a season, noticed that more than a few designers had used fur and pronounced the comeback of fur in magazines and newspapers, and on TV. Manufacturers and retailers, who read the fashion show wrap-ups, stepped up production of fur garments, anticipating an increase in demand. Other stores caught wind of the "news" that major retailers were stocking fur, so they followed suit. And finally, completing the chain, consumers, who had suddenly started spotting fur everywhere, caught on to the trend and bought more fur. The demand for fur had been slyly put in motion by the fur promoters themselves.

Once the first seed had been planted in the minds of the public, the marketing push intensified. PR-savvy celebrities may not have been brazen enough to attend pro-fur rallies, pose for pro-fur billboards, or speak out publicly about how much they adored fur, but pro-fur stars did indirectly show their support simply by being seen in it. At the 2000 Oscars, Jennifer Lopez created nearly as much of a buzz with her fur eyelashes as she did with her see-through Chanel gown. Fur groups wasted no time in milking the celebrity connection. The Fur Information Council of America (FICA) posted a list of cool young celebrities who'd been seen wearing fur—like 'N Sync, Kid Rock, Kate Hudson, and Britney Spears—on its website (apparently, both sides in this controversy want Ms. Spears in their camp—news had leaked that she also agreed to pose nude for PETA's "I'd rather go naked than wear fur" campaign in 2001, a claim her publicist later denied). Their campaign to appeal to the MTV crowd didn't stop at celebrity wannabe-ism. The organization also promoted wearing fur as an act of rebellion. Fur, according to FICA, wasn't just fashion—it was a fashion statement. "I choose what to wear: I set my own style," reads a section of the website. "If I want to pierce my tongue or get a tattoo, that's my choice and I expect others to respect it. I wear what I want whether it's wool, leather, fur or anything else. If it's OK with me, then I am wearing it."

Even older consumers began to see fur as an act of empowerment. When *Vogue* editor Anna Wintour sits front row at a fashion show wearing a massive fox jacket, she seems to be thumbing her nose at activists.

HAVE YOU HUGGED A TREE TODAY? THE BACKLASH AGAINST ACTIVISM

Ironically, a major catalyst behind the comeback of fur was the fur industry's own enemy: the anti-fur movement. "Based on the popularity of leather and fur products in the marketplace today, I think many consumers are rebelling against the 'politically correct' and animal activists," says Bonnie D. Belleau, Ph.D., professor and head of the Textiles, Apparel Design, and Merchandising Department at Louisiana State University. Since the eighties, the animal-rights cause had gradually acquired a bad reputation because of the actions of a few. By the end of the twentieth century, anti-fur activists had become widely stereotyped as either crunchy neo-hippies or as militant bullies. Many of those who made headlines didn't just debate the issue in public forums, hand out leaflets, and demonstrate quietly—they set buildings on fire, threw paint on designers, mailed animal entrails to magazine editors, paraded ridiculously in caveman outfits outside fur stores, and performed a host of other startling publicity stunts. Activists also began to target their enemies in more private ways. Teresa Platt of the Fur Commission USA (FCUSA), for example, has been targeted outside the normal realm of protests: she's been burned in effigy, compared to Hitler, received bomb threats, and had her home phone number and directions to her house distributed among activists. In January 1999, Brett Wyker, of the Coalition to Abolish the Fur Trade, reportedly sent Platt the following e-mail: "hey, what did oyu [sic] think of the Fur Farmers convention in WI? FUR IS DEAD AND YOU'LL BE SOON!" The personal attacks haven't deterred Platt, and have certainly not won the anti-fur movement any new fans.

The anti-fur cause even adopts unwitting spokespersons. In March 2002, Cindy Crawford angered PETA when she modeled a fur coat for Roberto Cavalli in her first catwalk appearance in years. In 1994, the supermodel had appeared in one of PETA's "I'd rather go naked than wear fur" ads wearing nothing but a faux fur hat. But as it turned out, Crawford had never agreed to be in that PETA ad in the first place. "It's time to set this straight," her spokesperson said. "A long time ago, Cindy did a favor for Todd Oldham. Todd had designed a fake fur hat, and she modeled it." But the photo was reused by PETA in a magazine ad. The public was led to believe Crawford worked with the group and believed in its animals-first philosophy, but she had never been associated with PETA.

Activists have grown increasingly creative, like the time in 2001 when Dutch fashion designer Frans Molenaar received several cards tucked in with his other Christmas greetings that showed a naked woman adorned with real tufts of pubic hair and the message, "If you really want to use the fur of a living being we are ready to lend you a hand." For fall 2002, PETA sponsored a non-fur Valentine's Day show by Marc Bouwer, who used fur early in his career but gave it up. The body that organizes the New York shows—7th on Sixth—considered it a way to neutralize PETA. In late 2001, a group called Against Fur Sluts doused Anna Wintour's house with red paint.

"People are sick and tired of being told what to do—there's definitely a backlash," says Betty Berger, of Berger Furriers in Marion, Iowa. Students from a nearby college travel twenty-five miles to march in front of her store; Berger says she hardly minds—she gets lots of free publicity. "People laugh at them," she says. "Passersby give them the finger." Some younger designers have turned to fur because they view the animal-rights issue itself as archaic. "For me, farmed fur is no different to leather, which I also specialize in," designer Tristan Webber once said. "The moral issues were worked through in the late 1980s."

Keith Kaplan of FICA agrees that the debate is old news. "Young people have moved on to other issues," he says. "PETA, as they've broadened their agenda and attempted to push people to stop eating meat, drinking milk, allowing animals for medical testing, etcetera, have alienated many and diluted their message." The younger generation never gained the sense of activism that their predecessors had developed toward the animal-rights issue because they didn't need to—the really contentious issues of endangered species and extreme cruelty had already been hammered out. "Consumers, especially the younger group, are tired of the rhetoric of animal-activist groups and tired of being told what to do," says Kaplan. "They'll wear what they want. And if they happen to like a particular fur garment, they'll wear it proudly."

In the 1999 compilation of essays *The Rights of Animals*, L. Neil Smith, publisher of the *Libertarian Enterprise*, wrote a piece entitled "Animals Are the Property of Humans," in which he described a term used to portray animal activists: "watermelons"—green on the outside, red on the inside—in other words, people who use environmental advocacy to abuse individualism and capitalism. He continued, "In my experience, those who profess to believe in animal rights usually don't believe in human rights." Much of the public echoed at least part of Smith's attitude, growing increasingly puzzled over activists: what was their motivation anyway? We used to think of animal-rights protesters as zealous animal lovers who would protect chimps and rabbits as if they were their family members. But some activists say they're simply fighting injustice, regardless of whether it's against an animal, a person, or a tree. In an interview for the *Toledo Blade*, the Michigan Five's Gary Yourofsky said, "I don't even like most animals," a comment that seems baffling considering his devotion to the cause.

In the ongoing war against fur, two internationally known animal-rights groups have played a significant role in shaping the public's opinions of the anti-fur movement: PETA and the Animal Liberation Front (ALF).

The Publicists: PETA

In early February 2000, twenty-two-year-old Kristie Phelps caught wind that Michael Kors's fall line, set to debut at New York Fashion Week on the eleventh, would be a virtual fur extravaganza. Phelps told her friends at PETA, where she works as a full-time campaign coordinator, and the wheels of protest were put into motion. For years, PETA had been sending Kors, who regularly uses fur, letters and videos with graphic scenes of fur-bearing animals having their necks broken and being electrocuted. Unsurprisingly, the designer never responded. "We decided the next best thing was to embarrass him in hopes that he would stop and pay attention to the issue," says Phelps.

The day of the show, Phelps dressed attractively (nonleather shoes, of course), then went over to the tents at Bryant Park, the illustrious site of Fashion Week. Carefully nestled under her jacket was a tofu cream pie she had whipped up earlier from a recipe of vegan pie crust and vegan Hip Whip whipped cream. Ticketless, she wasn't sure if she would get in the door or not. "All ticket-holders," ushers announced. In all the crowded chaos, a group of people managed to rush past the ushers, sweeping Phelps along with them to the standing-room-only area. She watched nervously as the models strutted the catwalk in glorious fur scarves and fur-trimmed coats. Having never attended a fashion show before, Phelps expected it to last at least an hour, so she was taken off guard when Kors came out to give his bow just fifteen minutes later. She rushed the runway, hurled the tofu pie at Kors, and shouted, "Fur shame!" The airborne soy barely hit the arm of the designer's jacket, and the rest flew into the crowd. "The next thing I knew, I was being led away by police," Phelps recalls. She spent the night in jail and was sentenced to serve seven days of community service.

Phelps pooh-poohed her brief incarceration as "nothing compared to the suffering that caged fur-bearers endure." The incident left the show's producers somewhat shaken, partly because an activist had managed to sneak in and partly because she had looked so much like *them*. Afterward, a security guard said it was difficult to identify potential culprits because the protesters were "young and beautiful." Evidently, Phelps didn't fit everyone's description of an activist. She wasn't a crunchy hippie chick with baggy clothes and overgrown eyebrows—she was a pretty, well-dressed young woman who, frighteningly, fit right in. Phelps seems like a nice girl . . . a nice girl who you'd suspect would never have set foot in a jail cell if she hadn't been involved with the animal-rights issue. In fact, the Kors incident wasn't the first time she had been in trouble with the law. She was arrested for taking off her clothes and sitting in a cage to protest animal cruelty at the circus once. "Nothing promotes discussion and dialogue better than a naked woman in a cage," she says. "It gives me perspective on the lifetime of suffering these animals endure." And in 1999, she and fellow female PETA member Alex Bury shocked an Alaskan crowd before Anchorage's Fur Rondy Grand Parade when they marched into the six-degree February chill with leopard-print body paint, bikini bottoms, black ankle boots, and a strategically placed banner that read "Only Animals Should Wear Fur." The women knew they'd be walking into hostile territory—the Fur Rondy, a celebration of the state's trapping tradition, had been taking place since 1935. "I was very nervous, and to this day, I get nervous before doing these kinds of events," says Phelps. "Our message was that tradition doesn't justify many of the cruel things that we do or have done in this country. You don't need fur to keep warm, even in Alaska." Another time, she and two fellow PETA members were arrested when they went into a Dolce & Gabbana boutique wearing donated fur coats, handcuffed themselves together, and smeared red paint on the window of the store. They held signs that read "Death Fur Sale" and chanted "Fur on your back is blood on your hands" until police dragged them away.

Shocking PR stunts have come to be expected from PETA. Founded in 1980 by Ingrid Newkirk and Alex Pacheco as a way to stop people from using animals for food, clothing, test subjects, and entertainment, PETA today boasts a membership list topping 750,000 worldwide. One of its many strengths over the years has been attracting a wide variety of members, from celebrities like Pamela Anderson and Chrissy Hynde to designers like Stella McCartney to college students, housewives, and businesspeople. They've staged several Rock Against Fur and Fur Is a Drag benefit concerts. In 1996, the group persuaded Boss Models to announce that its models would no longer wear fur and received pledges from filmmakers including Oliver Stone, Martin Scorsese, and Rob Reiner to keep fur off movie sets. The celebrity element has always been a vital one, says Dan Matthews, PETA's director of campaigns, for the simple reason that the organization doesn't have an advertising budget. "We don't have the money to run ads to get our message across, like our opposition does to promote their products," he says. The organization couldn't have asked for a better supporter than Stella McCartney, whose anti-fur antics became nearly as well publicized as her early designs for the house of Chloé. The designer had originally turned down a job at Gucci because of their strong link to leather and fur. She eventually inked a contract with the Italian fashion house in 2001 after negotiating a deal that would allow her to create her own line under their tutelage and without having to use materials taken from animals. The plum deal with her new employer didn't diminish her loyalty to the animal-rights movement, though. Two weeks before Gucci unveiled its winter 2001 collection, complete with full-length Mongolian fur coats and men's jackets trimmed with fox fur, McCartney was filming an anti-fur ad for PETA that ran in movie theaters.

As any advertising exec can tell you, sex sells, and that is part of PETA's modus operandi. But the group's flashy—and fleshy—tactics have angered feminists since the beginning of the anti-fur movement, raising the issue of whether you should battle one evil by replacing it with another. In addition to getting nude female models and celebrities to pose in ads and having female members sit nude in cages to protest the use of circus animals, PETA actions have included sexy young women ("chicks") dressing in revealing chicken costumes to oppose eating the birds; porn stars and Playmates in posters for pleather and vegetarianism; and pretty protesters traveling the U.S. wearing nothing but a banner that says "Human skin is in, animal skin is out." One of the reasons some people support PETA's use of sex to save animals is that they say it's for a good cause. But that, says feminist writer Nikki Craft, is like exploiting African Americans to convey a message about vegetarianism. "Should we be expected to take it as 'liberating' because it's framed as 'protest,' yet upon looking deeper it's just jacking up racial stereotypes and white privilege?" she once wrote. "Could we take PETA seriously? Yet some insist we ought to when they are jacking up sexual stereotypes, male privilege, and conservative politics."

Kristie Phelps doesn't see it as a sexist issue, since men have also participated in the campaigns (although, from news clippings from previous years, it's clear that men have only been involved in a handful of the protests). "Unlike women who are paid to pose nude or scantily dressed to sell a product, I receive no extra compensation for going naked," she says. "I participate because I want to do something that makes people stop and pay attention to learn the truth about the bloody fur trade. I've attended demonstrations fully clothed where we have a person in an animal costume and we hold posters and hand out fliers, and the fact is that no one really cares, unless we do something outlandish. Our Naked campaigns work."

PETA's strategies for attracting attention have both strengthened and weakened its effectiveness. To many people, the organization has helped make animal-rights activists seem like bullies. The vehemence of its detractors has often been just as intense as the group's own fervor. Anti-PETA websites, like Piss On PETA and People Eating Tasty Animals, litter the Internet. And more than a few PETA members have defected after only a short time, like Debra, a farmer in New Mexico. She had always been interested in the animal-rights issue, so she decided to join PETA in the early 1990s. "They kept sending me horrible pictures of caged lab animals and I basically got to the point where I couldn't open an envelope coming from them," she says. "I was a member for less than a year . . . I just couldn't take the graphic propaganda."

For every person it has initiated into its cause, PETA has turned off another with its abrasive tactics. "I found them quite violent and I wanted to dissociate myself from them," Naomi Campbell said of PETA after breaking ties with the organization in the late 1990s. She has publicly condemned organization spokesman Dan Matthews for his tasteless joke nomination of Andrew Cunanan for *Genre* magazine's 100 Men We Love list "because he got Versace to stop doing fur." And the supermodel came out in defense of *Vogue* editor Anna Wintour, who had suffered the horror of having a PETA member throw a dead raccoon on her plate while she was dining at the Four Seasons. At Randolph Duke's fall 2000 show, celebrity stylist Phillip Bloch was caught in the crossfire when he became the target of a PETA member's red paint. Immediately following the show, Bloch proclaimed, "I've never dressed anyone in fur, but I will now." A year later, it didn't take much to reawaken his anger about the incident. "If your show cost $100,000, how *dare* someone go ruin someone's day," he said. "Go demonstrate outside. And don't sit and throw red paint on *me*. I'm doing my job. Am I gonna go beat up the checkout girl at the supermarket because I don't like the price of cherries?" At the same time that he criticized PETA's methods, Bloch came out strongly on the side of their cause. "I have a good relationship with PETA," he said. "I'm very supportive of their beliefs, but how they follow through a lot of times is up to interpretation. They want to create awareness of cruelty

to animals; I think that's a very sound argument. Throwing paint on
people is not."

There's a growing group of people who can't stand PETA's tactics.
Take this Web posting from Chris, age nineteen: "Face it, there are too
many people out there who do stuff to be part of a community.
Mindless tree huggers are no different than people who buy a certain
brand of clothing that advertises the manufacturer on the front. Notice
how people who look alike and dress alike hang out together?" Others
are mixed. "For the most part I think PETA's issue is an important
one, but by going to such extremes, they're hurting their image," says
Erica, a twenty-six-year-old Web producer in Brooklyn. "I would
never participate or support their efforts because of the radical nature
of their organization, but all the same, I'm glad they exist—and only
partly because it's fun to see rich women get doused in red paint."

Some question how PETA attracts its protesters. Bill Eilers, owner
of Northwest Furs in Rapid City, South Dakota, once operated a Seattle
location, which attracted protests by the group every weekend. "PETA
paid protesters to picket," says Eilers. "For two years, every Saturday
from one to two—they stayed mostly on the sidewalks with signs and
talking to passersby and handed out literature. They chose us because
we had the best location in town. One time, activists put glue in our
locks and anti-fur graffiti on the windows, which caused about a thousand dollars in damage." Eilers says he once met a picketer in Las
Vegas who admitted that PETA had paid for his airline ticket, plus
room and board for the weekend: "He said he really wasn't against the
mink breeders, but the trip was too good to pass up."

The Extremists: The ALF

To some, Gary Yourofsky is a hero. To others, he's a dangerous kook. A
teacher by trade, the thirty-year-old has devoted every day of the past
five years to the cause of animal rights and has given lectures on the
topic at over eighty universities around the country. He was incarcer-
ated in a Canadian prison for seventy-seven days (as punishment for
the Eberts Farm mink raid). He went on a ten-day hunger strike while
in prison to protest animal cruelty. He's been arrested no fewer than

ten times. Yourofsky refuses to dine with anyone eating meat. To Yourofsky, PETA's publicity-driven actions are "bullshit." His own tactics are far more incendiary: he's prone to spouting things in his speeches and essays like "Do *not* be afraid to condone arson at places of animal torture" and "if an animal abuser who exerts hatred, cruelty, domination, and oppression against innocent animals were to perish accidentally or purposely during an arson or some other action, I would unequivocally support that, too."

Gary Yourofsky is one of very few people to ever publicly admit that he is a member of the underground eco-terrorist group the Animal Liberation Front (ALF). In fact, it doesn't take much arm-twisting to get him to own up to anything. On his arm, he sports a tattoo of himself, hooded and holding a bunny, with the letters ALF. When asked if he considers himself a leader of the ALF, he doesn't flinch, responding with a wholehearted yes. "No one has accomplished the things I've done," he says. If Yourofsky's dedication and tenacity at all represent the sentiment of the hundreds of other ALF members around the world, authorities are justified in feeling nervous.

If PETA's purpose is to instill fear of embarrassment, the ALF's purpose is to instill the fear of economic ruin and potential physical harm. Since its inception in 1976, the ALF has caused over $137 million in damage in the U.S. alone, according to a report by the departments of justice and agriculture. The purpose of the worldwide underground group is to carry out acts of economic sabotage (what many call terrorist acts) against the fur industry and others who use animals. Actions vary from mischievous pranks, like graffiti and gluing store locks shut, to full-fledged eco-terrorist acts of destruction. Some of the more severe actions for which the ALF has claimed credit include an arson at Minnesota's Alaskan Fur Company in 1996, which caused about $2 million in damage; a 1991 firebombing that ignited a fur supply barn, resulting in $150,000 in damage but even greater tolls in terms of safety; and a 1999 fire that inflicted $1.5 million in damage to the United Feeds Mill in Plymouth, Wisconsin. And countless other stories abound of fur industry folk receiving envelopes laced with razor blades and threatening phone calls, and being tailed back to their homes by strange cars.

No one is sure how many people consider themselves members of the ALF. An article in Britain's *Guardian* estimated an inner core of three to four hundred activists who are prepared to take part in illegal actions, along with a support base of thousands who send money, buy publications, and attend demonstrations. "There's no sort of hierarchy or membership list or physical face," says Portland, Oregon, activist Craig Rosebraugh, who acted as the group's spokesman in 1997. "Instead, the group operates under an ideology. If you believe in that ideology and you follow a certain set of widely published guidelines, then you can commit an action and then claim it as part of the ALF."

The ALF handbook, "Into the Nineties," is the *Anarchist's Cookbook* of the animal-rights movement. The anonymously penned book describes how to make timed incendiary devices and petrol bombs, and damage vehicles, locks, and telephone lines. It recommends tailing research scientists, furriers, and butchers to their homes, "where pressure also needs to be put." Yet in all its years of operation, the ALF claims, no human has been harmed (no human target of the ALF, that is: at a fur farm in Finland in 1997, a farmer shot and wounded an activist who was trying to free some animals). It's not that the ALF has no concern for human life, says Rosebraugh. "I will honestly state that it is a concern, but the modus operandi behind the actions is far more important than speculating the what-ifs. I don't think that's what the ALF or I or anybody else who believes in this would want. But keep in mind the absolute violence that goes on every day to all different life forms. The ALF is trying to *protect* life."

In late 1997, Ingrid Newkirk, cofounder and national director of PETA, admitted to the *New York Daily News* that her organization had funded the ALF at one time. "In the early nineties, it was a very different group, well organized, and generated a lot of sympathy. But they dissolved. . . . Now they're just angry, and act without planning," she said. In fact, Newkirk had been tied quite personally to the ALF. In 1992, she wrote *Free the Animals*, a flattering chronicle about the start of the American ALF and its founder, whom she calls "Valerie"—a former Maryland police officer who, at twenty-three, became an animal-rights activist after being called to duty at a lab where researchers were doing tests on monkeys in 1981.

Whereas PETA tends to target designers and consumers, the ALF frequently goes to the source of the fur: farmers, feed mills, auction houses. So in most cases people in the fashion industry are only indirectly affected by the guerrilla group's actions, through inflated prices. But the fanatical actions of the ALF have reverberated throughout the business, causing a low-level type of fear, like a milder version of the anxiety that abortion clinic workers feel on a daily basis. "The ALF is a terrorist group responsible for violence and the massive destruction of personal property," says Keith Kaplan of FICA. "Under the guise of compassion for animals they've determined they'll use whatever means necessary to draw attention to their agenda, even if it involves death or destruction. The hypocrisy of utilizing such means under the name of compassion astounds."

The ALF may have caused millions of dollars in physical damage to the fur industry, but it has cost the animal-rights movement far more in public opinion points. Amid all the destruction and mayhem, the animal-rights message gets swept aside in the turmoil.

IS MONEY AT THE ROOT OF ACTIVISM?

In February 2000, the *Los Angeles Times* printed a provocative and much-maligned commentary by senior fashion writer Valli Herman-Cohen titled "The Fur Fury: Is PETA driven by animal rights or resentment of the rich?" In it, Herman-Cohen wrote, "[PETA's] rage seems to also be about who has money and who doesn't. The choice of [Randolph] Duke, [Oscar] De la Renta and [Michael] Kors for the protests is notable because these designers have built their image up on an idea of wealth, luxury and status." She continued, "Protestors haven't splashed paint on runways that featured leather or the kind of elaborate beading that's available only from Third World countries with poorly paid laborers . . . they've gone after women—wealthy ones. No one feels sorry for rich people when they're attacked. An unpleasant part of us cheers."

When I talked to Herman-Cohen over a year later, she said the article had garnered more reader mail than any she could remember, most of it vitriolic. "A few writers took the time to thoughtfully reply to

my arguments, but most concentrated on the idea that PETA was justified in any actions to save animals from being murdered," she says.
Still, she stood by her motivation for writing it. In the seventies,
Herman-Cohen had owned a fur coat ("when no one under the age of
fifty wore fur") and feared she'd be attacked on her college campus
one night when she heard a threatening voice yell, "Get the fur coat!"
"It became clear to me that fur sparked envy in complete strangers,"
she says. "My campus encounter helped me understand that it's a lot
easier to scare a lady in a mink on Park Avenue than it is a biker in his
motorcycle leathers."

Many people immediately dismissed the argument that resentment of wealth plays any role in the anti-fur movement. After all, most
activists *are* motivated by good intentions. Dan Matthews of PETA says
resentment of wealth may be a problem in places like Great Britain,
where society is more stratified by class, but not in the U.S. "We have a
huge middle class here," says Matthews. "There are certainly people
who resent those who are ostentatious to some degree, but this is the
land of people aspiring to *have* things rather than people being bitter
about those that do. What [PETA has] sought to do is show that people
in the highest parts of society who can buy whatever they want, like
Kim Basinger or Pamela Anderson or Paul McCartney, choose a
lifestyle that doesn't harm animals."

But the money issue may not be completely off base. In the mid-
1980s, anti-fur groups Lynx and Greenpeace launched a British billboard campaign that juxtaposed a picture of a woman in a fur under
the title "Rich bitch" with a picture of a bleeding dead fox caught in a
trap under the title "Poor bitch." Misogynist overtones aside, the ads
played up the issue of money. The message wasn't just "If you wear fur,
you're cruel," but also "If you wear fur, you're a materialistic bitch."
The timing was right—the backlash against the excesses of the 1980s
was at its peak. Ostentation was on its way out. The image of the fur
wearer was starting to become Joan Collins from *Dynasty* and Cruella
De Vil in *101 Dalmatians:* the quintessential heartless bitch. In 1999,
an anti-fur faction attempted to pass an initiative in Beverly Hills that
would require warning labels the size of a credit card to be attached to

any fur product costing over $50 detailing how the animal died, unless the seller could guarantee that the animal hadn't been killed by electrocution, gassing, neck-breaking, poisoning, clubbing, stomping, drowning, or being caught in a steel leg-hold trap. Measure A, as it was called, was defeated by 3,363 votes to 1,908. The special election that gave everyone outside of Southern California a good laugh ended up costing the city $60,000. Those who opposed Measure A claimed that the community was targeted by activists simply because of its reputation as a place of wealth and luxury. In comparison, cities that aren't readily associated with money tend to experience far fewer protests. "There's the usual fur-free Friday that might make the news out here, or an occasional rodeo protest, but that's about it," says Kevin Syperda, a fur trapper in Pierson, Michigan. "I don't worry when I or my wife wear our fur coats or hats; we usually get a few compliments when we do. Some people have asked us about anti-fur problems, but that seems to be [centered] in the larger cities like New York, or out west where they can gain plenty of media play for themselves."

I would revise Valli Herman-Cohen's theory a bit. Perhaps the real issue isn't dollars and cents per se, but rather the distinction between waste versus usefulness. If humans couldn't survive without using animals, anti-fur sentiment would cease to exist. The Fashion Victim has grown to aspire to a life of luxury, yet she rails against the wastefulness of those who have achieved it. We roll our eyes at the middle-aged man who drains his bank account to buy a Porsche, gape at the rudeness of a woman who eats only the claws out of five lobsters at a buffet then tosses the rest, and sneer at pet owners who lavish gourmet goodies and trips to the doggy day spa on their pooches. We all waste, but we hate it when people who are wealthier than we are do it too. In the eyes of the middle-class spendthrift, a well-heeled squanderer is brashly flaunting her disposable income, like a millionaire who doesn't bat an eyelash over misplacing $5,000. It's unreasonable jealousy but difficult to escape nonetheless.

Fur has been made more available to the masses thanks to trends like the fur collar, but it has yet to lose its direct link with luxury. Like fine jewels and precious metals, a fur coat's value is in its exclusivity.

You can't have a fur . . . doesn't that make you want one? As with dia-
monds, pearls, caviar, precious gems, ivory, thoroughbreds, and saf-
fron, we ascribe worth to things that aren't inherently *worth* more.
With luxury comes the implication of wastefulness. No person today
needs a fur. Owning one is merely a symbol of the wearer's allegiance
to fashion and luxury.

Typically, areas where fur is needed the most are targeted by protesters the least, and vice versa. People in the perpetually mild weather
of Palm Beach don't *need* fur coats for warmth. People in Siberia
arguably do. Fashion designers don't *need* to kill seals to survive. Some
tribes of indigenous people in Alaska do. The perceived squandering
of an animal's life for the sake of something as trifling as fashion is
what makes so many people angry. Knowing that there was an additional reason for an animal's death makes it easier for the Fashion
Victim to stomach. Alicia, a twenty-year-old teacher in Dallas, Texas,
says, "I think it's only wrong to wear fur when there's not an alternate
use for the animal, like [food and medicine]. Leather, croc, snake are
okay, but mink or anything of the like is just murder in vain—who *eats*
mink?" Mink actually do serve alternate purposes, according to the fur
industry. The fur-bearers consume farm waste—the millions of tons of
leftover chicken parts that humans don't want on their grocery
shelves. After mink are skinned, their meat is used for animal feed.
So, says the industry, it's not as though millions of mink bodies are
being farmed for their fur alone. But these added uses don't necessarily make wearing fur more justifiable, they just detract from the real
issue of whether or not fur is wrong.

Since the 1970s, the pro-fur contingent has set out to prove fur's
usefulness. "Most people buy fur for its simple utilitarian value:
warmth," says Teresa Platt, of the Fur Commission USA. "It's estimated that half the world's fur goes to Russia, where winters are six
months long, for a simple hat to keep people warm. You can't get any
more utilitarian than that." True, in Russia, where frigid temperatures
start in November and don't let up until April, fur isn't just popular,
it's commonplace. According to Julia, a twenty-six-year-old inter-
preter in St. Petersburg, Russia, fur is abundant there, particularly in

hats and collars. "Fur is always fashionable and beautiful," she says. "A woman gets a very special style being in a fur coat. Moreover, it's a sign of her social and financial status. For sure, if you see a woman in a fur coat made of rabbit or goat and another one in a coat made of white mink, you'll think differently about their bank accounts. So very often it's used to express or to create an image. And, of course, fur is warm. When it's twenty degrees outside, even psychologically, it seems to be easier if you're in fur." In this colder environment, where fur is more accepted socially, activism is minimal. "Of course we have animal-protecting organizations, but their work is concentrated mostly around helping and protecting homeless and wild animals," says Julia. "The animals that are used in fur manufacturing are not hunted in the wild—it's prohibited by law. There are special farms for this. To protest against these farms is the same as to protest against cattle or chicken farms. Never in my life [have I] seen somebody protesting, actively or passively, against wearing fur. In Russia it's a matter of individual choice: if you are against wearing fur, simply don't buy it, but never press others [about it]."

Even the fur industry itself inadvertently perpetuates the attitude that wealth is evil. The International Fur Trade Federation reminds the public time and again that, in the fur industry, "Most [fur farms] (85 percent) are small, family-run businesses which have been passed from generation to generation," as if being big corporations would make them more evil. After all, it's easier for most of us to hate a giant corporation (just look at Philip Morris or Microsoft) than it is to throw rotten tomatoes at a small mom-and-pop operation.

WHY ARE WE STILL FIGHTING OVER FUR?

Over the decades, we've witnessed the "sinning-down" of society: things that were once considered immoral don't seem quite so sinful today. It was once thought that the bikini would be the downfall of society's moral values; now some women unabashedly wear barely-there thongs. Parents once thought that listening to the "sinful" rock 'n' roll of Elvis and the Beatles would surely lead their children down the footpath to hell; now bands like Coal Chamber and Slipknot make the King and the Fab Four seem like a boys' choir. Kissing on the first date today is far from the scandal it once was. And to some people today, wearing fur has gone the way of swearing—to them, wearing a mink scarf is only about as naughty as saying the word *damn*. But just as there are still traditionalists today who think rock music (even the most innocuous kind) and kissing are morally wrong, there will always be people who butt heads over the fur issue.

The Fashion Victim's appetite for more clothes whatever the cost has always been at the heart of the fur debate. If she doesn't have what's new, what's hot, what's in, she'll fall out of the loop. And when their hearts are set on wearing fur because it's in vogue, Fashion Victims rationalize their decision: "It's legal," "It's your right to wear what you want," "I eat meat; so what's the difference?" The battle also rages on because the pro-fur side does have a few valid arguments in its arsenal, beyond just maintaining that fur looks good. Fur supporters contend that natural fibers don't harm the environment as much as all those popular synthetic fibers that are on the market, which take generations to degrade in landfills. Faux fur, for instance, a plastic product made from petroleum, consumes natural resources and creates pollution in the manufacturing stage. Designer Mark Montano featured fur accessories like fox cuffs, stoles, and hand muffs in his fall 1999 collection, then debuted his first fur garment collection the next year. "I really think that in the long run our earth will be more damaged by people not wearing fur and leather and wearing plastics instead," he says. But again, that argument has a lot to do with the Fashion Victim's insatiable hunger for clothes—couldn't we reduce the need for both fur and synthetics if we bought less? And, supporters argue, trapping wild fur-bearers is sometimes necessary to maintain a viable balance of species within certain ecosystems, so fur obtained by trapping may be merely the by-product of a truly necessary activity. But in today's market, fur trapping is relatively inconsequential. Statistics show that 85 percent of the fur used today comes from farmed animals, so trapping makes up only a small percentage of the total.

When you boil down the true issue, these others don't even really matter. Regardless of how an animal is killed or what it's to be used for, the main issue of contention, which may never be resolved, remains: is it right to use animals for *anything?* As long as this question endures, so will the debate. After all, if fur ever totally disappears, the argument will switch to leather. And if leather vanishes, then the main thrust of the dispute will shift toward raising sheep for wool and so on. So at least for the foreseeable future, designers will continue to use skins, the Fashion Victim will continue to buy them, and the debate will live on . . . until, that is, fur simply falls out of fashion again.

Fur is certainly one of the most visible examples of how fashion straddles the line between socially acceptable and offensive. But it's not the only one.

WHEN CLOTHES ATTACK!

As with every juicy moral controversy (fur, cloning, euthanasia) the difference between right and wrong depends greatly on one thing—public opinion. A style's offensiveness is often measured in the amount of protest it receives. A jacket with the words "America Sucks" printed on the lapel will be pulled from a designer's line if more than one person objects. Of course, there's no finite number at which the tide turns—designers don't wait around for, say, the 153rd person to complain before taking a garment off shelves, but rather start to backpedal when there are just enough dissenters to make a big stink over the issue. To offend in a fashion show is one thing; to offend in the store is another. A designer may garner a bit of negative publicity from a show, but if customers are incensed by something they see on the rack, the designer's business will suffer. And that is simply intolerable. How can something as harmless as fashions arouse such strong feelings among so many? It's easier than you might think.

Fashion is inherently provocative. Or at least it should be. But there's a difference between pushing the envelope and being downright inconsiderate. In this age of political correctness, when we're hypersensitive over certain hot-button issues like religion and race, it's sometimes difficult for Fashion Victims to decide between right and wrong.

SACRILEGIOUS STYLE

In the 1980s, Madonna drove religious leaders into a tizzy by garnishing her racy lingerie look with rosaries and crucifixes. The icing on the cake? Thousands of girls, Christian or not, adopted the look—lace gloves, mesh shirts, blasphemous baubles and all. One of the major complaints about the use of religious symbols in fashion is that it waters down their spiritual meaning. In May 2002, Vatican news agency Fides issued a statement criticizing celebrities like Naomi Campbell, Jennifer Aniston, and Catherine Zeta-Jones for turning the cross into an expensive, jewel-encrusted "mania of the moment." The crucifix, once the hallowed symbol of an entire faith, had been reduced to a fashion statement.

Like Madonna, revolutionaries throughout the years have enjoyed using fashion to subvert religion. In 1999, French photographer Bettina Rheims caused an uproar when she displayed a photo of Jesus wearing a Helmut Lang T-shirt and Mary wearing Jean-Paul Gaultier and Manolo Blahnik in a Berlin exhibit. And the Church, generally less than pleased with the attention, rarely stands idly by. Rebel fashion team Imitation of Christ—who showed their spring 2001 collection at a funeral parlor, complete with a casket and mourning models—has fought a long-standing feud with Catholic League president Bill Donohue. In 2000, Donohue called the line "a cheap way to make a fast buck off rather stupid people" and made the bizarre offer to give them "his old pair of jeans with puke on them for a bachelor party." Designer Tara Subkoff fired back, "If you're the head of the Catholic League, why are you puking on your jeans at a bachelor party?" Fans realized that the religious imagery in all of these examples was done with a twist of humor. Imitation of Christ isn't really making a serious statement on the Church; Madonna was simply being, well, Madonna.

Interestingly, while designers typically offer no apologies for angering Christians, they do scramble to make amends when they've offended members of other faiths. Gaultier apologized after depicting models as Hasidic Jews with sequined yarmulkes and black robes in his 1993 collection. The next year, Chanel's Karl Lagerfeld issued an apology to the Muslim community after sending Claudia Schiffer down the catwalk in a tight, low-cut bodice with the word *Allah* embroidered over her right breast. He promised to destroy the dresses as well as any photos and negatives of the collection. And in 1997, Nike recalled thirty-eight thousand shoes featuring a flamelike logo that resembled the Arabic word for Allah. The company also promised to send design-ers to religious-sensitivity training and took its apology one step fur-ther. It agreed to sponsor a project that would build playgrounds in Islamic centers nationwide.

Why the discrepancy in the attitudes toward Christianity and other faiths? A lot of it boils down to *who* created the clothes. A Jewish designer who prints a verse from the Torah on a shirt will catch much less heat than a Protestant designer who does so. It's considered art when you rouse passions about your own religion; it's considered offensive when you stir emotions about someone else's. Even non-Christian designers who live in Western countries, just by virtue of liv-ing among a vast Christian population, seem to have more leeway to offend.

Just like designers who use fur in their collections, those who employ potentially controversial religious symbols have to be at least somewhat aware that their actions may draw protests. In 2000, DKNY recalled a line of pants with verses from the Koran running down the leg; had no one at the company suspected that this might anger Muslims? Unlikely. Again, it seems to be a case of wait and see: the DKNY pants could easily have slid under the radar if no Muslims had seen them or if no one complained. And some oblivious Fashion Victim in Argyle, Wisconsin, would have been the one to bear the brunt of the criticism when she wore the pants in front of a suddenly insulted person.

CULTURE KILLER

In April 2002, Abercrombie & Fitch promptly pulled three T-shirt designs from all of its 311 stores after receiving dozens of angry phone calls. Protesters charged that the shirts—one featuring two Chinese laundry workers wearing conical hats that said, "Wong Brothers

Laundry Service: Two Wongs Can Make It White"—promoted negative stereotypes of Asians. A spokesman said the company thought consumers, especially the Asian community, would like the shirts—an example of how oblivious some clothiers are when it comes to other cultures.

Once again, the level of offense greatly depends on *who* created the clothes. For instance, had Vivienne Tam created a campy shirt like the Two Wongs one, she might not have been criticized. Likewise, an African-American designer who splashed "Old School Niggaz" on the back of a jacket would run into fewer protests than, say, Karl Lagerfeld, if he were to do it. Abercrombie & Fitch's white suburban image didn't vibe with the image created by the Two Wongs shirt. I sometimes wonder: if the same shirt had been sold at a sassier store like Urban Outfitters, would red flags have ever been raised? One could argue that it's unfair, but that's the state of political correctness today.

It's long been popular for designers to borrow ethnic symbols, cultural traditions, and styles. Remember the Nehru jacket? Usually, the borrowing is called inspiration and few people complain. That doesn't mean the practice is without its critics. When bindi forehead dots and henna tattoos became an American fad in the late 1990s, many Indians seethed over the plunder of their culture for fashion profits. Celebrities like Madonna, Gwen Stefani, and Destiny's Child fueled the trend by showing up to awards shows decked out with the dots. "The bindi is no longer what it once was—a symbol of being Hindu and of having a symbolic union with God," says Sunita, a twenty-one-year-old Yale University senior. "Now, it's not only a fashionable item to wear but is also mass-produced specifically for export to other countries."

The true crime here is that fashion transforms meaningful symbols into watered-down products, not caring what the ramifications may be for their original cultures. "Assigning new cultural meanings to symbols with very old traditions or deep personal significance is inappropriate and insensitive," says Sunita. "It reduces the complexities of that culture to mere physical items, rather than the continual process that culture is." Thanks to this diluting effect, dreadlocks—a spiritual

Rastafarian symbol—can be transformed into a mere Western fashion statement. Hindu gods can be transformed into insignificant cartoon characters printed on pajama pants. Animals can be transformed into beautiful but otherwise meaningless coats. And all the while, Fashion Victims the world over will continue to buy into it.

Epilogue

While I was working on this book, fashion underwent a drastic change. As a result of the terrorist attacks of September 11, 2001, New York Fashion Week was called off for the first time ever; at no time in recent memory did fashion feel so frivolous. Sales figures and stock prices for some of the world's largest retailers plummeted. After a dizzying rise, Swedish retailer H&M announced in December 2001 that its U.S. sales were down about 12 percent after the attack. In 2002, Vanity Fair, which owns brands like Lee Jeans and The North Face, announced it would cut 13,000 jobs; Levi's cut 20 percent of its U.S. workforce; Gucci laid off 130 workers in its U.S. operation. SEC filings reported that Gap's then-CEO Millard Drexler took a voluntary 10 percent cut in salary in 2001 (taking him down to a paltry $2.2 million). In March 2002, luxury goods conglomerate LVMH, which owns such illustrious brands as Louis Vuitton, Christian Dior, and Celine, announced that its annual net income had been nearly wiped out as a result of lagging demand for designer labels after the terrorist attacks. At the same time, many discounters did a brisk business. Newark-based off-price apparel retailer Ross Stores saw a whopping 19 percent increase in third-quarter 2001 earnings. A sign of things to come?

Some cynics interpreted the downturn as the death of luxury, and even the demise of fashion itself. This just a few months after logo-splashed clothes, prized handbags from Italian fashion houses like Gucci and Fendi, massive flagship stores, and coveted shoes from Manolo Blahnik reigned—a time when the thought of luxury ever fading seemed unfathomable. It seemed that no one was willing to cut fashion a break. Some of the world's great designers declared their disgust at its current state. In January 2002, Giorgio Armani proclaimed in Italian newspapers, "I'll tell you something. Luxury disgusts me . . . I want young people to understand that today's world is false. They must understand that it is absurd to prostitute oneself or to steal just to get a designer bag because they think that without it they are nobody." Before Yves Saint Laurent took his final bow in early 2002, the sixty-five-year-old designer, in an interview in the French paper *Paris Match*, expressed his disdain for a modern-day fashion industry that puts commerce over art. "I have nothing in common with this new world of fashion, which has been reduced to mere window dressing," he said. "Elegance and beauty have been banished." Over the years, he had taken several jabs at the flashy young breed of designers like John Galliano and Jean-Paul Gaultier, once calling their work "a ridiculous spectacle better suited to a concert stage."

Don't sing fashion's funeral dirge just yet. "Nothing could be less truthful than the belief that luxury and/or fashion are ending," says David Wolfe, a prominent trend forecaster and creative director of the Doneger Group, a fashion-consulting firm in New York. It's not that fashion will ever come to an end—it's that our definition of it will evolve. "What we believe to be luxurious is subject to change as our society changes," says Wolfe. "Fashion can *never* end because it is always defined as 'the reflection of the society that wears it.' Therefore, whatever we wear becomes fashion."

Whether you rejoice over or bemoan fashion's staying power, hopefully some of the words in this book have opened your eyes to the way fashion affects your life and the lives of others. After spending the last year engrossed in the topic, my own outlook on shopping and dressing has certainly changed. Where once I felt no misgivings about dropping $80 on a shirt I'd wear once, now I often think twice before handing over $20 for a garment I know I'll get to use only a few times. I find myself reading the tags in my clothes, hand washing instead of dry cleaning, and seeing photos of ultra-thin models more for what they really are—artistic representations meant to sell clothes, and not blueprints for my own body. At the same time, I still occasionally look at Karolina Kurkova's thighs in a magazine, then switch to mine, then to hers, then to mine, and wonder why hers don't touch at the top the way mine do. I still wear leather shoes and don't investigate Bangladeshi labor laws before buying a tank top made in that country. And I still suffer from innumerable Bad Clothes Days, unable to shake the frustration that I don't have—and never *will* have—enough to wear. Just the other day, before meeting friends for dinner, I tried on ten outfits before settling on one. And even now, I see trends in *W, Vogue,* and *Harper's Bazaar* and feel compelled to buy into them in some adolescent hope that people who see me will think I'm cool. Most likely, I'll struggle with these issues for the rest of my life. But that's to be expected. After all, if there's one constant it's that fashion is a series of trade-offs, and that in the end, when we balance the good against the bad, fashion, with all its flaws, will always succeed in convincing us to love it more.

Index